The Origin and Development of the Pueblo Katsina Cult

The Origin and Development of the Pueblo Katsina Cult

E. Charles Adams

The University of Arizona Press
Tucson & London

THE UNIVERSITY OF ARIZONA PRESS

Copyright © 1991

The Arizona Board of Regents

All Rights Reserved

⊗ This book is printed on acid-free, archival-quality paper.
Manufactured in the United States of America.

96 95 94 93 92   6 5 4 3 2

Library of Congress Cataloging-in-Publication Data

Adams, E. Charles.

    The origin and development of the Pueblo Katsina cult / E. Charles Adams.

    p.   cm.

    Includes bibliographical references and index.

    ISBN 0-8165-1203-5 (cl : alk. paper); 0-8165-1358-9 (pb : alk. paper)

    1. Pueblo Indians—Religion and mythology.   2. Kachinas—History.

3. Pueblo Indians—Rites and ceremonies.   I. Title.

E99.P9A24   1991

299'.74—dc20   90-48047

                                                CIP

British Library Cataloguing in Publication data are available.

Dedicated to Ethan and Mary with love

Contents

Illustrations and Tables

Figures

Tables

Preface

The first time I saw a katsina, it was sitting with hundreds of others on a shelf in an arts and crafts store in southwestern Colorado. Of course it was a katsina doll. I was being paid fifty dollars a week as a first-year archaeology student on a dig in Mesa Verde National Park for the University of Colorado in the late 1960s, and I spent forty dollars on a ten-inch doll that I learned represented a corn katsina. I vaguely remembered hearing of katsinas in an undergraduate anthropology course, but I could not relate to the concept at the time. Now that I owned a doll, I had to know more. Over twenty years later, that process of attempting to understand the concept of katsina continues. This document measures that progress in some fashion.

Later that first summer doing archaeology, I saw my first katsina dance at Moenkopi Pueblo, a Hopi enclave on the Navajo Reservation just east of Tuba City, Arizona. Appropriately enough, it was a corn katsina dance. It was a hot, muggy day in early July. The summer monsoon season beckoned but had not yet loosened its annual rains. However, the mugginess of the air and the buildup of billowing clouds over the Mogollon Rim and San Francisco Peaks more than fifty miles away were sure harbingers of the monsoon season's impending arrival. I was only barely aware of these changing seasons and their significance to the Hopi and to the world of the katsina.

Our annual University of Colorado field trip had taken us through northeastern Arizona to excavations just beginning at the Peabody Coal Mine on the north end of Black Mesa, to the grandeur of Betatakin cliff dwelling in Navajo National Monument, and then finally to Moenkopi. As the field school arrived in a swirl of dust in ten-year-old, faded-green carryalls, I was struck by the setting. Moenkopi lay nestled in a spring-fed valley green with a dizzying array of irrigated crops. It struck me that the architecture of Moenkopi village differed little from the thirteenth-century Betatakin ruin I had seen earlier in the day. The pickups and cars, of course, made the setting of this century, but more importantly, Moenkopi teemed with people and animals. There were dogs and children everywhere!

I will never forget the sounds of this first visit to a Hopi village. There were the familiar sounds of people and children talking and laughing. There were the sounds of barking dogs and sputtering engines, as they pulled vehicles up and down the twisted, seemingly vertical, climb out of the old village up to the new highway. Rising above all of these familiar sounds was a very different one that attracted me like a songstress.

We parked the university vehicles at the upper end of the road before it twists down into Old Moenkopi, the part of the village established in the 1870s by farmers from Moenkopi's mother village on Third Mesa, Oraibi. We were told to leave our cameras because photographing the village and the katsina dance is forbidden. As we staggered down the slope toward the village, the rhythm of what I finally recognized as a song accompanied by a drum became louder. A cloud of dust emanated from the center of the village, the very source of this sound.

The crowd now grew. It consisted of mostly Hopi but also quite a few Navajo, in their traditional dress and hair styles, and even a few Anglos, or bahanas (pahoanam). Our group probably nearly doubled the number of bahanas. As I descended into the village, which is made of local sandstone with mud mortar and earth, brush, and beam roofs, I felt as if I were stepping back in time. Since that day I have often fantasized, as I wandered the Southwest looking for remains of the country's past inhabitants, about walking over a hill in some remote section of the land and finding a lost village still occupied by the Anasazi whom the Hopi call *hisatsinom*, the ancient people. For this scenario I always picture a village similar to Moenkopi without its modern trappings.

As we approached the singing, our group began to separate. A couple of my compatriots and I saw a crowd on a nearby roof with easy access via ladder. We figured to get a great view of the activities below us. As we scrambled toward this roof, I saw many faces. Some averted their eyes, many looked at me passively, but many were downright friendly. Suddenly I no longer felt like a complete stranger. I felt welcome.

I finally found a place on the roof where I could see. The vista was magnificent. I could see the Moenkopi Wash with its small, but regular, spring-fed flow of water winding like a shimmering spider's line from its source on Black Mesa to its final destination in the Little Colorado River just above the latter's confluence with the Colorado River. The valley below the village was filled with small farming plots, each watered with an elaborate system of ditches carrying water from the Moenkopi or from Pasture Canyon, the spring-fed drainage joining the Moenkopi at the village. I took in all of this as I quickly glanced at the surrounding countryside. My eyes, however, were immediately transfixed on the scene taking place in the plaza below.

The plaza of pueblo villages is central to day-to-day and spiritual activities. It is an open space, usually near the center of the village. A large village may have more than one. During most days and for generations in the past, these plazas have functioned as combinations of work areas, play areas for the children, market places, and centers for the public presentation of Pueblo ceremony. On this day the plaza was devoted to ritual. Although the perimeter was now packed with spectators, Hopi and non-Hopi alike, room was made for the dancers, the katsinas.

Details of the dancers' appearance escape me now. About thirty figures with masks covering their faces, their upper bodies bare, and their midsections covered with beautiful handwoven kilts stood in an open circle stamping their feet rhythmically to the beat of a large wooden drum covered with leather. A different katsina beat the drum. The dancers had turtle shells on the leg they stamped on the ground, adding a different but compelling sound. The dancers also sang a hypnotic song. The words to the katsinas' song were in Hopi and perhaps chanted rather than sung. Occasionally the rhythm would change, and the dancers would turn and face in the opposite direction. Then suddenly they stopped, walked counter-clockwise a quarter turn of the plaza and resumed their dance, repeating it identically to the one before. Elder Hopi men, unmasked, shouted encouragement and instructions to the dancers. These men would occasionally walk along the line of katsinas and sprinkle a white dust (that I later learned was corn meal and pollen) on each dancer. Also in the plaza and unmasked, with their bodies covered with a dark brown or black mud or soot, with black circles around their eyes and their hair covered with white clay, were several individuals that I later learned were clowns. These clowns became the center of attention once the katsinas finished their song and left the plaza. The clowns spoke mostly in Hopi, and the Hopi in attendance laughed with glee at the constant chatter provided by the clowns. In fact two of our group were forced to participate in a hilarious three-legged race staged by these clowns.

Many more details of the dancers' costumes and the general scene could be related, but they are of less importance to my purpose here. The important fact is that this ceremony, which I believed to have ancient roots, was still being enacted with such beauty and vitality. Katsinas fascinated me. Obviously, the symbolism of the ceremony was everywhere, from the markings on the katsinas, to the items they carried (rattles and pine boughs) or wore (kilts and sashes), to the clowns who alternately made fun of the katsinas and treated them with reverence, and finally to the wholesale, seemingly helter-skelter dispersal of food to the onlookers when the katsinas returned to the plaza for another round of dances. What did it all mean, and when did it all start? My questions were many, the answers were few and unsatisfying.

In the twenty-plus years since my first experience with katsinas, I have learned much. Each bit of knowledge gained has inevitably engendered twice as many questions. In the pages that follow I try to understand and to interpret katsina religion. I seek to decipher its origins and the basics of its function in Pueblo society. If I have established a beginning, then I have come a long way.

I still hold the same awe and respect for Hopi culture that I did upon that first encounter. The people have an amazing strength that is both derived from and imparted to their land. Their villages are made of the products of their land; so are their arts and crafts. Their spirituality comes from the earth and the sky. Whether by accident or intent, the Hopi have been my teachers. My thanks to all who have taught me.

Many individuals have contributed on a more specific level. Earlier drafts of this manuscript were read and commented upon by Emil Haury, Watson Smith, Keith Kintigh, David Wilcox, Peter Pilles, Kelley Hays, and Ekkehart Malotki. Your comments were all helpful and are appreciated. They have made the product much better.

Rose Slavin and Annette Cvitkovich helped type portions of many drafts of the manuscript. Ron Beckwith drafted the line drawings, except Figures 3.12, 3.18, 3.19, 3.20, 3.24, and 5.13, which were drafted by Kelley Hays. Sally Cole graciously allowed reproduction of her drawings of rock art for Figures 3.10 and 3.22. Mike Jacobs assisted me in locating artifacts for photography, and Helga Teiwes did the photography of the artifacts. I am indebted to you all for your valued assistance. The final product, for better or for worse, is my own responsibility.

Finally, special thanks to Jenny and Nathan Adams for their unswerving support and love, allowing us all to complete the nine-year odyssey to the publication of this manuscript. Thank you for sharing my dream.

E. CHARLES ADAMS

The Origin and Development of the Pueblo Katsina Cult

I

Introduction

Katsina dances are restricted to the Pueblo people of the southwestern United States. Today the Pueblo people occupy about 25 villages in Arizona and New Mexico. Pueblo people are often divided into language groups. In New Mexico these groups are Zuni, Keres, Towa, Tewa, and Tiwa and, up to the late 1600s, the Tompiro and Piro. In Arizona there are only the Hopi (Fig. 1.1).

The Pueblo people live on the Colorado Plateau landform that stretches over all of northwest New Mexico, northeast Arizona, southeast Utah, and the southwest corner of Colorado. This landform is typically a high, arid plateau dotted with isolated mountains or mountain chains and higher mesas where precipitation is more abundant. The Colorado Plateau is a land of contrast. Its superficially flat face is lined with deep canyons carved through rocks of red, brown, gray, yellow, and all of earth's hues. Vegetation is typically sparse and short, adaptations to the arid soils and prevailing southwest winds.

Precipitation frequently arrives in brief, powerful bursts brought by summer thunderstorms. The summer monsoon season in July, August, and early September means life or death to plant, animal, and human alike. The summer rains allow the corn to grow. Corn has been the primary food source to the Pueblo people and their ancestors stretching back over two millennia. Crops can be grown only where soils are adequate. People can live only where water is adequate. These two resources are in short supply on the Colorado Plateau and dictate where people relying on agriculture can survive.

Adaptation to this unforgiving environment gave the diverse prehistoric people of the Colorado Plateau the mutual basis that caused them to be lumped under the term "Pueblo." The word Pueblo is borrowed from the Spanish word for town or village. The Pueblo people are village dwellers.

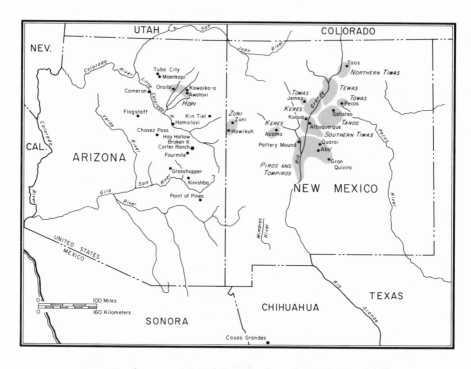

FIGURE I.I. Southwestern United States and northern Mexico showing
major modern and prehistoric towns or villages.
(Drawn by Ron Beckwith, Arizona State Museum)

Over 3,000 years ago the ancestors to the modern village dwellers were
introduced to maize, or corn, a plant domesticated in and brought from
Mexico. Slowly the people adapted the plant to the Plateau and adapted
themselves to its rich, dependable food source. Other domesticates sup-
plemented corn, but none replaced it. Thus, people throughout the Plateau obtained maize and developed village life as they became more dependent on its bounty.

But the Plateau is capricious. Droughts, windstorms, insects, floods, all
plagued these farmers. They developed religious values to give them the
feeling of control over their environment that every human seeks. Pueblo
religion is based on proper behavior in society, on cooperation with fellow villagers, on doing things correctly so that the deities who control
water, sun, and earth will be pleased and give the people bountiful harv-
ests. Perhaps the best-known and certainly the most colorful of Pueblo
ceremonies is the katsina dance. Katsinas are not gods, they are spirits.

They are ancestors who act as messengers between the people and their gods. They are also rainmakers, coming as clouds to the villages to which they are annually summoned.

This book is a study of the concept of katsina and the Pueblo religion that has developed around this concept. Ceremonies involving katsinas are relatively recent additions to Pueblo religion. Taken together, katsina ceremonies are frequently termed katsina religion. The focus of this book is more properly on defining what makes katsinas unique, why this concept was developed, and what adaptive value it had for prehistoric Pueblo culture. As a result, the attributes that made the concept of katsina successful will be emphasized. From this perspective and at its origin, katsina religion may be more properly considered a cult. This term will generally be used in the discussions that follow. The reasons for the development of katsina ceremonialism have never been adequately explored, although considerable discussion has focused on the age and origin of katsina religion. In this discussion the goals are to understand the cult in a more holistic manner. Not only is it desirable to know when and where the cult developed, it is perhaps more important to understand why and how it developed. If these goals are even partially fulfilled, a good start on understanding a very complex phenomenon, the katsina cult, will be accomplished.

Ceremonies involving katsinas are known worldwide. Although the Hopi of Arizona are best known for their katsinas both through their performances and the carving of katsina dolls (miniature representations of the performers in cottonwood root), katsina dances are held by the Zuni, the Keres-speaking villages, the Tewa, the Towa, and perhaps the southern Tiwa (Fig. 1.1). The 25 or so Pueblo villages remaining today once numbered over a hundred at Spanish contact (Schroeder 1979b). There are many indications that the katsina cult and dances were present among all the Pueblos prior to Spanish contact, with perhaps the exception of the northern Tiwa at Taos and Picuris. From earliest documents in the 1500s through the 1700s, masked dances called katsina were performed in Tewa, where it is much reduced today, as well as Keres, southern Tiwa, Piro, Tompiro, Towa, Zuni, and Hopi (cf. Dockstader 1954). The long-term effects of Spanish Catholicism and systematic attempts to exterminate Pueblo religion have disrupted many of the Rio Grande villages and their native ceremonialism. The missionizing forced the Pueblo to cloak much of their ceremonialism in veils of secrecy. Thus, the nature of the katsina cult in the eastern Pueblo villages is often poorly understood. As a result, much of the discussion on the modern cult and use of analogues for the prehistoric cult are drawn from comparisons to Hopi, Zuni, and Acoma katsina ritual.

The word katsina is borrowed from the Hopi word for really three interrelated concepts: dolls, masked dancers, and supernatural beings. Katsina (*ka tsína*) has been spelled most commonly in the literature as kachina, katchina, katcina, or katsina. I prefer katsina because it most closely represents the phonetic equivalent to the Hopi pronunciation using recognizable orthography. There is no translation for katsina. It is certainly a borrowed word (Emory Sekaquaptewa: personal communication). Foremost, there is no syllable initial *ka-* in Hopi (Malotki 1990). Evidence to suggest that it is a borrowed term from outside the Pueblo area, rather than being indigenous lies in the similarity of its pronunciation in the Zuni language and in Keresan as spoken in Acoma. At Zuni the word for katsina is *kó tikili* (Bunzel 1932) or *koko* (Dutton 1963: note 152). At Acoma katsinas are referred to as shiwanna or *k'atsina* (White 1932).

Bunzel (1932:901) suggests ancient roots to the cult because so many of the major ceremonies at Zuni are found in other Pueblos. Additionally, some of the katsinas have similar names in two or more of the villages. Similarities may be ancient, as Bunzel suggests, but substantial borrowing between Pueblos that is quite recent and could account for comparable katsinas or even ceremonies has also been documented (Bunzel 1932:901; Wright 1985). Nevertheless, if we assume that the major ceremonies are the oldest, Bunzel may be right.

What is the katsina cult, and why is it of concern to archaeologists? First, why do designs that appear to be katsinas appear in the art of the prehistoric people of the Colorado Plateau? Such developments are seldom accidental and without meaning. It is the meaning behind the evidence that most interests archaeologists. What is the evidence? Much of what modern observers of katsina ceremonies consider characteristic of the katsina cult would not survive to the present. What does survive are paintings or carvings of what are interpreted to be katsina masks. The best media for depicting masked figures are kiva murals (Dutton 1963; Hibben 1975; Peckham 1981; Smith 1952), rock art (Cole 1989b; Schaafsma 1972, 1980, 1981; Schaafsma and Schaafsma 1974), and ceramics (Ferg 1982; Hays 1989). The murals are the best medium because of the preservation of context involving the katsinas and the original colors. The discovery of extensive murals, some with masked figures, in the 1930s at Kuaua, a fifteenth-century pueblo north of Albuquerque, and at Awatovi and Kawaika-a, fourteenth- to sixteenth-century pueblos on the Hopi Mesas, set the stage for developing the concept that the katsina cult was prehistoric and not a Spanish introduction as first proposed by Parsons (1930). The perspective of archaeologists working on the murals was best stated by J. O. Brew who headed the Awatovi expedition of the Peabody Museum, Harvard University. In reference to decorations on ceramic vessels, he noted:

> In place of the relatively simple and static geometric designs of Pueblo III the new era was dynamic, characterized by sweeping figures, representations of birds (including the parrot), animals, insects, the human hand, and human figures often wearing ceremonial masks. . . . Associated with this vital change in design were equally startling developments in painting methods. . . .
>
> The change in ceramic art was duplicated in the ceremonial mural art. Paintings on the walls of kivas, . . . too, became dynamic. . . . Human representations and masked dancers were very common, much more so than on pottery. (Brew 1943:241–242)

Therefore, the prehistoric katsina cult is best recognized through icons that are similar to ones found in the modern religion. Iconography will be considered in detail in establishing the origins and age of the katsina cult later.

Appearing at about the same time in the prehistoric record are significant changes in size and layout of pueblos, major increases in trade between occupants of the pueblos, and additions to the material culture that seem to have their roots well to the south of the prehistoric pueblos. The second question before us then is, what relationship does the appearance of the katsina cult have with these other developments? Are the relationships merely fortuitous, are they a product of poor control of archaeological data making associations where spatial and temporal control are lacking, or are they related? If they are related, then understanding the role that katsina religion plays in modern Pueblo society may help archaeologists understand some of the changes discussed above.

The other key is understanding the environmental and cultural context of the time and place where the cult first appears. What factors caused a group to develop katsinas and the katsina cult? The cult is of particular interest to archaeologists because it crosscuts the material, social, and ideological domains of its modern practitioners and presumably its ancient participants. If so, it may provide some of the most readily identifiable artifacts, through its distinctive iconography, that archaeologists can use to infer social and ideological processes affecting prehistoric cultures in the southwestern United States. Inference of social and ideological processes in prehistoric archaeology is at best controversial (cf. Binford 1962). To have an archaeologically recognizable correlate to the katsina cult abetted by extensive ethnographic studies of the historic and modern katsina religion is a rare opportunity to conduct anthropology on a prehistoric society. For these reasons the cult is important to archaeologists.

The Concept of Katsina

Because of the author's familiarity with the Hopi, this discussion will emphasize katsina religion as it is practiced at Hopi but will more broadly consider the katsina religion as it is practiced and symbolized among western Pueblos, which for this paper include Acoma, Zuni, and Hopi. Masked dances are generally closed to non-Pueblo people in the eastern Pueblos; therefore, the data on katsina religion from eastern Pueblos is too spotty to consider in detail here. For a general discussion of pan-Pueblo katsina ceremony refer to Bunzel (1932) and Parsons (1939). Details of Zuni katsina ritual can be found in Bunzel (1932) and Wright (1985). White (1932) provides a detailed discussion of Acoma katsina ritual. The three aspects of Hopi katsinas, as dolls, as masked impersonators, and as supernatural beings, are generally shared by all other Pueblo people. The elaboration of the katsina in all three forms is unique to the Hopi; however, katsina ritual is equally elaborate at Zuni. Among the Hopi the carving of dolls has developed considerably and is a major craft item sold to tourists. An excellent history of the development of the Hopi katsina doll can be found in Erickson (1977). Although dolls are also carved at Zuni (Wright 1985) and at Acoma, until quite recently these have not been for sale to the public, but were available only for use within the community. The evolution of dolls from their internal use as toys for uninitiated girls to an art form has occurred at Hopi over the past century. Its development may be associated with the general stimulus to developing arts and crafts provided to the Hopi by Thomas Keam in the 1880s (Wade and McChesney 1980). The origin of the carved doll may be prehistoric, but evidence is scant. Their manufacture out of cottonwood root, if prehistoric or protohistoric, means dolls would not likely survive to the present. A detailed discussion of the subject will be presented later. The original function of katsina dolls is disputed as being either a teaching tool or a toy (Colton 1975:5; Malotki 1990; Whiting 1964:4). The dolls are given to girls until they are initiated at eight or nine. The dolls are initially the flat variety, and the first given is the Katsina Mother (*Hahay' iwuuti*) (Whiting 1964:4). The dolls allow the children to recognize katsinas and to begin to distinguish them. The importance placed on learning about katsinas for the child reflects the significance of katsinas to Hopi society.

The second form, the masked dancer, embodies the oneness of the traditional Hopi with their religion. Katsina ceremonies take place from late December to the end of July. Each ceremony involves most of the village where the ceremony will be held. Not only the participants are involved, but so are major segments of the village populace (minimally an extended family) who help to sponsor the dance by acquiring food for the katsinas to distribute at the ceremony. Every household in the village has, in effect, an open house on dance day where friends, relatives, or anyone can drop in to eat and chat.

Thus katsina dances are not only ceremonies, they are also social occasions for friends and relatives to gather. Katsina ceremonies can also serve to redistribute food. Katsinas can also be disciplinarians, such as the Sooso'yokt (or ogres), who come in February during the Bean Dance, or Powamuya. Individual katsinas can also help to organize work parties to clear springs. Numerous katsinas have warriors' marks, parallel painted stripes on the cheeks (Colton 1975:Fig. 19), suggesting that katsinas once aided the Hopi in war. Zuni oral traditions are filled with katsinas fighting one another and opposing or abetting the Zuni people in wars with their neighbors (Wright 1985). Similarly, at Acoma the people re-enact an attack on their village by katsinas (White 1932:88–94). The concept of war and its relation to the katsina cult is a theme that will be returned to later.

Katsina ceremonies are primarily celebrated to encourage rain, although they may be sponsored by an individual who has been ill or who has a sick relative. Whereas curing aspects to katsina ritual are poorly developed at Hopi, curing is the major focus of Keresan and eastern Pueblo katsina ceremonialism.

When a Hopi becomes a katsina impersonator, he does not look upon the mask that transforms him (all katsina, male and female, are impersonated by men) into a katsina as merely a mask, or something to cover his face to avoid recognition. Hopi katsina impersonators refer to their masks as friends. In fact to refer to one of these friends as a mask in the presence of a Hopi is to encourage correction and perhaps a lengthy lecture. The mask is a very sacred object and when donned is believed by the Hopi impersonator to transform him into a katsina. In other words, the mask represents the spirit of the katsina that, when donned, joins the spirit of the man. The performers are no longer mere men, but are katsina spirits who will take the prayers of the village populace for rain, healing, fertility, or whatever, to the gods who control such phenomena.

Thus we see the katsina in its third form, as a spirit. These spirits reside in the springs and the high country around the Hopi Mesas from about the winter solstice to late July. In late July at the end of katsina season the katsinas return to their homes in the Third World, beneath today's Fourth World, where all deceased reside. They enter the Third World via a ladder descending from the top of the San Francisco Peaks (Whiting 1964). Most Hopi believe this Third World is in or beneath what today we refer to as the Grand Canyon.

The katsina as a spirit is a complex phenomenon, often unclear in the minds of the Hopi. In their broadest consideration, katsinas are spiritual intermediaries or messengers to the Hopi deities that visit the villages from December to July. They are embodied in the masks and the men who don them. They take the prayers sung in the katsina songs and uttered in the days spent preparing for the public dance to the Hopi gods. This pantheon of gods controls the weather and the growth of the Hopi crops and ultimately holds the survival of the people in their collective hands. These gods may even be depicted in masked form or as dolls, such as the Masau-u katsina, who represents the ruler of earth and god of death and fire, but in reality they are not katsinas. It is vitally important that the prayers are performed and uttered correctly so that the gods will hear them and honor them.

But what is a katsina spirit and where does it come from? There are two levels of katsina, just as there are two levels in western Pueblo society, the priests, or leaders, and the nonpriests. The priestly class of katsina (Bunzel 1932) are referred to by Colton (1975) as mong or chief katsinas. The nonpriest katsinas are generally referred to as dancing katsinas recognizing their major functions in katsina ceremony. Among the Hopi, chief katsinas are totemic images to clans, each clan claiming descent or some ancient relationship to a specific chief katsina. At Acoma and Zuni, chief katsinas are more closely tied to one of the kivas. The specific chief katsina tied to a clan reflects the status of the clan in Hopi society. Thus the highest ranking chief katsina is associated with the highest ranking clan. The clan owns the mask to the specific chief katsina, and only a member of that clan can impersonate that katsina. These masks are quite old. Photographs of chief katsina masks in ceremonies in the 1870s through 1910s appear to show the same masks that one sees in modern ceremonies! The chief masks are stored in special rooms owned by the clan whose members care for them.

The chief katsinas perform only in one or more of the three major Hopi katsina ceremonies; Soyalang, Powamuya, and Nimanywu. Soyalang welcomes the katsinas back to Hopi at the winter solstice. Powamuya and the associated Patsavu ceremony are the initiation of young people into the cult. Nimanywu, just after the summer solstice, sends the katsinas home again. Each of these ceremonies is eight days versus the standard four days for other katsina dances. In general at Acoma, Zuni, and Hopi, chief katsinas do not dance but instead participate in specific functions during these most sacred of katsina ceremonies.

Each member of the katsina cult who participates also owns a mask for dancing katsinas that is prepared for each ceremony by repainting or otherwise modifying the basic mask to obtain the desired effect. These masks are stored at the individual's house or in his kiva. The nonchief katsinas, for example a corn katsina, can dance any weekend, although some katsinas are much more popular and are danced more frequently. Katsina dances can be either mixed or unmixed. Mixed katsina dances have many different katsinas dancing together. Unmixed dances have all katsinas identical with the exception of side dancers. Katsina dances are line dances, in contrast to circle dances that are more characteristic of Indian ritual and nonkatsina Pueblo ritual (Bunzel 1932:896–899). The dancers move rhythmically in coordinated movements but do not interact with one another. Bodily movements are restricted to the legs and arms. Songs are always sung accompanied by an instrument, either a drum or a resonated rasp. Additional sound effects are provided by the dancers who usually have rattles carried in one hand, turtle shells with hoof clappers that resonate with the rhythmic foot-stomping, and sometimes strings of bells.

Katsinas are most involved with the bringing of rain to Hopi fields. Katsinas live in the underworld, dancing in villages there during the time they are not in the modern Hopi world. According to Whiting (1964), when called by the priests at Soyalang, they ascend a ladder to the top of the San Francisco Peaks and travel as clouds to the Hopi villages. As cloud people katsinas become tied to ancestor worship and the concept of the katsina cult as the cult of the dead (Bunzel 1932:901; Titiev 1944). This concept applies to all three western Pueblos. When Hopis die their faces are covered with cotton, and they travel to the underworld to be born again as clouds to bring rain to their children. Therefore, katsinas are believed in part to be ancestors of the Hopi people. This complicated relationship leads to the Hopi-supported view of katsina spirits as deceased Hopi. Exceptions to these would probably include the priestly class of katsinas. Katsina religion is thus commonly viewed as involving ancestor worship.

The Katsina Cult as a Pan-Pueblo Phenomenon

For the Hopi the katsina cult is the only universal aspect of ceremonialism. When children reach the age of seven to eleven years, they select ceremonial parents of clans different from their own. These individuals are responsible for teaching them the ceremonial system, a first step being initiation into the katsina society. After initiation the individual may participate in ceremonies (if a boy) and gain understanding of the meaning and value of the katsina to the Hopi. Initiation, therefore, carries age-grading significance and marks a step on the ladder to adulthood. The soul of a child that dies before initiation cannot go to the underworld as a cloud or katsina but returns to the ceiling of its mother's home where it hovers until reborn in the next child (Titiev 1944:129). This is also the reason children might be buried in the floors of their homes.

The above characterization of the katsina society applies to the other western Pueblos, Zuni, Acoma, and Laguna. In the Tewa, southern Tiwa, and eastern Keresan villages the katsinas are associated with the moiety divisions (Eggan 1979:228), and moiety association is a prerequisite to dancing with masks. However, Dozier (1970:156) links katsina ceremonies at Zia and Santa Ana to the medicine societies and not to the moieties; and Goldfrank (1927:44) associates the katsina ceremonies with the noncuring Curdzi society at Cochiti. Moiety membership is generally through initiation of children ages seven to eleven.

In the Tewa villages, as a general rule, there are no katsina dances. Exceptions are Tesuque (Edelman and Ortiz 1979:331) and Santa Clara (Arnon and Hill 1979:301), although figures representative of katsinas are part of kiva paraphernalia at San Ildefonso (Edelman 1979:308). There are katsina-like groups, identified with oxua, in all Tewa villages with membership generally along the lines of moiety divisions. The southern Tiwa village of Isleta has katsina-like disciplinarians and ceremonies associated with the moieties; however, katsina ceremonialism is a late nineteenth century introduction to Isleta from Laguna (Parsons 1932, 1939:129, 349; Ellis 1979:445; Harvey 1963; Dozier 1970:156). So little is known about Sandia ceremonialism that no conclusions can be drawn (Brandt 1979).

Katsina ceremonialism apparently does not exist at the northern Tiwa villages of Picuris and Taos, although katsinas are recognized at Taos as dwellers in the underworld (Anderson 1951:216). Whether this has always been the case is not known. There is rock art in the vicinity dating to the fourteenth or fifteenth century that depicts katsinas and katsina masks, suggesting that katsina ceremonialism was present at that time. The situation among the Towa is similar to the western Pueblos with the katsina religion in operation at Jemez (Eggan 1950:308). Katsina representations are possible at Pecos which was abandoned in 1838 (Schroeder 1979a:434–435).

In the western Keresan villages of Laguna and Acoma, katsina ceremonies are well established. All of the youth are initiated into the cult at an early age (seven to eleven). The knowledge of village ceremonialism and responsibility gained at this time means the initiation is representative of an age-grade status. The katsina dances are performed in the spring, summer, and occasionally in the fall. Their purposes are rainmaking, fertility, and curing (Eggan 1950:243–244, 279–280; Ellis 1979:444–445). This latter purpose may be indigenous or borrowed from Zuni or Isleta (Ellis 1979:444–445).

At Zuni katsina religion is also well established. In order to become valuable to the village and people, all boys are initiated into the katsina society. Katsina initiation occurs in two stages, first when they are five to nine, and second when they are ten to fourteen. A boy participates in katsina ceremonies after being initiated into one of six men's groups or kivas. The members of the kiva sponsor and are responsible for his ceremonial knowledge. At this time the boys are whipped and learn about the katsinas. This is an age-grade status for Zuni boys. Formerly women were occasionally initiated into the katsina society in order to cure them of being frightened of the katsinas (Tedlock 1979:502). Katsinas are associated with rain, fertility, and curing (Tedlock 1979:502).

Thus at least for Zuni, and probably for Acoma and Laguna, the katsina religion is open to all (although women are not encouraged to join in Zuni) and is an age-grade status, much as at Hopi. None of these villages has the moiety system. All of these villages or village groups are organized around the matrilineage in terms of social structure and are crosscut by religious sodalities or societies, one of which is the katsina society, the only one open to all. In villages where a moiety system exists, it crosscuts and overrides the societies, in particular katsina rituals, often in village-specific fashion. Thus participation in moiety functions is an age-grade status replacing that of the katsina association in the western Pueblos. Generally, to participate in a katsina dance, one must be first initiated into a moiety.

One aspect of katsina religion that has been discussed extensively in the last few years and seems associated with the katsina ritual in all villages is its tie to the dead (Harvey 1972:203). Eggan (1950:91, 201, 203, 243) notes this association at Acoma, Zuni, and Hopi. Titiev (1944:129) notes this association among the Hopi and considers katsina religion to be a generalized kind of ancestor worship. This association among modern eastern Pueblos is more variable, probably due to the dilution caused by Spanish Catholicism. Nevertheless, wherever the katsina ritual is strong and operative, the association with ancestor worship is unmistakable. The association is present, but weak, in the eastern Keres villages and is much stronger in the Tewa-speaking villages and at Jemez. At Taos there appears to be a tie between the dead and katsinas, but this relationship is not apparent at Picuris or the southern Tiwa villages (Anderson 1951: 214–217). In summary, the themes of rain, fertility, (possibly curing), and association with the dead are universally associated with the katsina in the Pueblo world.

Modern Katsina Symbolism and Meaning

Katsinas are symbolic of Hopi and Zuni culture, and to a lesser extent at other Pueblos. This symbolism is true not only for the Pueblo culture, but also for outside cultures. The dominant American culture recognizes katsinas as readily as do the practitioners. Perhaps one of the original purposes of katsina symbolism and iconography was to separate practitioners from nonpractitioners, or us and them. This is most readily accomplished through the public performances that members of other cultures are welcome to witness. The color, the dramatic presentation, the group dynamics, the obvious esoteric knowledge involved all serve to reinforce this perception. What aspect of the public performance most distinguishes the katsinas? The mask. The katsina mask symbolizes the presence of the cult and reinforces the esoteric knowledge required to produce and wear the mask. Another major feature of a katsina dance is its group nature. Katsinas rarely dance in small groups or alone but in large groups. The public performances involve the dancing katsinas, not the priestly katsinas, perhaps because the risk of leaking esoteric knowledge is minimized and controlled by the practitioners. A third aspect of the public performance of katsina ceremonies is their setting. The dances are held in the major plaza of the village. Ideally, the plaza is surrounded on two or more sides by multiple-storied structures whose rooftops serve as viewing platforms for the ceremony.

But there are deeper levels of symbolism for the katsina cult used within Pueblo society. One of the purposes of these symbols is to differentiate members of the society. Only sponsors can plan and present a katsina ceremony. The specifics of this symbolism are so complex, variable, and poorly understood by nonpractitioners that they will not concern us except to note them. The critical notion is to recognize that katsina religion goes deep into the fabric of all Pueblo society, with the possible exception of Tiwa-speaking groups, and is the dominant ritual medium at Hopi, at Zuni, and at Acoma.

It has already been noted that the political structure of Hopi, Zuni, and, to a lesser extent, Acoma society is paralleled in the katsina world. It is equally important to note that katsina ceremony reflects and reinforces the fabric of Pueblo social structure. To make a village function most efficiently all segments (clans) must work together or cooperate for the better of the whole. This cooperation is developed through a theocracy of clan leaders (usually brothers of the female leaders of the clans, which are matrilineal and matrilocal). Each clan leader has a specific role, such as War "Chief," Sunwatcher (Sun) "Chief," or Village "Chief." Each role is performed as part of the whole to make the society and society's ritual work. The organization of katsina society closely parallels that of western Pueblo society.

Rule is by example rather than by force, for the only constituency each leader has is his own clan. The inherent divisiveness of the clan-based society is counteracted by the katsina cult. (For a different perspective on Hopi clans see Whiteley 1985, 1986). In order for the ceremony to be conducted properly, and thus for the katsinas to take the proper prayers to the gods, all segments of society must cooperate. Each clan plays a vital role in the proper functioning of katsina ceremony. By extension katsina ceremony is essential to maintaining cooperation within a Hopi village among all or most segments of the society. Many aspects of katsina ceremonialism involve interclan cooperation or sharing, such as food redistribution and initiation.

Thus in western Pueblos membership in the katsina cult is universal and is used to cement the divergent elements of the culture together. This is accomplished in part through required cooperation and sharing between clans in order to make the ceremonies work. Katsina ritual also sanctifies the structure of western Pueblo society. Encoded in this structure are the existence and essential nature of western Pueblo society built on the matrilineage, but also the two-level nature of western Pueblo society: the priests and the nonpriests, or common people. Thus katsina religion is a reflection of western Pueblo culture in microcosm, and as such, katsinas act as symbols of western Pueblo culture to outside observers as well as to their practitioners. In eastern Keresan, Tewa, and Jemez villages, all males are required to be members of a kiva group which works through moiety divisions to integrate village members. In general, katsina ritual is less pervasive in eastern Pueblos; nevertheless, it plays an important role in eastern Pueblo ritual, with the possible exception of Tiwa-speaking villages.

Material Correlates

Symbols of the katsina cult to the outside world have been noted above and include the mask, the performance in a group, and the setting in a plaza surrounded in part by rooms. Other activities or objects associated with katsina ceremony in Pueblo society include the kiva where the ceremony is planned, practiced, and occasionally staged; line dancing with songs and instruments; private rest areas used between public performances; food preparation and distribution; and association with rain or snow, fertility (usually equated with corn), and death.

In terms of costume, katsina dancers always wear a mask, and the male katsinas wear a belt or sash and a kilt woven (ideally) of cotton, carry implements in one or both hands, and have something tied to one or both legs that will produce sound as the performers move their legs in time to the song and drum or rasp. These are usually turtle shells with animal hoof clappers or shell tinklers. Female katsinas differ from males in wearing a manta (women's dress) instead of a kilt, in wearing the long white moccasins traditionally worn by women, and in seldom having objects tied to their legs because they usually do not dance. The sash/belt and kilt are woven in particular color schemes and designs among the Hopi. An integral part of the design scheme is a rectangle on a contrastive colored background with a small opening on one long side of the rectangle. The design is said to symbolize the katsina dance line. Another design occurring on sashes, belts, and kilts is the terraced "cloud" symbol. The katsinas themselves usually carry, wear, or are decorated with items rich with meaning. Douglas fir branches, which grow in cool damp places, are often worn or carried. Tadpoles, cloud and rain symbols, lightning, corn, all may be painted on the mask covering the head of the dancer. Lightning or snake designs can even be painted on the body.

A review of these associations reveals that few are unique to the katsina cult, although originally they could have been. Nonkatsina ceremonies can use kivas in much the same way, can stage public performances in the same plazas, can involve food preparation and redistribution, and can involve rain/snow, fertility, and be associated with afterlife (Titiev 1944). Seemingly unique to katsina ceremony are line (versus solitary, paired, or circle) dancing, rest areas, and costume (Bunzel 1932:896).

Summary

The discussion in this section on katsina symbolism has shown that the katsina cult functions in many different ways in western Pueblo culture both crosscutting and institutionalizing western Pueblo social structure. At the most general level the katsina cult serves to differentiate cultures that have the esoteric knowledge to stage the katsina cult from those that do not. To non-Pueblos katsinas symbolize Pueblo culture. Within western Pueblo society the cult is a mirror of western Pueblo political structure and social structure, but it also is the warp that holds the weft of western Pueblo society together, as represented by clans. Perhaps most importantly, katsinas are very personalized spirits. They represent ancestors, basically friendly spirits, that an individual can become one with when the mask is donned. This personal approach to ritual allowing the individual to communicate with his gods is *the* unique aspect of katsina ritual that distinguishes it from all other masked dancing among Indian tribes in North America (Bunzel 1932:902–903). Although individual expression is not encouraged, it is permitted within the katsina ritual drama. There is even achieved status among men who dance katsina. Better singers perform key roles in the katsina ritual drama needed in some performances.

The Archaeology of the Katsina Cult

Singular among all of the material attributes of the katsina cult of the Pueblo Indians is the mask. Although the mask is unlikely to be preserved in the archaeological record, it can be depicted as an art form and often was, as well as assume symbolic meaning. Altars associated with katsina ceremonies at Acoma use the cloud symbol to represent the katsina because they bring rain. A common name for Acoma katsina is shiwanna, also the Acoma word for storm cloud (White 1932:64). Terraced elements of design are often described as clouds by Pueblo informants. Such icons are frequently depicted on kilts or sashes worn by dancers and are part of some katsina masks in the form of tablitas. Examples are the Hemis Katsina, the Sa'lako Katsina, and the Butterfly Katsina at Hopi. Terraced rims to historic and modern Pueblo ceramic vessels signify a ritualistic function. These vessels are usually for aspersing the dancers during public performances to enhance the possibilities of rain. Although terraced vessels and cloud designs are associated with modern katsina religion, these designs are also used in association with other elements of western Pueblo ritual. Whether painted terraces on vessels, especially prehistoric ones, symbolize clouds or rain is a complex matter. Whether they symbolize the katsina cult is problematical and can only be interpreted in the context of discovery. In the total absence of other katsina cult or rainmaking artifacts, it is unlikely that terraced elements of design on prehistoric vessels always signified clouds. The other katsina cult icon, the open rectangle, is rarely seen on non-Hopi ceremonial attire, suggesting a restricted range of use. It has been depicted on Hopi ceramic bowls that were ritually associated (Adams 1979a:Plate 5; Wade and McChesney 1981:Plate IV-1).

With the exceptions of iconography, katsina cult material correlates fall into two categories: perishable and nonrestrictive. Perishable material remains include katsina dolls and masks made of wood, leather, gourd, or other perishable material. Preservation of perishable katsina cult material culture in pre-Hispanic contexts is not likely and none is known. Instances of nonperishable katsina-like dolls have been noted by Haury (1945) and in the collections of the Museum of Northern Arizona (Danson 1966:11), but neither is undeniably a katsina doll. In fact it is likely that neither is for reasons detailed later.

The nonrestrictive category includes items of material culture that, although associated with the cult, are not associated only with the cult. Prime examples in this category are kivas, plazas, prayer feathers, shell tinklers, turtle shells (carapaces), and the like. Nevertheless, some relationships in material culture not notable in the lists compiled from modern practice of the cult will be examined when the prehistoric cult is considered.

Because all katsina cult material culture outside iconography is either perishable or nonrestrictive, the only satisfactory beginning point to identifying the prehistoric katsina cult is to restrict our evidence to the katsina mask. Thus our evidence will be iconographic. Unless a mask is depicted, the assumption will be that the cult was not present. Once the evidence of depictions of the katsina mask have been presented, other aspects of material culture will be examined to determine the possible effect the cult had on the society it joined.

The recognition of material culture correlates to the cult are essential to identifying its presence in the prehistoric record. Development of the cult might correlate with changes in social, political, or ceremonial structure of prehistoric Pueblo culture. In other words, based on modern western Pueblo ethnographic studies, it is likely that the appearance of the katsina cult in the archaeological record is associated with other societal changes. Is the cult the cause or the result of these changes or do they codevelop? These relationships are the central concern of this book. The basis to the analysis is the assumption that the adoption of the katsina cult into pre-historic Pueblo society made the culture more adaptive and more likely to survive.

The Katsina Cult Hypothesis

Before looking at the archaeological record, it will be profitable to examine the effects on Hopi, and generally western Pueblo, culture of the katsina cult and to phrase these effects in terms of implications to our working hypothesis. As generally stated above, the *hypothesis* is:

If the katsina cult became integrated into the culture of a prehistoric group, then significant and recognizable changes in the material remains of that culture will be identifiable.

Assumptions

Basic assumptions underlying the hypothesis are: (1) that the katsina cult is a recognizable entity in the archaeological record, and (2) that the katsina mask is an undeniable indicator of the existence of the cult. Cole (1989a) has examined specific elements of katsina design and has concluded that the mask is the only reliable indicator of the presence of katsina ceremonialism. If the object on which the mask is depicted is portable, such as a stone slab or a ceramic vessel, then it will not be possible to suggest that the cult was present at the location where the artifact was found. If on the other hand, the depiction is not portable, such as rock art or kiva murals, then the argument for presence of the cult is considerably strengthened.

Implications

Implications derived from the hypothesis will detail the specific results expected by analog to the modern Pueblos. The implications are intended to outline the structure of katsina cultism for Pueblo society in the political, social, and ceremonial spheres of the culture.

(1) If the katsina cult is integrative, crosscutting the clan-based social structure of western Pueblo society, then habitation site size should either increase substantially when the cult is introduced and integrated or be present in already existing large habitation sites.

(2) If an important aspect of the katsina cult is public performances to bond the practitioners and separate them from the nonpractitioners,

then a plaza area surrounded on at least two sides by rooms should be present during or after the introduction of the cult.

(3) If the symbolic aspects of the katsina cult are important, then cult iconography should be present in and around the habitation site at readily visible points as rock art.

    (a) The most recognizable icon will be the katsina mask (Cole 1989a, 1989b).

    (b) Other icons, such as cloud symbols or open rectangles, may be present, but will be established only in association with the mask.

(4) If the katsina cult is present, then a rest area for katsinas between public performances will be present on the edge of the habitation site out of sight of the performance area and the audience.

(5) If the katsina cult is present, other material correlates should be present that cannot be defined using the modern cult. The following are possibilities:

    (a) Kivas of the western Pueblo are rectangular or square, quite different from eastern Pueblo kiva form which is round. Appearance of square or rectangular kivas is relatively late in the prehistory of northeastern Arizona and northwestern New Mexico and could be correlated with the katsina cult.

    (b) Food preparation and redistribution are associated with katsina cult, and all Pueblo, ritual. Development of new means of food preparation or communal food storage areas could be associated with the katsina cult.

Other changes in the material culture of habitation sites with the katsina cult can be predicted; however, these are the result of increased settlement size as much as due to the presence of the cult. Examples of such changes are expanded or improved agricultural systems, increased trade, and possibly craft or resource specialization. Such changes will be noted, if they seem appropriate to the discussion.

    In the pages to follow the discussion will fall into three basic categories. First will be a discussion of past work on the subject and historical evidence suggesting presence of the cult. After setting the stage, a detailed discussion of the evidence for the presence or absence of the cult throughout the Mogollon Rim and Colorado Plateau country will be reviewed. Finally, the meaning of the cult and consideration of the hypothesis and test implications will be presented.

2

Previous Documentation and Research

Under a variety of names and interpretations, it is evident that the katsina cult was widely distributed from the beginning of the Spanish period. The earliest mention was in 1582 by Luxan, the chronicler of the Espejo expedition (Hammond and Rey 1928:79; White 1934:626). A typical description by the Spanish, for example, is one following the Pueblo Revolt of 1680. The Pueblo leader Popé was accused of seeing to it that

> . . . [The Pueblos] at once erected and rebuilt their houses of idolatry called estufas, and made very ugly masks in imitation of the devil in order to dance the dance of the kachina; . . . (Hackett and Shelby, vol. II, 1970:237–238, 245–253).

The first written form of the word katsina was in 1625, Cacina (Dockstader 1954:59).

Fray Alonso de Benavides, during his three-year stay in New Spain from 1626–1629, ordered katsina masks burned (Kessell 1979:224). In addition nearly every Spanish account relates the problems the Franciscan missionaries had with the continued practice by the natives of their idolatrous religion despite all of the Spaniards' attempts at its suppression. Occasionally singled out were the masked katsina dances (Simmons 1979:181). This policy of suppression was the Spanish position throughout the 1598–1821 period of the New Spain colony, although their position ameliorated after the 1680 Pueblo Revolt. Such repression rarely succeeded in eliminating the practice, but did succeed in forcing it underground among the eastern Pueblo groups, and certainly resulted in a mixed native and Catholic religion among the eastern Pueblos. From documentary evidence, Dockstader (1954:59) has determined that in 1660 katsina dances were performed in Hopi, Zuni, Quarai, Tesuque, Chilili, Isleta, San Ildefonso, San Juan, Cochiti, Las Salinas, Tanos, Galisteo, Sandia, Jemez, San Marcos, La

Alameda, Puaray, Pojouque, and Santa Fe. These would involve, in addition to Hopi and Zuni, the southern Tiwa, Tano, Tewa, Keresan, Towa, and Tompiro speaking villages (see Fig. 1. 1).

The distribution of modern Pueblo groups having active katsina ceremonies is parallel to those groups least affected by the Spanish mission program. This is further brought home, as we shall see later, by the apparent distribution of the cult preceding Spanish contact. Although it seems unlikely that the katsina cult would be eliminated by the Spanish program in several villages, while other elements of the native religion survived, it is food for thought. As support for this argument, the Snake Dance was reported by the Spanish to have been performed in many of the New Mexico Pueblo villages. It was particularly repugnant to the Spanish, and its vigorous suppression resulted in its extinction everywhere today except the Hopi villages (Simmons 1979:179). Perhaps the public performances of the katsina dances were so egregious to the Spanish authorities that they were singled out. Again, it would seem likely that the Tewa and Tiwa would merely have gone underground with their katsina religion. One intriguing further possibility is that the katsina cult was less powerful among the Tiwa and Tewa. Its emphasis on rainfall may have held less significance to groups using irrigation along the Rio Grande River and more elaborate dry farming techniques than in the west. Also, as noted earlier, the eastern Pueblo moiety systems were the significant integrative institutions rather than the katsina cult, which is dominant in the western Pueblos. In either case, the cult may have been less difficult to dislodge than among groups where it was relatively much stronger (Cordell 1979:145–147, 150–151).

Among the non-Spanish Euroamericans, the earliest contact with the Pueblo came before 1820. During the period 1815–1840 the only contacts were by fur trappers and explorers. With the onset of the Mexican-American War, 1846–1848, the Euroamerican presence increased dramatically. Early expeditions sponsored by the federal government were primarily military reconnaissances. By the 1850s there were surveys for railroad routes, general mapping, missionary forays, and contacts by the United States Indian Bureau. The best early description of the katsina dances was by Dr. P. G. S. Ten Broeck, assistant surgeon to the U.S. Army, in 1852. He describes the ceremonies, masks, costumes, and dance rituals at Walpi, a Hopi village (Dockstader 1954:77). It remained for the early ethnographic accounts of the 1880s and 1890s by Stephen (1936) for the Hopi, by Cushing (1896) and Stevenson (1904) for the Zuni, and by Bandelier (1890–1892) for the other Pueblo groups to give us the first details of the depth and breadth of the cult. Dockstader (1954) presents a good account of the history of the katsina cult in documents.

Thus, although historic accounts are not available for every decade of this historic period (1600–1900), it is evident that the katsina cult was in existence and active throughout the area during early Spanish contact and continued unbroken in the villages in which it exists to this day.

Past Studies

Past studies of the origin, evolution, and meaning of the katsina cult have taken numerous tacks. For instance, Parsons (1930, 1933, 1939) suggested the cult was introduced by Mexicans who accompanied the Spanish conquistadors. This purely historical explanation seems unlikely from the weight of evidence of Spanish historical documents of the contact period and numerous lines of archaeological evidence.

The evidence for the katsina cult invariably rests with iconographic similarities between modern Pueblo katsina ceremony and dress and archaeological ones. Thus katsina masklike drawings are found in rock art (Cole 1989a, 1989b; Schaafsma 1972; Schaafsma and Schaafsma 1974), kiva murals (Dutton 1963; Hibben 1955, 1960, 1975; Smith 1952), and pottery (Adams 1981a; Carlson 1982b; Ferg 1982; Fewkes 1896, 1919; Hays 1989; Smith 1952; and various others).

As to origin of the cult, other than historical data, archaeologists compare iconographic similarities in the material record to historic counterparts to determine a source. Most recent archaeological evidence has authorities in agreement that the source is Mexican (Carlson 1970; Di Peso 1974; Dutton 1963; Hibben 1966, 1967; Smith 1952). Although the above all believe the incursion is recent, dating between 1150 and 1400, the source and the route are still much in debate. Casas Grandes or the Casas Grandes area has been cited by Di Peso (1974), Carlson (1970), and Adams (1981b). On the other hand, Schaafsma and Schaafsma (1974) seem to feel the development was indigenous to the Jornada of the southern New Mexico–El Paso area, although noting Mexican iconography and influence. Carlson (1982a) recently has also expressed the opinion that the cult developed in the Mimbres area citing the work of the Schaafsmas. In contrast to the others, he does not believe the source of the cult is Mexican, but views the similarities in iconography as coming from an ancient common root dating back to the coming of maize agriculture (1982a:153). Development of archaeological traits later associated with the cult, such as square kivas and large, plaza-oriented pueblos, has been discussed by Reed (1948; 1956) and by Johnson (1965).

Adams (1981a:5) has argued for two periods of influence from Mexico, one dating to the 1100s following the route through the Rio Grande Valley and a later one in the late 1200s following the San Pedro River Valley up to the Mogollon Rim and White Mountains. The latter route was first proposed by Carlson (1970:112) and supported by Di Peso (1974). The Rio Grande route is primarily used to justify the presence of new rock art motifs in the Jornada and Mimbres areas (cf. Schaafsma and Schaafsma 1974).

A third possible route along the west coast of Mexico and through the Hohokam region has also been suggested. This follows at least one route of Mexican influence and trade into the Hohokam heartland (Haury 1976:345; Riley 1987). The archaeological evidence for the latter is not compelling due first to lack of solid iconographic evidence and second, to lack of well-dated continuity in material culture across the needed areas. The reasoning for this suggested source is the obvious Mexican influence shared by the katsina cult and the Hohokam culture. In fact, however, the strength of Mesoamerican influence on the Hohokam faded after 1200 (Haury 1976:347–348). Additionally, during the classic period, A.D. 1100–1450, there was a contraction of Hohokam settlement (Gumerman and Haury 1979:86–90). By the time of the appearance of the katsina cult in the Pueblo area in the 14th century, the extension of the Salado to the north and east of the Hohokam area (although Kelley [1966:107] sees a possible west Mexican origin for the Salado), possibly related to the appearance of the katsina cult, had already disrupted any direct flow from the Hohokam area. (See Moulard [1984] for a discussion of possible early Hohokam influence in the Mimbres Mogollon and the ultimate reflection of this influence in Mimbres iconography.) Whatever Hohokam influence reached the Pueblo world of the fourteenth century did so through a Salado filter. The influence of the Salado on the Hohokam in fact suggests that cultural traits were moving from the east and north into the Hohokam area rather than to the north and east out of the Hohokam area.

In summary, then, there appear to be two possible archaeological sources for the cult, two routes of access to the Southwest, and three periods of appearance proposed by the various studies of the past 30 years. Sources are the Mimbres/Jornada area or Casas Grandes area. Routes are the Rio Grande Valley or the San Pedro River Valley. Periods of appearance in the Southwest are ancient (associated with maize), 1000–1200 (Jornada/Mimbres), and 1250–1350 (Casas Grandes and its interaction sphere, including the Salado). Each of these will be considered in more detail later. Additionally, the possibility of a relatively indigenous development is explored.

3

Distribution of Prehistoric Katsina Mask Iconography

As stressed in the first chapter, the goals of this book are to understand the concept of katsina and the framework of Pueblo culture that surrounds this concept; second, to be able to identify material correlates to the katsina that would be preserved in the archaeological record and to trace their distribution through time and space; third, to recognize other changes in the archaeological remains of groups that have or are in contact with katsina iconography; and fourth, to be able to draw upon the first three to understand why the katsina cult was developed where and when it was.

This chapter will focus on the second and third goals: the material correlates of the cult and associated changes in the cultures having or in contact with the cult. As noted in chapter 1, the katsina mask is the only clear-cut symbol of the katsina cult. Therefore, a starting point for looking at the distribution of the katsina cult prehistorically is to evaluate the distribution of motifs thought to be katsina masks or katsina figures in the archaeological record. The next task is to place these depictions in a temporal framework. Finally, in this chapter other changes in the archaeological record that seem to occur in conjunction with the appearance of katsina designs will be noted. To address the relations of katsina iconography to other changes in the archaeological record and ultimately to changes in the structure of prehistoric Pueblo society, it is not necessary to identify each katsina. No attempt is made to do so here. Wherever such observations have been made by previous researchers, native informants, or a strong resemblance to a modern katsina can be made, specific katsinas may be identified.

As developed in chapter 2, the documentary evidence and research of previous authorities suggest that the origin and early development of the katsina cult are pre-contact. Therefore, our search will focus on the archaeological record between A.D. 1000 and 1500 with particular attention paid to the 1250–1400 time period when, as we shall see, major changes in the archaeological record occur and the first widespread appearance of katsina iconography is recognized.

A number of approaches to this complex data base were considered with a geographic approach settled upon. The other choice was to look at the distribution of the katsina cult plus various changes in the archaeological record, such as village size, pottery design changes, and the like, individually as they vary through time and space. The geographical approach was chosen for two reasons. First, the focus of this chapter is an analysis of the distribution of katsina mask designs on various media. To communicate the cultural and environmental differences that play such an important role in understanding the development of the katsina cult to an audience not familiar with the details might prove confusing indeed. The secondary purpose of this chapter is to note other changes in the archaeological remains of various areas that co-occur with the appearance of katsina designs. Many of these changes are local and quite interdependent and can best be treated within a geographic framework. A product of this chapter will be the identification of several patterns that appear to be cross cultural and to cross geographic boundaries. These will be analyzed in terms of their particular distributions in chapter 5.

The study region has been divided into seven geographic areas. These areas are based primarily on natural boundaries, cultural boundaries, archaeological boundaries, or rarely on convenience dictated by the data. The divisions have been chosen to facilitate discussion of the cult and, for our purposes here, katsina mask iconography. The geographic areas are middle Rio Grande Valley (Socorro to El Paso, including the Mimbres and Jornada areas), upper Rio Grande Valley (Socorro to Taos), Zuni area (Cibola, White Mountains, upper Little Colorado River Valley above the Puerco River intercept), Mogollon Rim, middle Little Colorado River Valley (Puerco River to Oraibi Wash), Verde Valley/San Francisco Peaks, and the Hopi Mesas area (Fig. 3.1).

Middle Rio Grande Valley

This area includes the Mimbres River Valley area and the Jornada area from the Rio Grande east. It is characterized by the type, El Paso Polychrome, after about A.D. 1200 (Fig. 3.1). The most compelling archaeological evidence in this area for masks lies with the rock art described by Schaafsma and Schaafsma (1974:537–539) and Schaafsma (1972:95–122) as

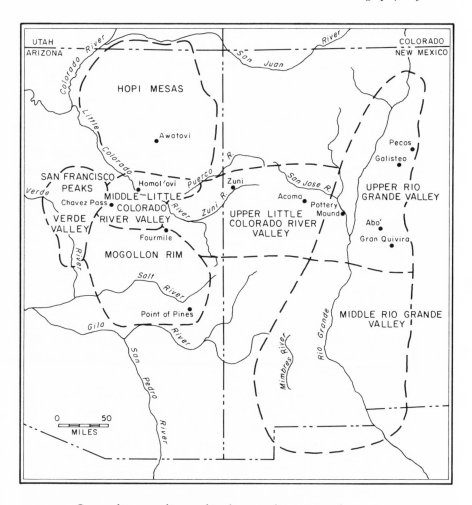

FIGURE 3.1. Geographic areas discussed in the text where potential
archaeological remains of the katsina cult have been located.
(Drawn by Ron Beckwith, Arizona State Museum)

Jornada style. This style has two areas of production, according to
Schaafsma (1972), the eastern area centering on the Rio Grande and
Jornada areas farther east, and the western area centering in the Mimbres
Valley. Many of these petroglyphs and pictographs are of masks, commonly shown with "almond-shaped eyes and a small triangular nose,
while the rest of the face may have abstract negative or positive decoration" (1974:538). One of the personages represented is described as having

the attributes of the Mexican deity, Quetzalcoatl (1974:538). As with this figure, many of the masked figures and anthropomorphs in the Mimbres area also have pointed headdresses or heads, or rounded heads, simply decorated or undecorated. These generally resemble the major, and perhaps early, deities of the Pueblos and some priestly katsinas. Best known and pan-Pueblo are the war gods, considered to be either twins or elder and younger brother. Among the Hopi the katsina chief, Ewtoto, and companion, Kokosori, are both round-headed. Ewtoto's lieutenant, Ahooli, has a pointed head. The solstice or Soyal katsina, is also round-headed. All of these are very simple and scantily adorned beings. These chief or priestly katsinas are in marked contrast to most of the other modern katsinas with elaborate headdresses and facial designs.

Other common depictions in the rock art throughout the middle Rio Grande Valley area are headdresses of animals or stepped headdresses (rain cloud symbols) resembling Hemis Katsinas. Cosgrove (1947) describes and illustrates several wooden tablitas recovered from caves in the upper Gila and Hueco areas of southwestern New Mexico. One tablita (1947:Fig. 1260) had a face with diamond eyes with eyebrows, a black triangular nose, and a rectangular toothed mouth. This figure is very similar to what are interpreted as katsina faces depicted in the rock art of the area and elsewhere. As noted by Cosgrove (1947:134), there is no indication that these were actually mounted on the head as tablitas are today. The katsina face tablita was apparently mounted on a stick and could have been carried as a standard or in front of the face. Crotty (1987) has also discussed hand-held masks and believes they need to be distinguished from face masks. Other katsinas, depicted in the Jornada area only, have facial characteristics resembling the Zuni and Hopi Shalako with the rainbow chin and horned headdress (Schaafsma 1972:116).

Rock art panels in the Mimbres area have been cross-dated to about A.D. 1000–1150 by their resemblance to forms and designs found on Mimbres Bold Face and Classic pottery types (Figs. 3.2 and 3.3). These types have recently been chronometrically dated (Anyon, Gilman, and LeBlanc 1981:219–220). The terminal dates for execution of the rock art in the eastern or Jornada area correspond with the close of the El Paso and San Andreas phases that are associated with elaborate, Jornada-like, polychrome pottery traditions (Schaafsma and Schaafsma 1974:538). When the rock art began is not as certain, but if associated with El Paso Polychrome pottery, it must date no earlier than A.D. 1200. Sites where the polychrome ceramic traditions flourished are generally large pueblos surrounding plazas.

FIGURE 3.2. Mimbres style rock art.
(Redrawn by Ron Beckwith, Arizona State Museum, from *Rock Art in New Mexico* by Polly Schaafsma, Fig. 86; permission granted by the Office of Cultural Affairs, Historic Preservation Division, State of New Mexico)

In summary, rounded- and pointed-head beings with either painted or masked faces are characteristic of the Mimbres area during the period 1000–1150. Dating perhaps as early, but probably not until the 1200s, are more elaborate faces, almost certainly masked, that are associated with the

FIGURE 3.3. Mimbres Classic Black-on-white pottery.
(Arizona State Museum collections; photograph by Helga Teiwes,
Arizona State Museum)

Jornada style in the Jornada area. These depict facial decoration and ear
and head attachments, such as tablitas, much like modern katsinas (cf.
Schaafsma 1972:102–103). As noted by Cosgrove (1947) and Crotty (1987),
there is some question whether some of the depictions are masks to be
worn on the face or are symbols and masks carried on sticks.

With the exception of Carlson (1982a), most authorities do not equate
Mimbres iconography to Pueblo katsinas (Brody 1977). Elements of a
more generalized southwestern ceremonialism including deities and the
war gods are the apparent foci of these depictions. Many of these elements, primarily nonkatsina, are the bases for modern Pueblo religion and
are shared throughout the Pueblo world.

In contrast, the later Jornada style does contain elements of masking clearly relatable to katsinas. The Jornada style differs in time and space from the earlier Mimbres style and is apparently the product of influence from the Casas Grandes area. El Paso Polychrome pottery is influenced by the Chihuahuan Polychrome of Casas Grandes and the surrounding areas. Increased size and changed layouts of settlements associated with the Jornada style are notable.

Upper Rio Grande Valley

This area includes most of the late prehistoric and historic Pueblo peoples, including the Piro, Tompiro, Keres, Tewa (including Tano), Tiwa, and Towa (Figs. 1.1 and 3.1). Although ceramic representations of katsina masks and masked figures do occur, they are not common (cf. Schaafsma and Schaafsma 1974:538). The preponderance of evidence comes from petroglyphs and painted kiva murals. The petroglyph sequence has been detailed by Schaafsma (1972) and is referred to as the Rio Grande style (Schaafsma and Schaafsma 1974:538–543). This style developed around 1325, using tree-ring dated ceramic types for cross-dating, and appears to be an extension of the Jornada style, with the Tompiro in the southeast Pueblo region sharing many characteristics with northern Jornada (1974:540). In addition to masks recognizable as antecedent to modern masks, the anthropomorphic figures are frequently shown dressed in sashes and kilts, much like modern katsinas (1974:540). Other ties to the Jornada style are the rainbow chin design, stepped or terraced tablita cloud motif, the four-pointed star, and plumed or horned serpent associated with Quetzalcoatl (Fig. 3.4).

The distribution of the petroglyphs as outlined by Schaafsma and Schaafsma (1974:543) extends into the Galisteo Basin, the Pajarito Plateau, and Frijoles Canyon. Isolated Rio Grande style glyphs have even been reported from the Taos Plateau area of the northern Rio Grande. If cult iconography can be equated to presence of the cult, then apparently the cult was strong among all Pueblo groups except the river Tewa and northern Tiwa. The cult was still strong among these groups when Spanish contact was made (Dockstader 1954).

Extensive excavation of kiva murals containing masked figures and other evidence of the cult have been uncovered, examined, and reported for Kuaua (Dutton 1963) and Pottery Mound (Hibben 1955, 1960, 1966, 1967, 1975). Mural panels have also been revealed at Gran Quivira (Peckham 1981) and Pueblo del Encierro near modern Cochiti (Schaafsma 1965).

FIGURE 3.4. Upper Rio Grande rock art.
(Photograph by E. Charles Adams)

Kuaua was excavated in the 1930s as a joint venture by the University of New Mexico, Museum of New Mexico, and School of American Research. Kuaua is now part of Coronado State Park and lies about 30 km north of Albuquerque on the west bank of the Rio Grande. Six kivas were located, two circular and four rectangular. One circular kiva and one square kiva belonged to the 1300–1400 occupation of Kuaua around the south plaza and contained no murals. A large circular kiva and three smaller rectangular kivas date to the 1450–1600 occupation. Two of the rectangular kivas, numbers III and VI, contained murals (Dutton 1963:22–33).

The murals depict altars, plants, animals, and anthropomorphs. The elements occur individually, in groups, and in scenes. All but five of the depictions are from Kiva III. The anthropomorphs are depicted in hair style, masks, and ritual paraphernalia bearing notable similarities to historic katsinas (Dutton 1963:34).

A total of 85 layers of plaster were on the walls of Kiva III of which 17 were painted (1963:49). Dutton (1963:201–203) gives a chronological rundown of the scenes depicted in Kiva III assuming one layer is equivalent to one year. Her interpretations are derived primarily from Zuni ethnography and using Zuni informants. According to these interpretations there are scenes of katsina initiation, katsinas involved in rabbit hunts, scalp dances involving the warrior society, and elaborate panels where both warrior and rain priests are involved in ceremonies (Fig. 3.5). The final portrayal is of the history myth from the time of emergence from the undermost world.

The square kiva and artistic continuity of the murals suggest association with the Jornada Mogollon to Dutton (1963:203). She sees two factions developing, the Warrior Society associated with the hunt, war, and fall and winter activities opposed by the Rain Society with which the katsina were associated and in power during the spring and summer

FIGURE 3.5. Kuaua kiva murals depicting the "Universe" with masked figures.
(Photography by Helga Teiwes, Arizona State Museum; originally published in *Sun Father's Way* by Bertha P. Dutton as Plate xv, by permission of the Laboratory of Anthropology, Museum of New Mexico)

(1963:203–204). The dual divisions by season are typical of moiety-based division of ritual power that is common in Pueblos in the area today. In terms of style the flat heads, striped chins, and terraced headdresses of many of the masked figures are more closely associated with Jornada style and differ considerably from the style of the Pottery Mound murals discussed below.

Whether the interpretations of the scenes by Dutton are correct or incorrect, there is little doubt that katsinas are present and some are very similar to historic or modern representatives. Depicted with fair certainty (Dutton 1963) are Paiyatima (Between the Sky), Kiaekapa (Corn Mother), Shulawitsi (Fire God), Kochininako (Yellow Corn Maiden), Kupishtaya (Lightning Man), Shumaikoli (Directional God), and Koyemshi (Mudhead). Also depicted are the Twin War Gods (Ahaiyuta), the White God (Shutsukya), the Black God (Kwelele), and the Horned Water Serpent (Kolowisi). All are Zuni identifications. Irrespective of the precise accuracy of the identity of specific katsinas, there is little doubt that major elements of katsina religion were known and present at Kuaua after A.D. 1450.

Pottery Mound was excavated from 1954 through the early 1960s by the University of New Mexico in conjunction with the School of American Research and the Museum of New Mexico under the direction of Frank Hibben. Pottery Mound is located on the Rio Puerco of the east, west of Los Lunas, New Mexico, about 50 km southwest of Albuquerque. It is a multiple-story, adobe village surrounding several plazas occupied from about 1300–1475, according to Hibben. At Pottery Mound, 17 kivas were found, all but one rectangular and all containing mural paintings. Some of the murals have been illustrated and discussed extensively by Hibben (1960, 1967, 1975). He dates the murals to about 1350–1450 on the basis of associated tree-ring dated pottery. Only four tree-ring dates on beams were obtained, all noncutting dates. Two are from Kiva 6 and date 1411 and 1427 (1975:10). Associated pottery types used to date murals elsewhere suggest that the beginning date for the Pottery Mound murals assigned by Hibben is probably too early and that more realistic dates for the murals may be closer to 1400–1500.

The murals depict subjects similar to those from Kuaua, but a wider range of subjects is presented due to the more extensive remains recovered. In contrast to the 20 mural paintings recovered from Kuaua, over 800 individual design fragments were recovered from Pottery Mound. The murals at Pottery Mound differ in style from those at Kuaua. Whereas the Kuaua murals are freely drawn and loosely arranged, in contrast, at Pot-

FIGURE 3.6. Pottery Mound kiva mural depicting the "Mosquito Man."
(Photograph by Helga Teiwes, Arizona State Museum; originally
published in *Kiva Art of the Anasazi at Pottery Mound* by Frank C.
Hibben as Fig. 86, by permission of K.C. Publications, Las Vegas)

tery Mound they are static, balanced, and carefully planned in execution
(Smith 1980:36–37), (Fig. 3.6). The Pottery Mound murals are quite similar
in style to those at the Hopi Mesas. Although Dutton concentrated on the
interpretation of the Kuaua murals using native informants, Hibben ac-
cented their connection to contemporary Mexican motifs, for example,
the plumed serpent and various Mexican birds (1975:59–63, Figs. 34, 42, 44,
45). He clearly sees the stimulus for the murals as Mexican (1975:59). He
also associates the murals with the arrival of the katsina cult among the
Pueblo people, noting similarities between modern katsinas and the
figures depicted on the walls (1975:80, 119). Although Hibben feels Pottery
Mound is probably Keresan and related to Acoma or Laguna (1975:54), he
also sees a close association, as noted by Smith, to the Hopi murals,
viewing Pottery Mound as possibly in part occupied by a contingent of

Hopi (1955:179; 1960:272), in contrast to later interpretations of Pottery Mound as ancestral to and stimulus for later Hopi achievements (Schaafsma and Schaafsma 1974:538–540).

Elements of design at Pottery Mound included katsinas and human figures, wild and domesticated plants, animals, altars, and secular and religious material culture of the people (Hibben 1960:272). In contrast to Kuaua, numerous pottery motifs and framing designs were found (Hibben 1975:Figs. 6, 13, 21, 22, 36, 50–54). Also depicted were figures carrying shields, according to Hibben (1975:130) a clear association to a war society. The war association is remindful of the Kuaua murals.

By 1475, decorations in glaze ware ceramic manufacturing areas of the Rio Grande developed curvilinear, abstract bird design styles similar to those on the Pottery Mound murals. Carlson (1970) calls this Fourmile style, and locally it is used to characterize Style IV glaze wares. In details, Style IV is almost identical to fifteenth century Sikyatki Polychrome designs, which were present at Pottery Mound. Additionally, about 1450, yellow-slipped glazes (Style III) were added to the red-slipped tradition. Thus, between 1450–1475 glaze ceramics very similar to Hopi yellow wares

FIGURE 3.7. Pottery Mound kiva mural showing macaws and masked dancer. (Photograph by Helga Teiwes, Arizona State Museum; originally published in *Kiva Art of the Anasazi at Pottery Mound* by Frank C. Hibben as Fig. 18, by permission of K.C. Publications, Las Vegas)

FIGURE 3.8. Pottery Mound kiva mural showing "soul faces."
(Photograph by Helga Teiwes, Arizona State Museum; originally
published in *Kiva Art of the Anasazi at Pottery Mound* by Frank C.
Hibben as Fig. 107, by permission of K.C. Publications, Las Vegas)

were manufactured and broadly traded in the upper Rio Grande area.
Manufacture apparently centered in the Galisteo Basin and at Tunque
Pueblo, southwest of modern Santa Fe (Snow 1982). The 1450–1475 date
attributed to this style change underscores the likelihood that the Pottery
Mound kiva murals are fifteenth century rather than fourteenth century.

Unfortunately, neither Hibben nor his Acoma informants would identify most of the specific figures, although their relation to modern Acoma
ritual was clear (1975:54–56). Depicted in the 109 murals published in 1975
were various masked figures including Mosquito Man (1975:Figs. 45, 86),
Squash Head (1975:Fig. 31), and Plumed Serpent (1975:Fig. 83); and unmasked figures, such as the Deer Dancer (1975:Fig. 55) and Butterfly Maidens (1975:Figs. 64–65). Several masked figures could not be identified
(1975:Figs. 18, 49, 61), (Fig. 3.7). Snakes and parrots or macaws were favor-
ite subjects either by themselves, with anthropomorphs, or in scenes.

Two interesting groups of figures are the "spirit figures" and "soul
faces" (1975:Figs. 89, 105–107). These are depicted with black, round heads
and simple eyes, mouths, and occasional noses that are either round,
elliptical, or rectangular. The soul faces occur within four pointed stars
(Fig. 3.8). These are probably spirits of the dead, and their frequency of
occurrence indicates that the cult-of-the-dead aspect of the presumed

katsina cult depicted in the Pottery Mound murals was a significant one. Their resemblance to rock art in the Rio Grande Valley and near Homol'ovi II in the middle Little Colorado River Valley is striking.

Numerous early Spanish accounts describe wall paintings in Piro, southern Tiwa, and possibly Tewa villages (cf. Dutton 1963:8–13). These could be descended from the tradition begun at Pottery Mound, a village abandoned less than 100 years before.

Excavations of the murals at Las Humanas (Gran Quivira) were conducted by the National Park Service under the direction of Alden Hayes from 1965–1967. Murals were found in two contexts: square rooms and circular kivas. The murals in the kivas are generally earlier than the rooms, which may explain in part the different iconography of the two structure types. The difference could also be related to use of the two structure types. Whatever the cause, the realistic moving figures, only one of which may be masked, are located in the rectangular rooms rather than in the circular kivas (Peckham 1981:33). Spanish documents of the seventeenth century indicate the katsina cult was active in the Gran Quivira area, so, it is interesting that the murals do not better suggest its presence (Hackett 1937:166).

In contrast the sixteenth and seventeenth century decorated pottery at Las Humanas, Tabira Black-on-white and Tabira Polychrome, were frequently decorated with katsina figures and katsina masks (Fig. 3.9). Hayes et al. (1981:89) describe details of these depictions and several of the katsinas present, recognizing the likelihood of variation in Pueblo katsinas across time and space. The Hopi Pot Carrier katsina or Cochiti Bloody Hand Katsina was identified as were the Hopi White Chin Katsina and Morning Star Deity. Interestingly, Morning Star is associated with war in the eastern Pueblos (1981:89). This association with war is a common theme in all of the northern Rio Grande murals. Hayes et al. (1981:89) see the stylistic influence on the Tabira ceramics as western Pueblo, probably Hopi or possibly Zuni, rather than Jornada or some other indigenous tradition of ritualistic iconography.

The murals at Pueblo del Encierro were discovered during salvage work associated with the construction of Cochiti dam (Lange 1968). Polly Schaafsma (1965) analyzed the only preserved painting found in a circular kiva at Pueblo del Encierro. The murals evidently date about 1500 and consist of up to 17 different layers of essentially the same motif, a pair of sun shields. Schaafsma (1965:16) notes that both sun and shield motifs are symbols in all Pueblos for war. In fact the closest similarity in wall paintings that she could find were in a late nineteenth century ceremonial room

FIGURE 3.9. Tabira Black-on-white pottery sherds showing human figures and katsinas.
(Redrawn by Ron Beckwith, Arizona State Museum, from *Excavation of Mound 7* by Alden C. Hayes, Jon Nathan Young, and A. Helene Warren, Figs. 118 & 119)

used by the War Chief at Walpi during the Winter Solstice ceremony (1965:14).

Schaafsma (1965:12–13) contrasts the paintings in the Pueblo del Encierro kiva to those at Kuaua, Pottery Mound, and at the Hopi Mesas, concluding that they bore little resemblance to the elaborate murals having masked figures. The lack of surrounding elements to the sun shields in the Cochiti area pueblo is also typical for this motif in the Pottery Mound and the Hopi Mesa murals and suggests that masked figures may not have been depicted in this particular kiva. It is interesting that the Pueblo del Encierro kiva is round and lacks masked anthropormorphs, the same pattern as Las Humanas, whereas the square kivas at Kuaua, Pottery Mound, and the square rooms at Las Humanas had more sophisticated and elaborate murals with masked beings as frequent themes. We shall return to this pattern later.

In summary, the extensive evidence from the rock art and kiva murals indicates the presence of katsinas and the katsina cult in the upper Rio Grande Valley, possibly first appearing during the fourteenth century. The rock art is dated as appearing about 1325 and the murals at Pottery Mound may date as early as 1350. Both of these dates are derived from association with tree-ring dated pottery and are in no way absolute. Although it is unlikely that either is earlier than the ascribed dates, both could be as much as 50–100 years later. The Kuaua murals, which date post-1450, more closely resemble the Jornada Mogollon style and could represent movement of these people from the middle Rio Grande Valley, which was abandoned about 1400.

The Pottery Mound murals differ considerably in style and are much more elaborate than their Kuaua counterparts. They also predate Kuaua by perhaps 50 years or more. This may indicate the presence of two related, but independent incursions of the cult into the Pueblo Southwest, or perhaps simply localized expression of the same phenomenon. We shall return to this question later.

Upper Little Colorado River (Zuni) Area

This area includes modern Zuni, Acoma, Laguna, and the upper Little Colorado River to the Puerco River (Fig. 3.1). The Zuni area was referred to by Spaniards as Cibola. Cibola is used by archaeologists to define this area of prehistoric Pueblo or Anasazi culture and will be used interchangeably with Zuni. Evidence of the katsina cult in this area comes principally from pottery and rock art. The area generally lies outside the Rio Grande style rock art associated with the katsina cult in the upper Rio Grande Valley as defined by Schaafsma (1972:129–131).

The best discussion of Zuni area rock art is by M. Jane Young (Young 1985, 1988; Young and Bartman 1981) who spent two years documenting Zuni rock art and updating the conclusions made by Schaafsma (1972) that were based on a much smaller sample. Young concludes that the katsinas and katsina masks are apparently part of the Rio Grande style for which she accepts the Schaafsma and Schaafsma (1974) date of post–1325. The iconography associated with the katsina masks and figures, however, is distinctive of a style separate from the pre–1300 Rio Grande style that has been referred to as the Little Colorado River tradition (Young and Bartman 1981:13), (Fig. 3.10). The source of the post–1300 iconographic influence is unclear. It could be from the east, as generally assumed, or from west to east, if in fact it is stylistically related to the Little Colorado River tradition. In either case it is evident that the style is intrusive into both the upper Rio Grande area and the Zuni area and is unrelated to the previous rock art traditions of either area.

In the area and expanding well beyond the assigned borders, numerous design styles on pottery have been outlined by Carlson (1970) in his analysis of White Mountain Red Wares. Of concern to this study are the Pinedale style, dominant from 1275 to 1325 and lasting to about 1400, and the Fourmile style, dominant from about 1325 to 1400, first appearing about 1300 and lasting to 1450. Both styles appear only on red ware as

FIGURE 3.10. Katsina mask rock art from the Zuni area.
(Redrawn by Ron Beckwith, Arizona State Museum, from original
drawings by Sally J. Cole; originally published in *Rock Art Evidence for
the Presence and Significance of the Katsina Cult at 13th–14th Century
Homol'ovi in the Central Little Colorado River Valley, Northeastern
Arizona*, Master's thesis by Sarah J. Cole, Fig. 35a, used with
permission)

black-and-white designs on red slips or black-and-red designs on white
slips, thus producing polychromes. The white-slipped surfaces (interiors
of bowls and exteriors of jars) of some red wares are not common in the
Cibola–White Mountain region as here defined, but are the dominant
color style below the Mogollon Rim in Salado Polychromes (Roosevelt
Red Wares).

The Pinedale style is a hybrid of the local ceramic tradition (defined by
Carlson [1970] as Puerco–Wingate–Tularosa styles) and influence of the
Kayenta-Tusayan (Hopi) ceramic tradition from the north (Carlson
1970:108), (Fig. 3.11). The most common layout is an unsectioned band
with decoration focused on the walls of bowls. It never focuses on the
interior (1970:91). Motifs consist of interlocked solid and hatched units,
with solid units as preeminent, or more so than hatched (Fig. 3.11). Negative designs are common, and bird or parrot figures are commonly made

FIGURE 3.11. Pinedale Polychrome showing the Pinedale (early Fourmile)
decoration style.
(Arizona State Museum collections; photograph by Helga Teiwes,
Arizona State Museum)

by adding a beak, legs, and tail to a triangle (1970:91). Patterns are symmetrical and comprised of either alternating or repeated motifs. In every
way Pinedale style follows the Anasazi tradition of decoration with the use
of geometric motifs in a symmetrical layout.

Fourmile style provides a dramatic contrast to Pinedale style. The focus
of decoration changes to the center of the bowl from the sides. The center
areas are often filled with a single design motif rather than a repeated or

alternated series. The central motifs are often biomorphs (1970:94). This motif can also appear on contemporary black-on-white vessels. Ferg (1982:19) notes two "katsina mask" motifs on a Pinedale Black-on-white that dates A.D. 1250–1350 (Fig. 3.12). The motif on the bowl bottom is often a curvilinear bird suspended from the interior band that is more centered than in Pinedale style. The most common bowl motif, however, remained geometric (Fig. 3.13). In contrast to Pinedale Polychrome, geometric elements in Fourmile Polychrome designs rarely interlock.

The Fourmile style bowl decorations are defined as having curvilinear, asymmetrical, centered motifs. This style is found not only on Fourmile Polychrome, but also on contemporary prehistoric Hopi ceramics, such as Sikyatki Polychrome and Jeddito Black-on-yellow, where the designs are frequently interpreted as abstract birds (Fewkes 1919), and on

FIGURE 3.12. Katsina depictions on Fourmile Polychrome and on Pinedale Black-on-white: (a,c) Fourmile Polychrome from Homol'ovi I in the Field Museum of Natural History collections; (b) Pinedale Black-on-white from a private collection.
(Drawn by Kelley A. Hays, Arizona State Museum)

FIGURE 3.13. Example of Fourmile style design on Fourmile Polychrome.
(Arizona State Museum collections; photograph by Helga Teiwes,
Arizona State Museum)

contemporary Zuni types (Woodbury et al. 1966). The Fourmile motifs
also appear on ancestral Hopi and Pottery Mound kiva murals (Fig. 3.14).
In these murals these motifs are associated with katsina figures and, presumably, the katsina cult. Although no direct associations of pottery with
murals have been found in the upper Little Colorado River area, the
appearance of katsina masks on rock art and the appearance and spread of
Fourmile Polychrome about 1325 make it reasonable to speculate that the
Fourmile design style is associated with the katsina cult. Additionally,
katsina figures appear on Fourmile Polychrome, as noted by Ferg (1982),
Kenaghy (1986:401), Martin and Willis (1940:Plate 105), and Martin et al.
(1961:Fig. 80).

Contemporary with or slightly later than Fourmile Polychrome is Kechipawan Polychrome (1375–1475), a black and red-on-white style bearing similarity to Sikyatki Polychrome (and Fourmile Polychrome) both in design style and vessel form that was made in the prehistoric Zuni villages (Fig. 3.15). The most detailed study of this type is associated with the excavation of the prehistoric and historic Zuni site of Hawikuh (Smith, Woodbury, and Woodbury 1966). At Hawikuh 40% to 50% of Kechipawan bowls and jars had Fourmile style motifs and layouts, many asymmetrical bird or feather motifs.

Matsaki Polychrome, dated A.D. 1475–1700 according to Woodbury and Woodbury (1966:329) and A.D. 1400–1700 by Kintigh (1985), is an attempt to copy Sikyatki Polychrome, a frequent import to the area from the Hopi Mesas, by the six Zuni villages of the period. Matsaki Polychrome has black-and-red designs (rarely massed white areas) on a slipped buff background (Fig. 3.15). Matsaki ceramics illustrate poorer control of design execution, interior surface finish, and crumblier paste than Sikyatki. Vessel forms with the continuously curving bowl and squat, strongly everted, neckless jars also copy Sikyatki forms. A shoe or slipper pot form is also noted (1966:328). However, figurative and katsina designs were rare to absent on the Matsaki Polychrome and Black-on-buff types found at Hawikuh (Smith et al. 1966:Figs. 51–73).

Interestingly, Matsaki vessels were the predominant types in Hawikuh inhumations and cremations (1966:235–236) and with Fourmile style Kechipawan types comprised two-thirds of the burial vessels. It should be noted that many of the historic Hawikuh Polychrome (1630–1700) vessels associated with burials also had Fourmile style layouts and motifs. Matsaki Polychrome was the most common decorated vessel associated with the cremations at Hawikuh with 66 of 117 showing "killing" (a hole punched in the vessel bottom), like Mimbres vessels. The killing included both holes in the bowl bottom and notching of the rim (Riley 1975:150). Refer to Moulard (1984) for an interesting perspective on the function of punching a hole in the bottom of a bowl or notching the rim on Mimbres vessels.

Thus it appears that the Fourmile style first appeared on Zuni pottery about 1375, becoming predominant after 1400 with the development of Matsaki Polychrome, which was strongly influenced by Hopi-manufactured Sikyatki Polychrome, also bearing Fourmile styles. As noted, Hopi pottery was frequently, if not commonly, found in the six late prehistoric and historic Zuni villages. In addition to Jeddito Yellow Ware (Jeddito Black-on-yellow and Sikyatki Polychrome) in the Zuni villages, Danson (1957:68) found this ware on late prehistoric sites to the south of Zuni.

FIGURE 3.14. Example of Fourmile style design in a kiva mural at Awatovi,
   Hopi Mesas.
   (*Kiva Mural Decorations at Awatovi and Kawaika-a* by Watson Smith,
   Fig. 49; reprinted courtesy of the Peabody Museum, Harvard
   University)

A possible earlier direction of influence for the Fourmile motif, as
discussed by Riley (1975:149–150), is from the southwest from the Salt–Gila
River or Tonto Basin area. This Salado influx noted in Hawikuh is best
indicated by Gila Polychrome (Smith et al. 1966:47–48). Whether the
Salado pottery was made locally or in the Tonto Basin is less important
than the influence the people or their ideas may have had on the indigenous Cibola population (cf. Johnson 1965). This influence could be as
early as 1300. Of course the significant number of cremations at Hawikuh
strongly indicates influence via the Salado from the Hohokam country.
Dittert (1959:236) also attributes major changes in the assemblages at
Cebolleta Mesa near Acoma to influences from the south or southwest.
Whether these are Mogollon or Salado (or the archaeologically amor-

phous cultural entity termed Western Pueblo that combines elements of both of these groups), Dittert does not specify. The changes Dittert recognizes for the thirteenth and fourteenth centuries in his Kowina Phase near Acoma include coursed adobe architecture, rectangular kivas, aggregated villages, enclosing walls, polychrome pottery, and piki stones (1959:553–562). The polychrome ceramics include Roosevelt Red Ware, White Mountain Red Ware, and Zuni ceramics.

In terms of wall murals, a few are mentioned in historical documents. Coronado reports paintings on the walls of Zuni kivas in 1540 (Smith 1952:78). However, during the excavation of Hawikuh by Hodge in the 1910s, no evidence of murals was found (1952:79). In Acoma the only reports of murals on walls date to the 1930s (1952:90), and no reports of kiva or other murals are reported for Laguna. It should be noted that such negative evidence hardly supports the thesis that little or no mural painting occurred. Because most murals were apparently drawn specifically for and during religious ceremonies and visitors were rarely allowed in kivas

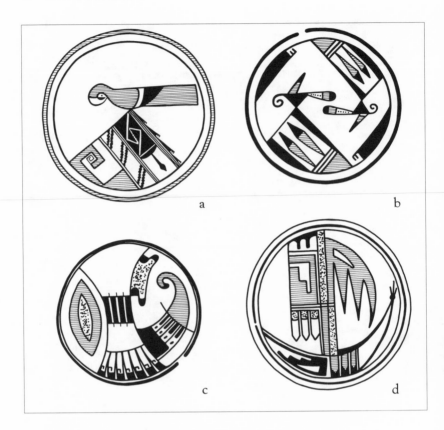

a   b

c   d

FIGURE 3.15. Zuni ceramics showing Fourmile style designs: (a,b)
Kechipawan Polychrome; (c,d) Matsaki Polychrome.
(Redrawn by Ron Beckwith, Arizona State Museum, from *The
Excavation of Hawikuh by Frederick Webb Hodge: Report of the
Hendricks-Hodge Expedition, 1917–1923* by Watson Smith, Richard B.
Woodbury, and Natalie F. S. Woodbury, Figs. 47d & g, 51d, 52a by
permission of the Museum of the American Indian Haye Foundation,
New York)

during these periods in Pueblos, it is likely that the absence of murals in
historical documents is due as much to these circumstances as to their
nonexistence. Wall plaster is a fragile commodity. Poor preservation combined with limited excavations must also be considered in evaluating the
lack of evidence. Kintigh (1985) notes the presence of both square and
rectangular kivas at the large Zuni area sites of Atsinna and Pueblo de los
Muertos, dating A.D. 1280–1325. Kiva murals were discovered at Atsinna,

but all of the motifs were geometric rather than having life forms and other traits characteristic of the katsina cult kiva murals of the following century uncovered at such villages as Pottery Mound and Kuaua.

In summary, prehistoric evidence for the coming of the katsina cult to the upper Little Colorado River area rests both with ceramic and rock art evidence. The association of Fourmile design styles with the katsina cult stems from the depiction of katsinas in some of the pottery (Ferg 1982; Kenaghy 1986:401; Martin et al. 1961). Corroborative evidence for associating Fourmile style (or Sikyatki style from the perspective of the Hopi Mesas) ceramic motifs with the katsina cult is their use in kiva murals also depicting katsinas (Smith 1952; Hibben 1960:272). Thus whereas the association of sudden design style change on pottery, as seen on Fourmile, Kechipawan, and possibly Matsaki Polychromes, with the appearance of the katsina cult is probably well founded, it is substantiated by the contemporaneous appearance of katsina masks in rock art in the Zuni area and slightly later on kiva murals elsewhere. A date of 1300 to 1350 for the arrival of the cult seems well supported with both Fourmile Polychrome and Rio Grande style rock art dating to about this time in the area. Although absence of katsina cult kiva murals at Atsinna would seem to bracket the cult's arrival between 1325 (Atsinna's abandonment) and 1350, it will be argued below that katsina icons on kiva murals probably postdate 1375. Coronado's 1540 report of wall murals at Zuni certainly supports a prehistoric development of the cult.

At this point it should be noted that at modern Zuni and Hopi, wall murals are found on kiva and nonkiva walls (Smith 1952:92–93, 97–98). The nonkiva rooms are also ceremonial and are the scene of initiations or nonkiva aspects of some of the Zuni or Hopi ceremonies. Such nonkiva ritual uses certainly could account for the murals in rectangular rooms found at Las Humanas (Peckham 1981) in the upper Rio Grande area. It is uncertain if all are directly tied to the katsina cult today, but Dutton's (1963) analysis would indicate that although they may not be, the elaboration of mural painting is associated with the arrival of the katsina cult. It is certain that the kiva mural designs are solely ceremonial (Dutton 1963; Hibben 1975; Smith 1952:321).

Rectangular kivas and plaza-oriented pueblos seem to be associated with and probably anticipate the arrival of the katsina cult. The presence of both in post–1250 pueblos throughout this area may indicate that they were necessary elements before the arrival of the cult. Increase in village size begins at Acoma about 1300 and at Zuni about 1280, predating the Fourmile style pottery designs by at least 25 years. However, Kintigh (1985) notes that the large late thirteenth- and fourteenth-century pueblos at Zuni were unstable and short-lived. It was not until about 1400 that the six historic Zuni pueblos were founded. Is the appearance of Fourmile style iconography on Zuni pottery about 1375 purely coincidental, or does it imply that the cult was influential in stabilizing the social structure of the villages?

Mogollon Rim

Following Carlson's (1970:1–4) definition, this area includes the section from Roosevelt Lake (including the Tonto Basin) on the west to the White River on the east and from the southern reaches of the Silver Creek drainage on the north to the Gila River on the south. This last boundary extends the region farther south than did Carlson (Fig. 3.1). The early culture to about 1200–1250 is Mogollon with Anasazi becoming a major influence resulting in a mixed culture after 1250 (cf. Johnson 1965), although other investigators would place the transition to a mixed or "Western Pueblo" culture at A.D. 1000 (Martin 1979:65). The issue of terminology is not of concern for our analysis. This area includes the prehistoric sites of Pinedale, Showlow, and Fourmile above the Mogollon Rim and due west of the White Mountains. These large late Pueblo III and Pueblo IV sites (1200–1400) are the type sites for the ceramic types and derived styles discussed in the previous section. The Chicago Field Museum under the direction of Paul S. Martin conducted major research in the Hay Hollow Valley, as well as in the upper Little Colorado River, including thirteenth century Broken K Pueblo (Hill 1970). Broken K was abandoned about 1280 but is significant to our discussion here in that it has both an enclosed plaza area and rectangular kivas. These attributes will be discussed in detail later. Dominant ceramics at Broken K included St. Johns Polychrome, a thirteenth-century White Mountain Red Ware. There is no indication of katsina cult icons at Broken K.

Below the Mogollon Rim the major sites date about 1300–1450 and include Forestdale, Kinishba, Gila Pueblo, Grasshopper, and Point of Pines. The characteristic decorated ceramic types (the Roosevelt Red Wares) and styles for this area seem to derive out of Pinedale Polychrome. The earliest of these types is Pinto Polychrome and Pinto Black-on-red, which are similar to Cedar Creek Polychrome and can be classed as Pinedale style (Fig. 3.16). Developing out of Pinto are Gila Polychrome and Tonto Polychrome, which are similar to the Fourmile style with a central focus to their design (Carlson 1970:105–108), but stylistically were influenced by Casas Grandes Polychromes.

FIGURE 3.16. Roosevelt Red Ware vessels with early Fourmile and
   Escondida styles: (*a,d*) Pinto Polychrome; (*b,c,e*) Gila Polychrome;
   (*f,g*) Tonto Polychrome.
   (Arizona State Museum collections; photographed by Helga Teiwes,
   Arizona State Museum)

Gila Polychrome differs from Fourmile Polychrome in that bowl interiors are slipped white with black designs applied, rather than the red interior of Fourmile Polychrome with black and white designs (Fig. 3.16). Tonto Polychrome adds red to the black designs of Gila Polychrome. In terms of design styles, figurative motifs on Gila Polychrome and Tonto Polychrome are very rare in contrast to their relative frequency on Fourmile Polychrome (Ferg 1982:18). Design styles and layout appears to be strongly influenced by Escondida Polychrome, whose appearance at Casas Grandes probably dates about 1300, or slightly earlier.

Point of Pines Polychrome, a degenerate form of Fourmile Polychrome made after about 1400 in the Point of Pines region (Carlson 1970:77–82), provides stylistic continuity with Fourmile style in contrast to contemporary Salado Polychromes.

In between Point of Pines and the western development of Gila Polychrome emerged Showlow Polychrome. Both Kinishba and Forestdale sites witness this development. Showlow is quite similar to Gila Polychrome in having white (or part white) bowl interiors and red exteriors; however, Fourmile style designs predominate. Black-and-red or black only designs are used. Showlow Polychrome develops into Kinishba Polychrome between 1350 and 1400. Kinishba Polychrome bears the same motifs and forms, differing only in having a yellow or brown paste and an unslipped surface (1970:75). This black and red-on-yellow color scheme is quite remindful of Sikyatki Polychrome manufactured on the Hopi Mesas. Thus the Fourmile style has a broad distribution from the Cibola area south to the Point of Pines area. The late Salado Polychromes develop about the same time as Fourmile style, but diverge in terms of style toward Casas Grandes Polychromes. These traditions overlap in the upper Little Colorado and nearby Mogollon Rim areas. The depiction of katsina masks on Salado Polychromes, as noted by Ferg (1982), is much more restricted than on the Fourmile style. It seems to be most frequent above the rim on the Fourmile Polychrome type. This would date the most prominent display of katsina masks on Mogollon Rim pottery at post–1300 or post–1325.

As with the upper Little Colorado River–Cibola area, with the exception of the Canyon Creek cliff dwelling, excavation has not turned up any painted murals. The Canyon Creek murals are in a probable ceremonial room and consist only of the stepped triangular "cloud" motifs noted before (Haury 1934:Plate 33). The murals probably date to the middle third of the fourteenth century. The rock art of the area is poorly known and described. The pictographs at Canyon Creek may or may not be typical.

They rarely depict the human form. Most notable are a textile pictograph, possibly a sash, at the Canyon Creek Ruin (Haury 1934:Plate 1) and what may be shields (1934:Fig. 26). Two of the shields apparently depict the sun (1934:Fig. 26a,d) and could be related to the sun shield motif described by Schaafsma (1965) for the Pueblo del Encierro kiva murals. The other two murals (1934:Fig. 26b,c) either associate or incorporate anthropomorphic features; however, neither could be interpreted as a katsina or katsina mask, although Canyon Creek clearly dates to the fourteenth century. Whether the sun shields are associated with war iconography, as at Pueblo del Encierro, is unclear and requires a much broader data base. The Canyon Creek sun shields are depicted in pictograph form and date pre–1350, whereas the Pueblo del Encierro sun shields date about 1500 and are depicted as murals on kiva walls.

Cummings (1940:Plate 34) has only one plate showing katsina-like motifs in rock art from Kinishba. These are significant for their probable date to the fourteenth century and the association of yellow ware pottery (Kinishba Polychrome) having Fourmile style motifs. Several painted stone slabs with katsina mask depictions on them from Kinishba and Point of Pines have been recovered (Cummings 1953:226, Plate 29; Di Peso 1950). Thus, with the exception of Kinishba and Point of Pines, no direct evidence corroborative of katsina cult iconography is known below the Mogollon Rim (Turner 1963:31).

In summary, the evidence for the katsina cult in the Mogollon Rim area is based on classic Fourmile style ceramics. The justification for this association was presented in the preceding section. It is worthy of mention that the classic Fourmile style has a broad distribution from the Point of Pines area on the south, to the Hopi Mesas on the northwest, to the Acoma/Laguna area on the northeast. In this immense area, every major pueblo site dating 1300–1450 has a ceramic assemblage comprised of a local variant with Fourmile design style. Ferg (1982) has plotted the distribution of katsina masklike motifs on numerous ceramic types including Pinedale Polychrome, Fourmile Polychrome, Cedar Creek Polychrome, Jeddito Black-on-yellow, Sikyatki Polychrome, Pinedale Black-on-white, Gila Polychrome, two from the Rio Grande area, and from the Casas Grandes area on, Ramos Polychrome and Escondida Polychrome.

The early development of Fourmile style and its broad dissemination in the Mogollon Rim country certainly bespeak its popularity as a design style. But this popularity characterized earlier White Mountain Red Wares as well. Some researchers have suggested that White Mountain Red Ware was produced at only a few large sites and was a status item

(Lightfoot and Jewett 1984). Upham (1982) has accorded similar status to Jeddito Yellow Wares. Although it might be useful to have a one-to-one association between the Fourmile design style and the katsina cult, without corroborative murals and rock art in the Mogollon Rim country, this cannot be made, although Ferg's (1982) katsina mask motifs as a variant of Fourmile style certainly makes the link stronger. The association of the "Sikyatki variant" of the Fourmile style with the katsina cult in the Hopi country and the probable earlier date of this style in the upper Little Colorado River–Cibola–Mogollon Rim areas lead to the conclusion that elements of the cult may have come into the Mogollon Rim country before arriving in Hopi and that perhaps the cult's origin lies either in the region in which Fourmile style developed and flourished or farther to the south or southeast.

This brings up the question of the relationship of Fourmile style to the Mimbres/Jornada ceramic and rock art tradition. Although this will be explored in depth later, a few anticipatory comments can be made at this time. In terms of central focus of decoration on bowls and use of life forms, Mimbres style clearly resembles Fourmile style. However, the subject matter is quite different as is the style, which is more clearly integrated into other elements of the decoration and into the vessel form in Fourmile and Sikyatki (Brody 1977:107–108). The dating is also a problem. Mimbres style ceramics apparently were no longer manufactured after 1150, whereas Fourmile style did not develop until after 1300 (Carlson 1970:112). The associated rock art tradition of Mimbres also does not characterize the Fourmile style area.

The rise of Casas Grandes in northern Chihuahua in the thirteenth century with ceramic iconography very similar to the Fourmile style may suggest a regional interaction sphere, if the style is not an indigenous development (Brody 1977:109–110; Carlson 1970:112). As noted by Ferg (1982) and Di Peso (1974), abstract bird motifs and katsina masklike designs clearly of the Fourmile style occur in fourteenth-century Casas Grandes ceramics (Fig. 3.17). A possible intermediate, locally made version of Chihuahua Polychrome, showing Casas Grandes influence as far northwest as the San Pedro River Valley, has been described by Di Peso (1951:124–129) and named Babocomari Polychrome. Carlson (1970:112–114) sees the development of yellow ware traditions in the Mogollon Rim and Hopi country and intervening points as a result of this Mexican stimulus. Although it is possible that Casas Grandes ceramic iconography was the source of the Fourmile style, the latter's stylistic roots seem more clearly tied to developments above the Mogollon Rim. The marriage of Mogollon

FIGURE 3.17. Casas Grandes ceramics showing parrot and curvilinear
designs similar to Fourmile style: (a,c,e) Escondida Polychrome;
(b,d,f) Ramos Polychrome.
(Arizona State Museum collections; photograph by Helga Teiwes,
Arizona State Museum)

Rim (Tularosa) style and Plateau (Kayenta) style that resulted in Pinedale style in the late 1200s is clearly altered into divergent stylistic traditions after 1300. Gila and Tonto Polychromes are stylistically strongly influenced by Casas Grandes Polychrome. The Fourmile style, on the other hand, clearly derives from Pinedale style in the upper Little Colorado River area. Common bases of Anasazi and indigenous populations probably led to increased interaction throughout the Salado-Fourmile areas during the fourteenth century. This regional dynamic was almost certainly influential, if not causal, in the development of the katsina cult.

Middle Little Colorado River Valley

This trapezoidal area is bounded by the Petrified Forest National Park on the northeast, by the painted desert on the north, by the junction of Oraibi Wash with the Little Colorado River on the northwest, and by the drainage area of Chevelon Creek above the Mogollon Rim to the south (Fig. 3.1). This area includes several sites occupied during the 1250 to 1400/1450 period. These include Puerco Ruin in Petrified Forest National Park, Wallace Tanks or Stone Axe Pueblo near Petrified Forest, Chavez Pass (Nuvakwewtaqa) southwest of Winslow, and the Chevelon Ruin, Cottonwood Creek Ruin, and Homol'ovi I–IV near the town of Winslow. Other Pueblo IV sites are located in this area, but are not as well known or as completely studied as the above.

Research in the area began in 1896 when J. Walter Fewkes (1898, 1904) visited the Homol'ovi sites, Chevelon Ruin, and Chavez Pass. In 1901 Walter Hough (1903) visited Wallace Tanks and Puerco Ruin. Hough's collections were quite small, and no subsequent research has taken place at Wallace Tanks. Numerous excavations at Puerco Ruin (called Adamana by Hough) by Cosgrove (1934), Schroeder (1961), and Jennings (1980) have failed to produce any ceramics or kiva murals suggesting the presence of the katsina cult at the pueblo. However, Cole (1989b:201–208), Jennings (1980:Fig. 39), and Martynec (1985) do identify several masked figures represented in the rock art below Puerco Ruin that are in the Rio Grande style. Research at Homol'ovi III by the Arizona State Museum suggests that Puerco Ruin was established before 1300, or prior to the development of the katsina cult, and may have served as a seasonal site for Wallace Tanks after 1300 (Adams 1989). Jennings (1980:162) compares the rock art figures to those found near Homol'ovi II by Pilles (1975) and notes that they are nearly identical. If Jennings' (1980:24) dating of Puerco Ruin as 1250–1350 is correct, this would suggest the rock art and the presence of the katsina cult predates 1350. If Puerco Ruin is indeed a seasonal site of Wallace Tanks, the rock art could have been carved by occupants from Wallace Tanks which was occupied to at least 1400. This would rectify the seeming inconsistency of Jennings' dates for the pueblo, the absence of ceramics indicative of the katsina cult, and the presence of Rio Grande style rock art. This problem will be considered in depth in chapter 7.

Fewkes excavated in the cemeteries of Chevelon and Homol'ovi I while barely testing the other Homol'ovi sites or Chavez Pass. He supported the contention of the Hopi people that these were ancestral sites associated with specific Hopi clans on their migration to the present villages. Fewkes (1898, 1904) published brief descriptions of his work and photographs of some of the artifacts he had recovered. Among these were painted stone tablets with tablita-like forms depicting clouds from Chevelon and numerous ceramic vessels in the Fourmile style from Homol'ovi I, Homol'ovi II, Chevelon, and Chavez Pass depicting natural and supernatural animals and man-animal forms, with several depicting katsinas.

Some of the katsina forms on vessels have been identified by Hopi informants as Chakwaina (Tsa'kwayna), which also appears early at Zuni. These show the broad band of teeth, lines or crescents for eyes, and partial to total black face that could indicate the black face, hair, or beard of this katsina (Fig. 3.18) (cf. Smith 1952:296–298; Fewkes 1904:Plate 27b). Wright (1977:34), Colton (1975:57), and Fewkes (1903:64, Plate 4) indicate the Tsa'kwayna came to Hopi via Zuni and may have originated farther east. These vessels would contradict this interpretation. The katsina on the vessels also closely resembles Hee'e'e and So'yokwuuti. Hee'e'e is often equated to Tsa'kwayna Mana, or an unmarried female Tsa'kwayna. These katsinas also have black faces, hair, and beard; a broad, toothy mouth; but have round eyes. Smith (1952:296–298) notes these personages depicted on the Awatovi kiva murals. This would indicate that whoever the katsina, it was widely known and a central figure of the early cult.

Pilles (1982:5) notes a vessel from Chavez Pass that portrays a Shalako figure. Such figures with rainbow chins and horned headdresses were common subjects in the Jornada style of the middle Rio Grande Valley. The occurrence of this style east of the Rio Grande Valley and especially east of Zuni before 1400 is seemingly unique in the Chavez Pass vessel. Sa'lako, Tsa'kwayna, and Hee'e'e are all priest or chief katsinas (Wright 1977:29; Colton 1975:7). Western Pueblo groups generally perceive priest katsinas as among the oldest katsinas, which would fit with the archaeological data just presented. Pilles (1987:117) also documents the presence of several petroglyphs at Chavez Pass that depict masked beings that he

FIGURE 3.18. Tsa'kwayna Katsina depicted on an Awatovi Black-on-yellow
   bowl probably from Homol'ovi I.
   (U.S. National Museum collections; drawn by Kelley A. Hays,
   Arizona State Museum)

interprets as katsinas or some other class of masked personages.

Other beings depicted on the Homol'ovi area ceramics, termed Winslow Orange Wares, are abstract and realistic birds, probably representing
raptors and parrots or macaws, and reptiles or serpents with arrowlike
tongues, legs, and wings (Fig. 3.19). Although it might be convenient to
associate the latter with the horned serpent, the similarity is remote.
Similar creatures were found by Fewkes (1898, 1919) at Sikyatki Pueblo on
the Hopi Mesas (Fig. 3.20).

In terms of typological systems, one ceramic tradition influencing the
Winslow Orange Wares made in the Winslow, Chavez Pass, and Petrified
Forest areas employed traditional geometric designs on a standard radial
and offset quartered layout characteristic of the Anasazi (ancestral Pueblo)
with abundant use of diagonal or horizontal hachures and long solid tri-

angles. On bowls these motifs are frequently repeated along the sides of the vessels contained within bounded lines with the bottom of the bowl left undecorated (Fig. 3.21). This Pinedale style apparently derives from upper Little Colorado River groups. This style also characterizes the Jeddito Orange Ware tradition in northeastern Arizona associated with the Anasazi on the Hopi Mesas. Designs on Jeddito Orange Wares are different from those manufactured by their neighbors to the north and appear to have been influenced by manufacturers of White Mountain Red Ware. This relationship suggests early ties between the thirteenth century Hopi Mesa groups and their counterparts along the upper Little Colorado River.

A second ceramic tradition influencing Winslow Orange Wares directly is the White Mountain Red Ware tradition. Whether later than the Jeddito style influence, or contemporary, both Pinedale and Fourmile

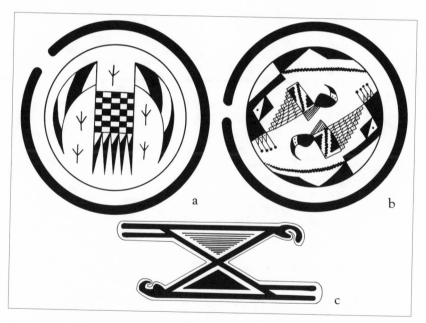

FIGURE 3.19. Abstract macaw or parrot forms representing Fourmile style on pottery: (*a*) Jeddito Black-on-yellow from Homol'ovi II from a private collection; (*b*) Jeddito Black-on-yellow from the Field Museum of Natural History collections; (*c*) Homolovi Polychrome from Chevelon Ruin from the U.S. National Museum.
(Drawn by Kelley A. Hays, Arizona State Museum, by permission of the Field Museum of Natural History, Chicago)

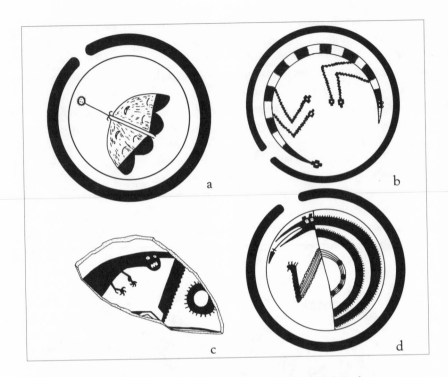

FIGURE 3.20. Stylized zoomorphic figures representing Fourmile style on pottery: (*a*) Jeddito Stippled from Homol'ovi II from the Field Museum of Natural History collections; (*b*) Jeddito Black-on-yellow from Homol'ovi II from the Field Museum of Natural History collections; (*c*) Jeddito Black-on-yellow from Chevelon Ruin from the U.S. National Museum collections; (*d*) Awatovi Black-on-yellow from Homol'ovi I from the Field Museum of Natural History collections. (Drawn by Kelley A. Hays, Arizona State Museum, by permission of the Field Museum of Natural History, Chicago)

styles are apparent (Fig. 3.21). Some of the Fourmile styles depict katsinas (Fewkes 1904). Recent excavations at Homol'ovi II with calibrated radiocarbon dates of 610+/−85 years (calibrated to A.D. 1340–1397; mean + 1350) and 600+/−75 years (calibrated to A.D. 1337–1373; mean + 1352) (Hays and Adams 1985:Appendix E) yielded an assemblage comprised of 50% Jeddito Yellow Ware with over 95% of the restorable vessels being Jeddito Yellow Ware (Hays 1985). One restorable bowl with a possible Sun Forehead katsina mask was recovered. Recent compositional analysis of yellow ware sherds from Homol'ovi II by the Conservation Analytical Laboratory of the Smithsonian Institution indicates that some of the sherds were manu-

FIGURE 3.21. Examples of geometric and Fourmile style designs on
    Winslow Orange Ware: (a,d) Homolovi Polychrome in early
    Fourmile style; (b,c) Homolovi Polychrome in Fourmile style;
    (e) Homolovi Polychrome; (f) Tuwiuca Black-on-orange.
    (Arizona State Museum collections; photograph by Helga Teiwes,
    Arizona State Museum)

factured at the Hopi village of Awatovi and that of those that could be sourced, all were manufactured at villages on the Hopi Mesas (Bishop et al. 1988). Thus the indigenous Winslow Orange Ware varieties were almost totally replaced in the Little Colorado River area by 1350 by yellow wares traded from the Hopi Mesas. Based on tree-ring dated and seriated pottery in the region, the dates of Winslow Orange Ware and early Jeddito Yellow Ware (Awatovi Black-on-yellow) in the Little Colorado River Valley can be bracketed as 1275–1350. The quantity of ceramic trade indicates there were strong ties between the two population centers, certainly on an economic level and judging from Hopi oral traditions (Courlander 1971:72–73; Fewkes 1898:584, 608–609), probably also on a sociocultural level.

The appearance of Fourmile style motifs, including some with katsina masks, on indigenous pottery types, such as Homolovi Polychrome and Chavez Pass Polychrome, suggest the presence of the katsina cult at the local villages. These ceramic motifs probably were contemporary with those depicted on the imported Fourmile Polychrome vessels, because they closely resemble Fourmile Polychrome designs, as if they had been copied.

The preponderance of late Jeddito Yellow Ware, Fourmile Polychrome, and Fourmile style Winslow Orange Ware with the burials at Homol'ovi I excavated by Fewkes (1898, 1904) may indicate the primary use of these vessels was as funerary offerings and that the katsina cult was already associated with death. Association of icons on burial ceramics with a cult of the dead was first indicated from the Mimbres area (Brody 1977; Moulard 1984).

Additional evidence of the cult at Homol'ovi II is in two forms. First, Pond (1966) excavated a rectangular kiva in the western plaza that contained a mural of two dancing figures in full ceremonial regalia, much like modern katsinas. The absence of the head area due to erosion cannot substantiate that they were katsinas, but their resemblance to figures in other contemporary painted kivas at Awatovi and elsewhere is suggestive. It is unfortunate that Pond did not better document the figures, nor investigate the possibility of additional murals on other layers of the kiva's plaster. All but one of the 24 whole or restorable vessels recovered from the kiva were Jeddito Yellow Wares (Pond 1966:557–558).

More compelling evidence of the cult at Homol'ovi II can be found in the petroglyphs to the west and south of the site. A total of 199 panels containing over 1,000 elements were recorded by the Museum of Northern Arizona in association with the assessment of Homol'ovi II (Weaver et al.

1982). Cole (1989b:106–108) has since completely documented the rock art of the Homol'ovi area. She identified 499 panels with 57 (11.4%) having katsina figures. A total of 89 mask and katsina representations are present on the panels (Fig. 3.22). Forty-nine of the panels with 72 examples of katsina iconography have been recorded at Homol'ovi II alone (Cole 1989a:321). The katsina figures or masks occur singly or in groups up to four.

The petroglyph figures are generally simple with standard eyes. Nose features are rarely represented. Variation comes principally in the mouth or head ornaments, such as ears or antennae. The meaning of these beings can be interpreted in three ways. They could be analog forms to Tlaloc (Schaafsma 1980), although the considerable variation depicted and the absence of large circular eyes on most does not entirely fit this interpretation. The figures do not give the sense of being human; they convey a

FIGURE 3.22. Rio Grande style rock art from the vicinity of Homol'ovi II. (Redrawn by Ron Beckwith, Arizona State Museum, from original drawings by Sally J. Cole; originally published in *Rock Art Evidence for the Presence and Significance of the Katsina Cult at 13th–14th Century Homol'ovi in the Central Little Colorado River Valley, Northeastern Arizona*, Master's thesis by Sarah J. Cole, Figs. 25c & 19, used with permission)

spirit or death quality. Similar figures called "spirit figures" and "soul faces" were depicted on the Pottery Mound murals and, using informants from Acoma Pueblo, were interpreted as spirits or ghosts (Hibben 1975:118, 134). Therefore, these faces could be of the deceased, or they could be of katsinas in an early simplified form. Hibben (1975:118, 134) interpreted similar figures as ghosts or spirits of the dead. Both katsina and spirit forms could be depicted, with the simpler, featureless forms being spirits and the others, especially with bodies, being katsinas. The most plausible explanation, though, combines these two thoughts into one. If the katsina cult is the cult of the dead, then katsinas and spirits, or the deceased, are portrayed and considered as one. The dead become katsinas and take human messages to the deities.

The grouping of the figures and their physical relation to Homol'ovi II, at least in some cases, must have had some meaning. General meaning will be discussed later. With more research and additional informant data, specific meanings may be decipherable, or at least better guessed. Rock art still figures into modern Hopi ceremonial drama. Hopi informants identified the following katsinas in the rock art of Homol'ovi II: Taawa (Sun Katsina), Tseeveyo (Giant Ogre Katsina), Kooyemsi (Mudhead), and Tsa'kwayna.

There is also considerable rock art associated with Homol'ovi IV (Tuwiuca). Cole (1989a:321) recorded five katsina figures at a panel about 400 m northwest of the pueblo. Tuwiuca is the earliest of the Homol'ovi group sites, ceramically dated 1250–1300 (Andrews 1982; Hantman 1982). It is noteworthy that the katsinas are not depicted in direct association with the pueblo, but at a considerable distance from it. Cole (1989b) believes that the katsina masks near Homol'ovi IV could have been carved by its occupants, that is between 1250–1300 and that their remoteness was intentional. If so, the pre–1300 date would be the earliest documented katsina rock art known.

In summary, the figurative pottery, kiva mural, and rock art all depict katsina-like figures, considerably at variance with even the depiction of figures before 1300 in any medium except rock art. The katsina petroglyphs differ from those of the Jornada style, as defined by Schaafsma (1972), that commonly depict eye or chin striping. They more closely resemble the glyphs found in the Galisteo Basin area south of Santa Fe (Schaafsma 1972:Figs. 120–121) that characterize the style distinctive of the area between San Marcial on the south to the Pajarito Plateau on the north (1972:141). This style is a subdivision of the Rio Grande style described earlier. Schaafsma (1972:142–144) describes this style as having fairly simple masks, usually round, rectangular, or triangular faces with eyes and mouth indicated by single dots. Elaborations are simple headgear or a forehead mark. The cheek, chin, and eye markings of farther south are notably absent. The body form is rectangular or boxlike. Simple snakes and the horned serpent are commonly depicted, as they are at Homol'ovi II.

Pilles (1975), however, has defined the rock art of Homol'ovi and the middle Little Colorado River area having katsina depictions as the Pueblo IV style. He notes that the highly stylized birds and quadrupeds are not as well represented at Homol'ovi II and other areas of the Little Colorado River as they are in the Rio Grande. Cole (1989a:326) further notes that shields and highly decorative masks of the Rio Grande style are also missing from the middle Little Colorado River tradition, but that this style has many continuities of style with earlier rock art of the area. Thus the middle Little Colorado River Pueblo IV style is distinctive and may predate the 1325 date proposed by Schaafsma and Schaafsma (1974) for the Rio Grande style.

As to meaning, it seems likely that the Warrior Society or war elements were integral parts to the ritual system of the culture of the people of the middle Little Colorado River Valley after 1300. Whether the Warrior Society was crosscut by the katsina cult, autonomous from the cult, or closely integrated to the cult is difficult to determine. The predominance of possible katsinas with warrior overtones, such as Tsa'kwayna, Hee'e'e, Hu, Hon, and Wuyaqqötö, in the mask assemblage at Homol'ovi II, suggests that the katsina cult and the Warrior Society were somehow integrated. The Kuaua kiva murals studied by Dutton (1963) seem to indicate that during the fifteenth century in the Albuquerque area, the Warrior Society and katsina cult usually maintained separate rituals, but occasionally shared ceremonies. Hibben (1975) notes Warrior Society attributes in the murals at Pottery Mound as well, as does Schaafsma (1965) for the murals at Pueblo del Encierro. Both of these pueblos probably also postdate 1400.

Thus katsina cult iconography can be found in the rock art, on the pottery, and also probably in kiva murals of the middle Little Colorado River Valley. As in other areas, the kiva murals occur on the walls of a rectangular kiva. (All fourteenth century kivas in the Homol'ovi group are square or rectangular.) The kivas are within a large plaza area, just as at Kuaua and Pottery Mound. At Las Humanas the round kivas are in plaza areas, but the rectangular ceremonial rooms are in the roomblock. The relation of cult iconography to the development of enclosed plazas and adoption of rectangular kivas will be explored later.

Verde Valley and San Francisco Peaks

This area includes the San Francisco Peaks volcanic field and the middle and part of the lower Verde Valley (Fig. 3.1). On the southwest corner is Perry Mesa on the landform dividing the Verde River from the Agua Fria River where the New River and Cave Creek head. On the southeast corner is the Tonto Basin. The early culture in the San Francisco Peaks area beginning between A.D. 500 and 700 is Sinagua. This cultural tradition is characterized by paddle-and-anvil brown ware ceramics with none decorated (Pilles 1979:459). By 1300 the area was mostly abandoned except for a few sites where in addition to the native brown wares and the white wares that had been traded from the Anasazi for 300 or more years, there also occurred yellow pottery. The sites of Old Caves, Grapevine, Pollock, Kinnikinnick, and Chavez Pass are good examples. Due to the high frequency of Winslow Orange Ware ceramics at Chavez Pass, which are used to define the thirteenth and fourteenth century occupation of the middle Little Colorado River Valley, and its close proximity to the Homol'ovi pueblos, Chavez Pass is considered part of the middle Little Colorado River Valley area for this discussion.

In the upper Verde Valley the Sinagua were present only at low levels, if at all, until 1100 when population expanded, and migration into the area from the Mogollon Rim and San Francisco Peaks areas occurred. These sites were mostly small and scattered. After 1300 there is a marked contraction into about 40 large pueblos and cliff dwellings. This process also occurred in the lower Verde Valley with the pueblos not only along the Verde River, but also extending as far westward as the New River and the Agua Fria River. All of the areas were abandoned by 1425 (Pilles 1976:114–116).

The period 1300–1425 is known as the Tuzigoot Phase in the middle Verde Valley and as the Roosevelt Phase in the lower Verde Valley. Especially in the lower Verde there is a mixture of indigenous Sinagua and intrusive Salado traits. In terms of ceramics the Salado culture is represented by Gila and Tonto Polychromes in addition to the indigenous Salado type, Roosevelt Black-on-white. Other pottery of the indigenous culture is San Carlos Red-on-brown and various plain wares. Tuzigoot White-on-red and Verde White-on-red are the decorated types for the middle Verde (Pilles 1976:119). These middle Verde red wares have crudely executed geometric designs, rarely being symmetrical (Colton and Hargrave 1937:171). There is no ceramic evidence in the designs of the Tuzigoot Phase red wares to suggest the presence of the katsina cult.

Yellow wares are relatively common (over 2% of sherds) at several sites on Perry Mesa and in frequencies of less than 2% at most Tuzigoot Phase sites of the middle Verde. These are apparently Jeddito Yellow Wares and not of local manufacture. The common occurrence of buff to yellow paste in Tuzigoot Red Wares does, however, admit the possibility of local manufacture, although the generally finer temper of the yellow wares contrasts quite markedly with the medium temper of the indigenous decorated types, both in the middle and in the lower Verde. Although the difference between the Tuzigoot Red Wares and Awatovi Black-on-yellow would be less drastic, the micaeous red and black inclusions in Tuzigoot Red Wares are absent in Awatovi Black-on-yellow. Analyses of several yellow ware ceramics from the Verde Valley by the Conservation Analytical Laboratory of the Smithsonian Institution using neutron activation analysis should settle most questions about whether the yellow wares were manufactured at the Hopi Mesa villages, or elsewhere.

In all likelihood the yellow wares are trade items originating at the Hopi Mesas. Early Spanish reports of Hopi textile and ceramic trade items throughout southwestern Arizona bolster the contention that trade was the likely prehistoric vehicle (Garces 1775–1776 in Coues 1900). A prehistoric and historic trail into the Verde Valley from the Hopi Mesas via Homol'ovi, Chavez Pass, and Stoneman Lake has been identified by Colton (1957). Interestingly, at several Verde Valley sites containing yellow ware, Winslow Orange Wares are also present, principally Homol'ovi Polychrome. This would seem to link the source of Jeddito Yellow Ware for the Verde Valley to sites in the middle Little Colorado River Valley rather than directly to sites on the Hopi Mesas. It also indicates that a long-distance exchange system existed prior to 1300, assuming Winslow Orange Wares are slightly earlier than Jeddito Yellow Wares, anticipating the more far-reaching system of the fourteenth century, partly documented by Upham (1982).

Although yellow wares are present in low frequencies at all late pueblos in the San Francisco Peaks/Anderson Mesa area, neither murals nor rock art with katsinas or katsina masks are known from the Flagstaff area. The yellow ware ceramics were traded either directly from Hopi or via Homol'ovi or Chavez Pass. Presence of obsidian at all of these sites from sources near the Peaks suggests it was traded for the yellow ware. The frequency of obsidian on post–1300 pueblos along the middle Little Colorado River and in the Hopi Mesas area increases severalfold over pre–1300 sites suggesting obsidian was a key element in exchange (Harry 1989). Thus the yellow ware was probably only a trade item and was unrelated to katsina cult ritual.

The yellow wares both in the Verde Valley and around the San Francisco Peaks are all Awatovi Black-on-yellow and Jeddito Black-on-yellow. The absence of Sikyatki Polychrome (yellow ware having black and red designs), which was manufactured after 1350–1375, indicates yellow ware exchange occurred between 1300 and 1350–1375. No figurative or Fourmile style designs are known on these vessels, or on the indigenous types, suggesting the katsina cult probably was not present.

No kiva murals are known from either the Verde Valley or the Peaks areas. This may be due to relative infrequency of excavation and poorer preservation; however, the rarity of kivalike structures in the Verde Valley is probably the real cause of the lack of kiva murals. The Verde Valley may have had a different ceremonial basis from that on the Colorado Plateau (cf. Pilles 1976:117). This difference could certainly explain the absence of the katsina cult. The rarity of Fourmile style motifs on the Salado types in the Tonto Basin where kivas are also rare or absent is consistent with this pattern.

Possible Maasaw (Hopi Earth Deity) or Kooyemsi (Mudhead Katsina) figures were found at Honanki, a twelfth to thirteenth century cliff dwelling below the Mogollon Rim near Sycamore Canyon in the middle Verde. These figures are remindful of those at Homol'ovi II. A katsina-like petroglyph is known from Fossil Creek in the middle Verde. The figure from Fossil Creek has a circular face with a band across the eyes and one perpendicular line dividing the lower face in half. It is horned. It also has a rectangular body with a zigzag line and circles. The division of the face into three parts is similar to masks in the Hopi Mesa murals (Smith 1952:307), although there the upper face is divided. The Fossil Creek figure does not resemble any contemporary Hopi katsina.

If these figures are katsinas, they are very rare and could postdate the archaeological sites, perhaps being made by later travelers and traders. Historically, the Hopi have visited Tuzigoot, and nearby Bill Williams Mountain and the Chevelon Cliffs are considered boundaries to the modern Hopi homeland and were visited periodically, as they have been recently (Page 1982). The Stoneman Lake trail used to trade items into southwestern Arizona has already been mentioned. Use of the Peaks and vicinity by the Hopi is well documented (Nequatewa 1936:103–110; Whiting 1939:49). The Peaks contain the passage to the underworld for Hopi katsinas and are the sources of many plants and some animals important to everyday Hopi use and ritual.

In summary, the evidence for the katsina cult in the Verde Valley and around the San Francisco Peaks is scanty and can be attributed to more recent use by the Hopi. The rarity of the kiva in Verde Valley sites can explain the absence of the cult there. In the Peaks area there are very few sites postdating 1300. Sites dating to this period may have been marginal to the cult, or indications of its presence have yet to be recognized or found.

The Hopi Mesas

This area includes all of northeastern Arizona, north and east of the Little Colorado River Valley and the Puerco River Valley, and southeast Utah south of the San Juan and Colorado rivers (Fig. 3.1). Principal archaeological sites of the post–1275 period are those on and around the Hopi Mesas and the Jeddito Wash area, Steamboat Canyon, Bidahochi, and Kintiel (Wide Ruins). There is a very thin scatter of pottery and rock art from this period in such widespread areas as Canyon de Chelly, the Moenkopi Wash area, Klethla and Long House valleys north of Black Mesa, and the various canyons draining north into the San Juan and Colorado rivers (Adams and Adams 1987). For the most part this latter group consists of small, temporary settlements and for our purposes, except for the rock art, will not be of concern to this analysis.

Archaeological work in the area in sites postdating 1275 is not substantial, and much is poorly or incompletely reported. Fewkes (1896), excavated Sikyatki below First Mesa and tested in several other sites in the area, the Peabody Museum of Harvard University excavated parts of Awatovi and Kawaika-a on Antelope Mesa (Brew 1937, 1939, 1941), Hough (1903) tested several sites, and Hargrave (1931) tested Kokopnyama and Kintiel. Adams (1979b:40) notes a 1250–1350 village below present Walpi, but it was too disturbed to allow any conclusions concerning the katsina cult.

Prior to 1300 much of this area was occupied by the Anasazi who made a gray culinary ware and white ware decorated with black designs. As noted earlier, in both the White Mountain area in east central Arizona and through much of the area north and west of Black Mesa, red and orange ware traditions were established and fully developed by the eleventh century. On the Hopi Mesas orange wares replaced white wares as the dominant decorated color combination in the 1200s (Smith 1971). The clays producing the red or orange colored vessels are high in iron oxide and when fired in an oxygen-rich atmosphere, produce the orange and red colors. The clays for the white wares are low in iron oxide and are fired in a neutral or reduction atmosphere, one with little or no oxygen.

By 1300 much of northeastern Arizona was severely depopulated, if not abandoned, except for the area around the Hopi Mesas and Jeddito

Valley, the Bidahochi villages, and perhaps three or four others along valleys southeast of the Hopi Mesas. After 1300 in the Hopi area the white ware clays began to be fired in oxygen-rich atmospheres giving buff, tan, or yellow colors. The designs on the early yellow ware types, Antelope Black-on-straw and Awatovi Black-on-yellow (Smith 1971), are identical to the local orange ware, Jeddito Black-on-orange which was earlier and contemporary (Fig. 3.23). Kintiel Black-on-yellow, Kintiel Polychrome, Klageto Black-on-orange, and Klageto Black-on-yellow are all believed by Smith (1971:473) to be merely variants of Jeddito Black-on-orange and Jeddito Polychrome. Jeddito Polychrome has white designs added to the black ones. The Kintiel and Klageto pottery types date about 1250–1300 (Breternitz 1966:80–81) after which the upper Puerco River and Leroux Wash areas were apparently abandoned. The appearance of these types south of the Zuni area (Danson 1957:74) could explain the destination of the inhabitants, or they could have been absorbed into Zuni, Hopi Mesa, Bidahochi, or Little Colorado River Valley villages postdating 1300. In any case there is no indication of the katsina cult at Kintiel or other contemporary villages in the pottery or any other remains prior to their abandonment, although at Kintiel there is a large, plaza-oriented village, and a rectangular kiva has been tree-ring dated to 1276 (Smith 1972). The village layout and the rectangular kiva also characterize the Zuni area at the same time (Kintigh 1985).

About 1300–1325 sand replaced sherd temper, transforming Antelope Black-on-straw to Awatovi Black-on-yellow (Smith 1971:601). As in Jeddito Polychrome, white designs were added to black paint on yellow wares and are called Bidahochi Polychrome. At about the same time as the appearance of the yellow wares, coal replaced juniper wood as the firing fuel (Hack 1942a; Shepard 1971:183). Due to the higher firing temperature of coal, this gave a harder ware. About 1350–1400 changes in design layout motifs appeared (Fig. 3.23). Those with only black designs are typed Jeddito Black-on-yellow; with the addition of red, Sikyatki Polychrome; with the further addition of white in massed areas, Kawaika-a Polychrome; with black and red designs and engraving in the painted areas, Awatovi Polychrome; and with only black but engraved, Jeddito Engraved (Colton and Hargrave 1937:150–156). These later types all employ the Fourmile style in some percentage of their decorations. In design the Hopi Fourmile style resembles Fourmile Polychrome in being asymmetrical in layout with abstract birds; however, the Hopi Fourmile style is considerably more dynamic than Fourmile Polychrome, especially in depicting life forms, such as animals, insects, plants, and mythological creatures reminiscent of serpents and dragons (Figs. 3.20, 3.24). Because the Hopi Fourmile style

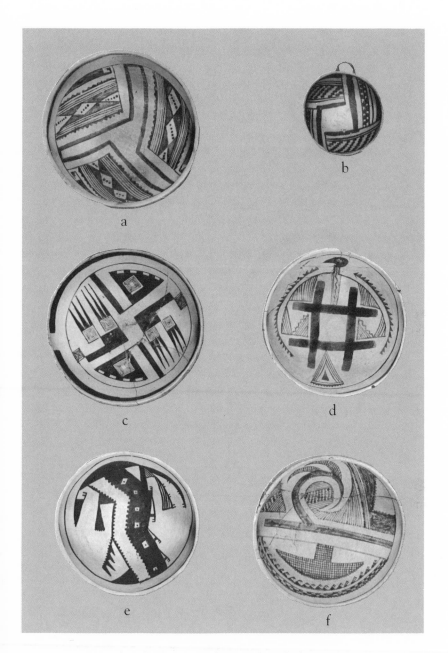

FIGURE 3.23. Examples of geometric and Fourmile style designs on
ceramics from the Hopi Mesa villages: (*a*) Awatovi Black-on-yellow;
(*b*) Huckovi Black-on-orange; (*c*) Jeddito Black-on-yellow;
(*d–f*) Jeddito Black-on-yellow in Fourmile style.
(Arizona State Museum collections; photograph by Helga Teiwes,
Arizona State Museum)

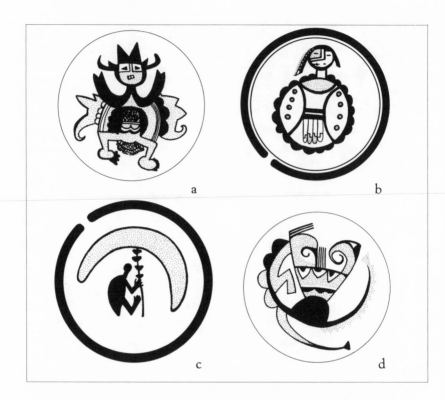

FIGURE 3.24. Asymmetric, Sikyatki style designs typical of post-1400
ceramics from the Hopi Mesa villages: (a,b,d) Sikyatki Polychrome
from Sikyatki Pueblo; (c) Sikyatki Polychrome from Old Shongopavi.
(Field Museum of Natural History collections; drawn by Kelley A.
Hays, Arizona State Museum, by permission of the Field Museum of
Natural History, Chicago)

does differ in detail from the Fourmile style of the upper Little Colorado
River and Mogollon Rim areas, to facilitate discussion it will be referred
to as Sikyatki style. The Sikyatki style designs resemble the Mimbres
tradition except they are more closely integrated to their framing design
and are drawn with consideration of the vessel form and layout (Brody
1977). Large, squat, neckless jars and large bowls with curved sides and an
incurving rim characterize Sikyatki style forms. As with Matsaki Polychrome, a shoe or slipper pot form is known (Fewkes 1898:Plate 120).
Rectangular medicine box forms also appear during this period, both at
Sikyatki Pueblo and at Hawikuh (Fewkes 1898:Plate 128; Smith et al.
1966:Fig. 80).

The fine sand temper to temperless paste, hard fired from coal, and light yellow color make the Hopi Mesa yellow ware pottery very distinctive. Such a ceramic tradition did not evolve in the Little Colorado River Valley, at the Homol'ovis, in the Verde Valley, or elsewhere that yellow ware pottery is found. It is likely that almost all such "Hopi" yellow pottery was indeed manufactured on and exported from the Mesas, a contention recently supported by nuclear and compositional analyses of some of the exported yellow wares (Bishop et al. 1988). Such trade preceded the adoption of the katsina cult and Sikyatki style, but was continued into areas occupied to or beyond 1350 when the Sikyatki style was adopted. If the Sikyatki style motifs are associated primarily with mortuary offerings, as suggested in the excavations of Fewkes (1904) at Homol'ovi I and Chevelon Ruin, this could restrict their flow in trade to only villages practicing the cult. Similarly, if exchange were only between village elite or leaders (Lightfoot 1984; Upham 1982), the cult could have provided a powerful new medium of elite access to esoteric knowledge, further restricting the flow of status-oriented yellow ware. Such associations should be explored in future excavations in ancestral Hopi sites, that is, those containing yellow ware with Sikyatki style motifs and layouts.

In terms of figurative designs the most spectacular in the Southwest outside the Mimbres Valley area certainly came from Sikyatki Pueblo, northeast of the modern First Mesa Hopi villages. Fewkes (1898, 1919) has grouped and described these vessels by decoration. He identifies as depicted on these vessels: a twin war god, feathered serpents, prayer feathers, cloud symbols, unmarried women with hair whorls, insects, quadrupeds, lizards, human parts, and especially birds (Fewkes 1898:Figs. 263, 266, 355; Wade and McChesney 1981:20). Notably lacking, however, are katsina masks common in murals and rock art of the Hopi Mesas area, and on pottery from the middle Little Colorado River Valley, Mogollon Rim, and elsewhere (Ferg 1982). Photographs of some of the Sikyatki Polychrome vessels excavated from Awatovi by the Peabody Museum Expedition and collected by Thomas Keam, a local trader, from other of the post-1300 villages have been published by Wade and McChesney (1981). As with the Fewkes vessels, katsina masks or figures are rarely depicted. Their rarity may suggest that there was a proscription against their depiction on ceramics from Hopi Mesa villages, or at least on their use in those villages, for the kiva mural evidence, discussed below, leaves no doubt that the katsina cult was being practiced at the Hopi Mesa villages in the 1400s. Perhaps, as Kenaghy (1986:561) notes, ceramics were used as devices to signal the presence of symbolic, in this case katsina, information. At Hopi, vessel form or other decorations may have filled the role that masks did elsewhere.

At Awatovi and Kawaika-a on Antelope Mesa just east of First Mesa, the Awatovi Expedition of 1935–1939, sponsored by the Peabody Museum of Harvard University, recovered more than 200 individual mural paintings from about 20 kivas (Smith 1980:30). All of these kivas were rectangular, very similar to modern Hopi kivas and kivas found associated with yellow pottery and having murals at Pottery Mound and Homol'ovi II. Many of the Antelope Mesa kivas have panels displaying abstract designs identical to those used on contemporary pottery that have been termed the Sikyatki style (Smith 1980:35) and that is clearly related to the Four-mile style. Others of the murals depict katsinas and Hopi deities in conjunction with the Sikyatki style design. For this reason it is asserted that the Sikyatki style on pottery and murals is associated with the katsina cult. Because these motifs appear on pottery between 1350 and 1400 (Smith 1971:601), it is believed the cult arrived at the Hopi Mesas area about this time. Although Jeddito Yellow Ware pottery characterizes the assemblage at Bidahochi, 30 km southeast of the Antelope Mesa pueblos, Sikyatki style pottery is not found there. Jeddito Yellow Ware is not found at all at Kintiel, 50 km east of Bidahochi. Thus Kintiel and other contemporary villages were probably abandoned shortly after 1300, before the manufacture of the Jeddito Yellow Wares; whereas, Bidahochi was occupied until about 1350. After 1350 only Antelope Mesa and the Hopi Mesas were occupied.

Smith (1952, 1980) has identified several of the figures depicted in the Awatovi and Kawaika-a murals (Fig. 3.25). Among the katsinas identified are Pooko (Dog), Ahöla (The Solstice Katsina representing the Germ God), Kokopölmana (Kokopelli Mana), and possibly Avatshoya, the Spotted Corn Katsina (1980:35–36; 1952:296–298). All of these figures are prehistoric, or pre-1630 when the Spanish erected a mission at Awatovi. A non-katsina male Kookopölö, one of the Hopi Twin War Gods, and Aaloosaka, the Germ God, are also depicted. As noted earlier, the very common masked figure of Hee'e'e, Tsa'kwayna Mana, or So'yokwuuti could also be intended instead of the Kokopölmana listed above. This group of similar looking katsinas is also commonly a subject of rock art as noted both in the Homol'ovi II glyphs and in the Rio Grande Valley. Their depiction in color, full figure, and fully dressed in the murals, make their identification a much easier matter than with the petroglyphs.

The kiva murals are very similar to those found by Hibben (1960) at Pottery Mound. So much so that Smith (1980:37) declared some could be the work of a single artist or at least belong to the same school. In this vein it is interesting to note the Hopi and Zuni stories retold by Hodge (Smith

FIGURE 3.25. Kiva mural from Awatovi showing katsinas.
(*Kiva Mural Decorations at Awatovi and Kawaika-a* by Watson Smith,
Fig. 65a; reprinted courtesy of the Peabody Museum, Harvard
University)

1966:51). The Hopi say the people of Sikyatki and Awatovi came late in
prehistoric times from the Rio Grande country. They stopped at Zuni and
lived there for some time. The descendants of these people in Hopi country are at Sichomovi on First Mesa and belong to the Asa or Tansy
Mustard Clan. Their descendants at Zuni also belong to the Mustard Clan
(Ai'yaho kw). The Awatovi clans are not specified. This legend certainly
could tie the Pottery Mound people, who had pottery and kiva murals
identical to those at Hopi, to a group in Hopi and could also explain the
abundance of Jeddito Yellow Ware pottery early in all the Zuni villages. It
should be noted that local legends or stories often rearrange historical
events to suit their own people's needs. Further discussion of this subject
will be presented later.

   In the vicinity of the Hopi Mesas it is difficult to separate the fourteenth
to sixteenth century rock art from that of the historic and contemporary
periods. Katsina masks, feathered serpents, and snakes have been recorded in abundance or observed by Turner (1963) and others. At shrines

away from the mesas, such as Tutuventiwukwa (Newspaper Rock) near modern Tuba City on the Hopi Salt Trail to the Grand Canyon, there are scores of pictographs. These too, for the most part, were used historically. One area that has not been used historically by Pueblo people, based on ceramic evidence, is the Glen Canyon area of southeastern Utah. Turner (1963) has done a significant analysis of the rock art of the Glen Canyon region. His style 2 is associated with Pueblo IV Hopi (1963:6, 11–13) and is probably concentrated in the fourteenth century (1963:32). Turner had Hopi informants identify the petroglyphs, and they listed the following katsinas and deities: Ahŏla (Germination Katsina), Hu (Whipper Katsina), possibly a Buffalo Horn Katsina (Mosayur Katsina), and the Snake Warrior God. Serpents and snakes are also depicted. With the exception of a dance group consisting of informant-identified Hopi maidens and a Hu Katsina that are shown with dance kilts and the Hu with a necklace, the figures, as is typical at Homol'ovi II, show only the head or head and shoulders (Fig. 3.26).

Turner (1963:31) also provides a list of style 2 petroglyphs in the Southwest. These include in addition to the Glen Canyon area in southeastern Utah, Canyon de Chelly/Canyon del Muerto, Ford House in Chinle Wash, Tolchaco (northwest of Leupp along the Little Colorado River), Willow Springs (Tutuventiwuqwu), Inscription Point, Crack-in-the-Rock at Wupatki National Monument, and the Hopi Mesas, which also contain later prehistoric and historic Hopi glyphs. With Turner's (1963:31) assumption of equivalency between his style 2 and what Schaafsma (1972) later calls the Rio Grande style, the association of style 2 with the Hopi outside northeastern Arizona and southeastern Utah can be questioned. For the Glen Canyon and other nearby areas, prehistoric Hopi manufacture is probable, given the association of yellow ware probably manufactured on the Hopi Mesas. Because of the precise definition and extensive documentation of the Rio Grande rock art style by Schaafsma (1972) and its use by other researchers, the Rio Grande style name will be retained in this and following discussions on rock art. It will include Turner's style 2 and Pilles's (1975) and Cole's (1989a, 1989b) Pueblo IV style defined for the Little Colorado River area.

In summary kiva murals, ceramics, and rock art all bear katsina cult iconography indicating the cult was present and quite strong in the villages on the Hopi Mesas and along the Jeddito Valley of Antelope Mesa. Of course the historic records and modern ethnographies on the Hopi testify to its significance among the Hopi for the past 300 years. The time of arrival on the mesas is dated 1350–1400 based on tree-ring dates, tree-ring

FIGURE 3.26. Rock art from the Glen Canyon area of southeastern Utah
showing a katsina mask.
(Photograph by Christy G. Turner II, courtesy of the Museum of
Northern Arizona archives; originally published in *Petrographs of the
Glen Canyon Region* by Christy G. Turner II, Fig. 9)

dated ceramics, stratigraphic studies at Awatovi, and seriation of the
Awatovi ceramics (Adams 1981a; Breternitz 1966; Smith 1952, 1971; Wade
and McChesney 1981). The Sikyatki style, based on Hopi yellow ware
ceramics, therefore apparently postdates the Fourmile style in the White
Mountains by 25–75 years. The implications of these relative dates will be
explored in the following chapters. The distribution of the Rio Grande
style rock art is thin, but widespread, in northeastern Arizona and southeastern Utah north of the Hopi Mesas. These areas, however, apparently
were little used by Pueblo people after 1400.

Table 3.1 *Katsina Mask Representations and Associations by Geographic Area*

Geographic Area	Rock Art/ Period	Pottery/ Period	Kiva Murals/ Period
Middle Rio Grande	Jornada Style Post-1200	None	None
Upper Rio Grande	Rio Grande Style Post-1325	Rare 1350–1450	Jornada Style Post-1450 (Kuaua)
		Fourmile Style Post-1450/1475	Hopi Style Post-1400 (P. Mound)
Cibola Area	Rio Grande Style Post-1325	Fourmile Style Post-1325/1350	None documented
Mogollon Rim	None documented	Fourmile Style Post-1300/1325	None
Middle Little Colorado River	Pueblo IV Style Post-1250/1300	Fourmile Style Post-1325	Hopi Style? Post-1350
Verde Valley/ San Francisco Peaks	Rare, Post-1300	None	None
Hopi	Style 2 Post-1300	Sikyatki Style Post-1350	Hopi Style Post-1375/1400

Summary

The broad nature of the foregoing discussion has been summarized in Table 3.1. Three patterns are notable and will be treated extensively in the chapters to follow: (1) katsina designs appear broadly in rock art and on ceramics about 1300–1325, and later on kivas, about 1375–1400; (2) village size increases at about the same time, or slightly earlier; (3) enclosed plazas are characteristic of these late thirteenth-century aggregated pueblos, and rectangular kivas are the only or nearly only kiva form on which murals with katsinas are painted. The distribution of these changes by geographic area is also informative and will be treated in detail in chapters 4 and 5.

Katsina designs on rock art occur broadly along the Rio Grande Valley from El Paso north to Taos, although details of these styles do vary. The Jornada style characterizes the middle Rio Grande Valley, the Rio Grande style the upper Rio Grande Valley and parts of Cibola, the Little Colorado River style in the middle Little Colorado River area and western

Cibola, and style 2 in the Hopi area. The Rio Grande style is the most complex, perhaps combining styles from both the Jornada area and areas to the west. Katsina designs on rock art are very rare along and below the Mogollon Rim. Those that exist, as in the Verde Valley, may be products of visitation by Hopi or middle Little Colorado River residents participating in the cult.

Ceramics depicting katsinas in any but rare instances during the fourteenth century are limited to the upper Little Colorado River, Mogollon, and middle Little Colorado River areas. However, the related Fourmile style is also characteristic of the Hopi Mesas area, as Sikyatki style.

The distribution of kiva murals is also interesting but much more difficult to interpret due to problems of sampling error and preservation. In other words, absence of kiva murals from the known archaeological record of an area is not capable of proving that murals with katsinas do not or did not exist in the considerably unexplored archaeological record. Nevertheless, the kiva murals at Hopi Mesa villages and Homol'ovi II slightly predate those at Pottery Mound and are definitely earlier than those at Kuaua and Las Humanas.

The broadest assemblage of media bearing katsina designs is clearly in the west, especially for the fourteenth century remains. The relationship of katsina designs to changes in village size, enclosed plazas, and rectangular kivas is not as clearcut, although the latter are clearly favored for murals having katsina masks and figures. The broader distribution of the architectural and settlement changes beyond the katsina cult design distribution will be examined in the next two chapters.

4

Characteristics and Associations of the Katsina Cult

In the large post-1300 (Pueblo IV) villages near the Hopi Mesas several characteristics are shared with the large contemporary villages along the middle and upper Little Colorado River Valley, the Zuni area, the Rio Grande area, and the Mogollon Rim area. In addition to variably dated, but shared, characteristics of designs depicting katsina masks or katsina figures, there are artifacts and architectural features that seem associated with this period in these far-flung areas. Beyond the specific designs bearing katsinas there appear to be other icons that develop in the decorative repertoire of the prehistoric artists. The assemblage of repeated designs will be argued to represent an iconography or style that is in some fashion symbolically tied to the katsina cult. These motifs are also found in the Rio Grande style rock art (Schaafsma 1972:Figs. 117, 128, 130). In brief the iconography of this style is comprised of elaborate, curvilinear motifs of abstract birds, of realistic quadrupeds, lizards, insects, and other life forms. Specifics of this style in subject matter and layout differ from the Mimbres Classic Black-on-white life forms. Masked beings, probably katsinas or deities, are also depicted, less frequently on pottery and more so on murals and rock art. These anthropomorphic figures are usually solitary or unconnected small groups on rock art. On murals, in contrast, they usually involve several anthropomorphs (human and superhuman), perhaps plants, animals, and pottery designs, the latter possibly used primarily as filler (cf. Brody 1989). Pottery designs characteristic of Sikyatki Polychrome and Fourmile Polychrome are found in the Pottery Mound, Awatovi, and Kawaika-a kiva murals (Figs. 4.1, 3.14). All who have studied these murals believe most are ceremonial. Some are associated with or are altars (Smith 1952) and some are identifiable to specific ceremonies (Dutton 1963; Hibben 1960; Smith 1952).

FIGURE 4.1. Sikyatki style design on a Pottery Mound kiva mural.
(Photograph by Helga Teiwes, Arizona State Museum; originally
published in *Kiva Art of the Anasazi at Pottery Mound* by Frank C.
Hibben as Fig. 52, permission granted by K.C. Publications,
Las Vegas)

Artifactual Associations

There are several artifacts that are possibly associated with the arrival of
the cult. The first is the shoe or slipper pot found at Hopi in Sikyatki
(Fewkes 1898), at Zuni (Smith et al. 1966), and probably elsewhere (Fig.
4.2). It first appears at Hopi in association with Sikyatki Polychrome and
at Zuni with Matsaki Polychrome. Thus it is possible that the Matsaki
Polychrome shoe form was borrowed from Hopi, as was Matsaki Polychrome itself, rather than developed independently. Dixon (1963, 1976) has
discussed the distribution of the ceramic shoe form at length. It is a utility
or culinary ware, and its form allowed it to be shoved between hearth-
stones over hot coals. Its handle remained cool while the contents were
allowed to simmer for a long time (1976:387). Its earliest appearance is in
Mesoamerica and according to Dixon (1976:387) it did not reach the
southwestern United States until after 1200. For example, Di Peso
(1951:117–118) recovered six "duck" vessels from the Babocomari village
along the Arizona-Mexico border in southeastern Arizona, which he dates
1200–1450. It is interesting that Sisson (1975:475–476) reports the use of
shoe-form vessels in late post-classic Tehuacan Valley sites for holding
cremated human remains. The 1200–1600 dates of this occurrence correspond exactly with their appearance in the southwestern U.S. Although
there is no evidence of shoe pot use in the Southwest associated with
cremations, there is some association with burials. Very little data are

available to consider the relation in the detail it requires. Both the Sikyatki and Hawikuh shoe pot vessels were associated with burials and several burials at Hawikuh were cremations. It is unclear if the shoe pot at Hawikuh was involved with a cremation.

Piki is a thin, wafer-like cornbread that at one time constituted a major portion of Hopi diet. It is cooked on a griddle called a piki stone. The piki stone as used at Hopi is a carefully selected and prepared slab of sandstone. It is made by grinding and smoothing the tabular slab and seasoning it with cotton seed, watermelon seed, or (recently) corn oil (J. Adams 1979:23). The piki stone is placed on slabs surrounding three sides of a firepit. During its "seasoning" and with use, the surface of the stone turns black and shiny due to the carbonizing of the heated oil that has penetrated the stone's surface. In discussing the origin of the katsina cult many years ago with Emil Haury (1977), he commented on the association of the piki stone with the constellation of traits from the south that had recently been associated with the cult. Haury noted the similarity between clay griddles (comals) at Los Muertos and piki stones at Hopi and Zuni in his report on Los Muertos in the Salt River Valley (1945:109–111).

Kidder (1932:75) reports stone griddles at Pecos Pueblo that have highly polished surfaces made lustrous black by constant rubbing and greasing. These surely are piki stones. They are associated with Glaze III and later ceramics or post–1350. Dittert (1959:562) also noted the appearance of piki stones in sites dating to the fourteenth century near Acoma and relates their appearance to other characteristics associated with Salado that appear at the same time.

a   b

FIGURE 4.2. The slipper or shoe-form vessel: (a,b) Jeddito Plain.
   (Arizona State Museum collections; photograph by Helga Teiwes,
   Arizona State Museum)

FIGURE 4.3. Piki stone fragments from the Homol'ovi sites.
(Arizona State Museum collections; photograph by Helga Teiwes,
Arizona State Museum)

During surface studies at both Homol'ovi I and Homol'ovi II, dating about 1300–1400, fragments to several piki stones were observed. Some were weathered so that the characteristics of the stone, other than being fire-reddened tabular sandstone, could not be discerned. Excavations at Homol'ovi II in 1984, at Homol'ovi III from 1985 to 1989, and at Homol'ovi IV in 1989 by the Arizona State Museum, University of Arizona, uncovered piki stone fragments in room floor or feature context in all three pueblos. At Homol'ovi III the piki stone has been found in the earliest occupation levels in the pueblo, all dating 1275–1300 (Fig. 4.3). The Homol'ovi III founders emigrated from the upper Little Colorado River or Mogollon Rim area where White Mountain Red Wares were the predominant decorated type (Adams 1989:222–223). It seems likely that knowledge of the piki stone may have been introduced into the Homol'ovi area from the source area of the Homol'ovi III immigrants. The paucity of yellow ware pottery on the surface and in the fill of excavated units at Homol'ovi IV suggests a pre-1300 date for its occupation. The ceramic assemblage and layout of Homol'ovi IV are very similar to villages in the Hopi Mesas area. Presence of piki stone fragments at Homol'ovi IV could indicate a northern origin or borrowing from Homol'ovi III occupants. Additional research on the ground stone assemblages of excavated thirteenth century sites in both the upper Little Colorado River area and the Hopi Mesas area are needed to clarify this early development of a new corn processing artifactual assemblage. The presence of three-sided, slab-lined hearths in addition to four-sided ones may offer additional clues to the presence of piki stone food processing. Because the piki stone completely covers the hearth stones, air and fuel can be fed only from an open fourth side which is unnecessary in a hearth used for traditional food preparation.

Piki stones have not been reported from earlier sites in the American Southwest, although some of those described as griddles might qualify. At present the Homol'ovi III and Homol'ovi IV specimens are the earliest piki stones in well-dated proveniences. Distribution, as with shoe pots, is not known due to problems of identifying the stone and the paucity of work and reporting from excavations of sites from this period. The timing and place of the appearance of the piki stone ties it to the development of cult iconography on Fourmile Polychrome, although its roots seemingly lie to the south in the southern Mogollon (Salado) or Hohokam region of what is today southern Arizona and northern Mexico. Nevertheless, it seems that both the shoe pot and the cooking griddle have similar origins and appear in the study area after 1250.

Piki bread was a food staple of the Hopi into the twentieth century and is still made in quantity for ceremonial occasions. It is commonly distributed by the katsinas to the audience during dances. This mechanism for food distribution is reported in early ethnographies (Stephen 1936). Piki is commonly blue, but can also be red, yellow, or nearly white depending on the color of the cornmeal and other additives. This form of food preparation is similar to the corn tortilla, a Mexican innovation (cf. Haury 1945:110). The piki stone was part of each Hopi home. Prehistorically, piki was probably a new method of corn preparation and was unlikely primarily a ceremonial aspect of the katsina cult, although it could have been part of prehistoric katsina dances and food distribution. The addition of lime through ash to piki (and Pueblo hominy) provides needed nutrients to the Pueblo diet and would also have favored its spread.

Other artifact types that could be associated with thirteenth and fourteenth century influences from Mexico are stone paint palettes and rectangular medicine bowls (Fewkes 1898:Plate 128). The only known earlier occurrences of palettes are in the Hohokam area (cf. Haury 1976:286–289) and in Chaco Canyon (Judd 1954:285), another area showing marked early exchange for materials originating in Mexico. The latter date in the 1030–

1130 period. The Hohokam have palettes with rims or edges that date as early as A.D. 500.

Historic and modern medicine bowls usually have terraced sides, symbolic of clouds and rain, and figures associated with water, such as frogs and pollywogs painted on their sides. These crenellate bowls in modern Hopi and Zuni ceremony are used for aspersing and to hold medicine water on altars (Stephen 1936:603, Fig. 24). The crenellate or terraced rim seems to have developed about 1800, and did not appear on the rectangular vessels found by Fewkes at Sikyatki (Adams 1979a; Fewkes 1898). Although rectangular bowls with less vertical sides also occur in the Hohokam area dating to the Colonial and Sedentary periods, about 700–1100 (Haury 1976:176–183), adoption of this shape in the Anasazi area for this period apparently did not occur. Small square or rectangular vessels with effigy heads, usually aquatic birds, are known in the Anasazi area at least by the 1100s, and predominate into the 1300s, adding a polychrome turkey/macaw/parrot form after 1300. A subrectangular vessel form with sloping sides is also relatively common in fourteenth century Roosevelt Red Wares. Except in general shape, however, these do not seem antecedent to the post–1400 forms. The fifteenth century date at Sikyatki is the earliest known prehistoric occurrence. The designs on the Sikyatki vessels give no hint of ceremonial use, unlike their successors.

A possible fourteenth century flat katsina doll, possibly the Hemis Katsina, was reported by Haury (1945:198–200) from Double Butte Cave near Tempe, Arizona. Eighteenth century specimens are known from Walpi (J. Adams 1980). A southern origin seems likely, given the above; however, the Double Butte specimen is more likely a nonkatsina ritual effigy, similar to ones still used by Hopi and other Pueblo groups, usually on altars (Stephen 1936:Figs. 22, 62, 484). A set of six "statuettes" excavated in 1959 near the Puerco River in eastern Arizona were given to the Museum of Northern Arizona (Danson 1966). About 10–13 cm in height, they also do not resemble masked katsinas. Thus to date, no prehistoric examples of katsina dolls are known. If the prehistoric dolls were made of wood, as are the historic examples, poor preservation could explain their absence in the archaeological record. It is also possible that katsina dolls were developed after contact with Euroamerican cultures.

Architectural Associations

Several elements of architecture and village-plan change in the Southwest about the time and in the areas of the development or appearance of the katsina cult. Characteristics to be examined include the development of enclosed plazas, increased site size, and the appearance of rectangular kivas.

For the period 1250–1450, in almost every major site occupied by Puebloan people in the Zuni, Rio Grande Valley, Mogollon Rim, Little Colorado River Valley, and Hopi Mesas areas, there was a large, often multiple-story village many times the size of the average site for the preceding period (cf. Cordell 1984:328–337; Kintigh 1985; Lipe 1983:471; Martin and Plog 1973; Stuart and Gauthier 1981:411–425). Associated with the appearance of these large sites was the development of enclosed plazas (Fig. 4.4).

Rectangular kivas are part of Mogollon Rim and Cibola architecture of the 1200s and are present in all sites of north-central and northeastern Arizona postdating 1275 (possibly even 1250) in association with the large sites with enclosed plazas (Gumerman and Skinner 1968; Hargrave 1931; Johnson 1965). Gumerman and Skinner (1968) note rectangular kivas in the Hopi Buttes area dating to the McDonald Phase, A.D. 1100–1250. As in the Mogollon area, the form is apparently derived from local pit house form modified by some kiva characteristics, such as addition of a bench and a firepit-ventilator system. This conclusion was also reached by Johnson in his dissertation study of the western Pueblo (1965:76). Rectangular kivas are virtually the only ones decorated with katsina cult style (katsina figures and Fourmile style pottery design) murals. This is the case at Kuaua, where round kivas are also present; at Pottery Mound, where 16 or 17 kivas with murals are rectangular; at Las Humanas; at Awatovi; at Kawaika-a; and probably at Homol'ovi II (Table 4.1). The murals postdate the appearance of rectangular kivas in areas where circular kivas were the standard, by less than 100 years and in most by 50 years or less.

What is apparent is the relationship between increasing village size, the appearance of the plaza enclosed by a wall or rooms, and the rectangular kiva (Table 4.2). Concentration of population into fewer and larger sites and the appearance of enclosed plazas were noted as common architectural results of changing demographic, economic, and possibly environmental factors (cf. Plog et al. 1982). Plazas, so common in prehistoric and historic Mexico, could merely be a logical development for centers of trade and commerce for the staging of markets. Plazas or central open spaces develop in the large Chaco Canyon sites about the same time (A.D. 1050), or slightly earlier, than in the Mimbres area. Some intermediate village layouts of post-Chaco great houses dating to the A.D. 1175–1250 period include a walled-in area with rooms on one side that mimic plaza areas. These have been noted by Kintigh (1990) in the upper Little Colo-

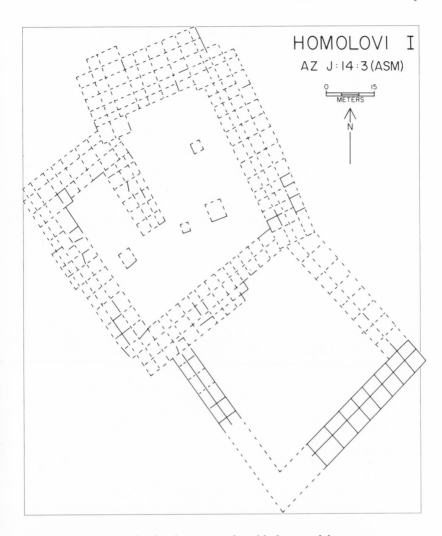

FIGURE 4.4. An example of a plaza-oriented pueblo layout of the 1300s.
(Adapted from *The Emergency Protection of Homolovi I Ruin* by Steven
G. Dosh, Fig. 2; redrawn by Ron Beckwith, Arizona State Museum,
by permission of the Museum of Northern Arizona, Flagstaff)

rado/Cibola area. Perhaps this is the intermediate form that ties plaza
development to indigenous roots. Large, thirteenth century pueblos associated with Tularosa-style ceramic designs (antecedent to the Pinedale
style), some with enclosed plazas, also develop in the Cibola area. The
relationship of various architectural trends will be explored later.

It is also during these periods (1000–1300) that agricultural features first appear in variety and complexity in the Anasazi and Mogollon areas (cf. Herrington 1982:75–90). Perhaps these are logical outgrowths of the concentration of large populations into single villages. Herrington (1982:75–90) points out the diversity and complexity of water control and agricultural features employed by classic Mimbres cultures in association with the classic period pueblos already discussed. In the 1300s, covered ditches occur near such large Rio Grande Valley villages as Sipawe and Tijeras (Judge 1975:44).

Other Characteristics and Associations

From his study of Mimbres painted pottery, Brody (1977:109–110) believes that Mimbres influence on the later Sikyatki and other polychrome traditions is slight and probably derived secondhand through Casas Grandes. These conclusions are based on differences in the iconography of Classic

Table 4.1 *Prehistoric and Historic Sites Having Kivas with Murals of Masked Anthropomorphs*

Site	Probable Age of Painted Kiva	No. Painted	Site Size	Room: Kiva Ratio	Painted Kiva Shape	References
Awatovi	1375–1630	10	1000+ rooms	50+:1	square	Smith 1952, 1972
Frijoles Canyon	1400–1500+?	3	N/A	N/A	round	Hewett 1938 Chapman 1938
Las Humanas*	1545–1672	7	225+ rooms	30+:1	square	Peckham 1981
Kawaika-a	1400–1500+	12	500+ rooms	40+:1	square	Smith 1952, 1972
Kuaua	1450–1575	2	1200+ rooms	200+:1	square	Dutton 1963
Pottery Mound	1400–1475	17	500+ rooms	30+:1	16 sq. 1 rd., no masked figure	Hibben 1975

*Las Humanas has 7 round kivas and 7 square rooms. Only the rooms have masked figures.

Table 4.2 Comparison of Changes in Village Size to Appearance of Plazas and Rectangular Kivas during the 1250–1400 Period

Area	Average 1100–1250 Hab. Site Size	Average 1300–1400 Hab. Site Size	Length of Occup. 1300–1400	Plaza-Oriented Layout 1250–1400	Rectang. Kiva Present 1250–1400	Average 1400–1600 Hab. Site Size	Length of Occup. 1400–1600	References
Middle Rio Grande	20–50; 100+ Mimbres	>125	50–100	yes	yes*	N/A	N/A	Stuart & Gautier 1981
North Rio Grande	<20	>300	<100	yes	yes†	500+	200+	Stuart & Gautier 1981
Zuni	10–20	500	<50	yes	yes	650	200+	Kintigh 1985 Plog 1978
Mogollon Rim	10	>250	<50	yes	yes	N/A	N/A	Longacre 1964 Johnson 1965
Middle Little Colorado R.	10	500	<100	yes	yes	N/A	N/A	Adams, Stark, & Dosh 1990
San Francisco Pks/Verde Valley	<20	150	<100	no	no	N/A	N/A	Pilles 1987
Hopi Mesas	20	500	100	yes	yes	500	200+	Adams, Stark, & Dosh 1990

*Rectangular kivas occur along the northern and northeastern fringes, but are unknown in the core area.
†Rectangular kivas occur in many villages, but not in all.

Mimbres Black-on-white from Sikyatki Polychrome. The subject matter differs and the layouts differ, with the Sikyatki style more closely allied to local Anasazi styles and the Mimbres style to its own roots. Brody (1977:110) does note the same forms and linear precision of Mimbres design in some Casas Grandes pottery. This suggests to him that the Mimbres figurative tradition influenced Casas Grandes and that Casas Grandes in turn influenced the later Pueblo cultures at Cibola, Hopi, and the Rio Grande Valley.

Although apparently the ceramic figurative tradition of the Mimbres died out, rock art contemporary with the figurative ceramics did not, or did it? The Mimbres rock art (Jornada style, western area) (Schaafsma 1972) is stylistically distinctive from the Jornada rock art of the middle Rio Grande Valley (Jornada style, eastern area). The Mimbres area style dates about 1000–1150. The simple pointed- and round-headed figures of this style more closely resemble modern Pueblo deities rather than katsinas. The Jornada glyphs (eastern area) are dated by Schaafsma (1972:119) to about the same time as the western glyphs because they are similar. She therefore places them under the same style. The distinctiveness of the eastern style and of its geographic location from the west would seem to argue against this idea. Jornada eastern style appears to be associated with Animas, El Paso, and San Andreas Phase sites in the middle Rio Grande Valley and west (1972:119) dating after 1200. If the eastern style were in vogue prior to 1150–1200, it certainly is likely that some of the elaborate and innovative designs, compared to the western phase, would have been incorporated in the western region. The eastern style glyphs more closely resemble masked beings, or katsinas (Fig. 4.5), but differ from the Rio Grande rock art style to the north in having flat-topped heads rather than rounded ones; striped or decorated chins rather than undecorated; oval or lenticular eyes rather than rounded; a nose present rather than absent; and simple mouths drawn as a line rather than rectangular ones, often having teeth. It is suggested that two traditions, both contributing to Pueblo ceremonialism and iconography, are represented in the western and eastern styles. The early ritual complex in the Mimbres developed about 1000–1100, whereas the elaborate, distinctive cult of the eastern phase Jornada developed after 1200 and spread northward and eastward. To simplify matters for future reference, the western style rock art will be termed Mimbres style and the eastern style, Jornada style. The relationship of both these styles to other contemporary rock art styles and to katsina cult iconography will be taken up in detail in chapter 5. The discussions by Brody (1977) and Schaafsma (1972) comparing Mimbres rock art to Pueblo

FIGURE 4.5. Jornada style rock art.
(Redrawn by Ron Beckwith, Arizona State Museum, from *Rock Art in New Mexico* by Polly Schaafsma , Fig. 86; permission granted by the Office of Cultural Affairs, Historic Preservation Division, State of New Mexico)

IV rock art conclude that the Mimbres figurative rock art is unrelated or only extremely tangential to katsina rock art.

The modern katsina cult is closely tied to rain, or more exactly, to moisture or precipitation. This has been discussed in chapter 1. A second association of the cult is war. In modern Pueblo society where war has been eliminated for the past century or more following Euroamerican dominance and subjugation of the Navajo, the Warrior Societies have died out or are greatly reduced. Among the Hopi on Third Mesa (Titiev 1944:156–157) and First Mesa (Stephen 1936:85, 89), a Warrior Society existed that was associated with the Kookop and Spider Clans on Third Mesa and the Sun and Eagle Clan on First Mesa. Deities associated with this society are the War Gods (Warrior Brothers), Maasaw, and Spider Woman. Elsewhere in Pueblo society the sun is associated with war (Schaafsma 1965). In either case, there is no direct association with the katsina cult. However, the war gods and perhaps Maasaw are represented on Mimbres rock art and pottery and are associated with the early unmasked anthropomorphic iconography first evident in the eleventh century. This warrior theme, also a common Mesoamerican theme (Schaafsma and Schaafsma 1974), thus predates the masked katsina cult and may have developed or been accepted as the villages grew larger, population became more concentrated, and resources may have been scarcer. Thus among the Mimbres people it is possible a Warrior Society existed with associated supernatural beings as early as the eleventh or twelfth century.

Is it only fortuitous that most of the rock art associated with the appearance of the katsina cult that can be identified is associated with beings having strong ties to Pueblo Warrior Societies, such as Tsa'kwayna, Hu, Hee'e'e, and others? These are masked figures who may be warrior figures rather than katsinas. Dutton (1963:200–201) also notes the predominance of war themes in the early kiva murals at Kuaua, alternated with initiations into the katsina society. Schaafsma (1965) points out that the sun shield murals on the fifteenth century kiva walls at Pueblo del Encierro were probably war-associated. No katsina murals were recovered from Pueblo del Encierro. Thus in rock art and kiva murals there are indications of an early(ier) and separate Warrior Society. Their shared use of the Kuaua kiva and the existence of warrior katsinas, many of which apparently were quite early, indicate early ties between the katsina cult and a Warrior Society. Perhaps an indication of warrior themes with early katsinas is the present universal nature of the masked whipper (Whipper Katsina) among the Pueblos from Taos to Hopi (Ortiz 1969:19). The Whipper is also commonly depicted in the rock art.

The Mimbres-associated Warrior Society developed in the eleventh century and the Warrior Society is also preeminent in fifteenth century pueblos in the upper Rio Grande Valley. On the other hand, katsina cult icons do not appear until the thirteenth or fourteenth century in the middle Rio Grande Valley and the Mogollon Rim. Thus it is possible that the katsina cult had some association with the Warrior Society during its development in the late 1200s or 1300s. The katsinas most likely represented in fourteenth century katsina iconography generally have war associations in present-day Pueblo ritual; however, this is no guarantee that this association existed six centuries earlier. This would suggest the two societies were integrated prior to A.D. 1300. According to Dutton's (1963) interpretation of the murals at Kuaua, though, the katsina cult apparently became integrated with the Warrior Society in the fifteenth century in the upper Rio Grande Valley. Whether integration was achieved in the thirteenth century or not until the fifteenth century will be considered in detail later.

5

Origin and Age of the Katsina Cult

The preceding discussions have established the possible distribution of the katsina cult in the southwestern United States on the basis of existing evidence, and suggested some sources for the cult. Several possibilities have been discussed for both age and source of the cult.

In terms of origins, the following have been discussed: (1) the cult is Mexican in origin coming from Casas Grandes or farther south; (2) it originated in the Mimbres area identifiable by the classic Mimbres figurative pottery; (3) the Mimbres culture is indirectly related to the cult having influenced the Casa Grandes people who in turn developed the cult; (4) the Jornada rock art style corresponds with the origin of the cult influenced either by the Mimbrenos or the Casas Grandes people; (5) the cult was introduced by Mexicans accompanying the Spanish; or (6) the cult developed in the areas where the Fourmile style designs first appeared, that is along the Mogollon Rim and upper Little Colorado River.

The dating of the cult dismisses number 5. How can a choice be made from among the other five? It is quite possible that parts to more than one may be correct. A reexamination of the data will be useful at this time. The points that have been established so far can be summarized below:

(1) In the eleventh century large villages with central open spaces similar to plazas and possible rectangular kivas appear in the Mimbres area. Farming systems also are associated with these, including irrigation ditches, grids, and others (Herrington 1982).

(2) Figurative pottery and rock art appear at the same time in the Mimbres area. As Brody (1977:206–207) points out, however, the subjects and layouts differ from later pottery, rock art, and kiva mural artistry. The associations are strongest with Mesoamerican death ideologies or underworld characters. Deities such as Tlaloc, the rain god, and Quetzalcoatl, the horned water serpent, are also represented. Many of the icons have war equivalents in modern Pueblo society suggesting the

development of a Warrior Society among the Mimbres people during the eleventh and early twelfth centuries.

(3) Masked beings reminiscent of some modern katsinas depicted in rock art and a brown ware polychrome pottery tradition characterize the Jornada region (middle Rio Grande area) by the 1200s.

(4) Brown and red ware polychrome pottery flourishes in the Mogollon Rim and upper Little Colorado River Valley in the 1100s. These White Mountain Red Wares influenced or at least shared iconography with groups to the south as Salado Polychrome (Roosevelt Red Ware) and north into the Cibola, middle Little Colorado River, and Hopi Mesas in the 1200s. Yellow wares are added to the polychrome tradition after 1300.

(5) In all of the areas in (4), except western Salado areas below the Rim, there are concentrations of population in large villages with enclosed plazas and rectangular kivas by 1250 to 1300. The western Salado area, for example the Tonto Basin, does have compound enclosures that may be related to enclosed plazas. Rather than kivas or great kivas as foci for community ritual, however, Salado groups in large aggregated communities apparently used platform mounds, a concept probably borrowed from Hohokam groups to the south.

(6) Masked beings (katsinas) appear in rock art as the Rio Grande style in the Rio Grande Valley, Zuni, and middle Little Colorado River areas by 1350. As the Fourmile style, katsinas appear on pottery by 1325 in the Mogollon Rim area and before 1350 in the upper and middle Little Colorado River areas. In the Hopi Mesas area katsina motifs apparently postdate 1350 on ceramics and possibly on rock art. Kiva murals with katsinas may date as early as 1350 at Hopi and Homol'ovi, but probably date 1375–1400. Kivas murals along the Rio Grande all postdate 1400 and, except for Pottery Mound, apparently postdate 1450. If shared iconography of late Glaze III and Glaze IV ceramics with ceramic depictions on the Pottery Mound kiva murals can be used for cross-dating, than a post-1450 date could even be applied to the Pottery Mound kiva murals.

(7) Large areas of Pueblo occupation along the Mogollon Rim, Pajarito Plateau, Little Colorado River Valley, and elsewhere are abandoned between 1400–1450.

Thus during the eleventh century, Mogollon (and especially Mimbres) culture underwent substantial change. Village size grew, surface rooms appeared and developed into pueblos of stone and adobe that enclosed plazas, and rectangular kivalike structures appeared in these plazas (LeBlanc 1983). At one time when Di Peso (1974) proposed a beginning date of 1060 for his expansive, Mexican-inspired, Medio Period at Casas Grandes, major influence on Mimbres Culture (and Chaco) was attributed to Casas Grandes. Revised dates for Medio Phase developments to the thirteenth century (Ravesloot et al. 1986) make the strength of such influences impossible. It now seems more plausible that population growth, possibly through immigration of Anasazi people as well as through natural increase, resulted (or caused) from successful agricultural intensification techniques in many Mogollon culture areas, including Mimbres. Concentration of population around agriculturally productive areas resulted in or encouraged increased trade with the Anasazi to the north, the Hohokam to the west, and to other nearby Mogollon groups; elaboration in craft specialization; and elaboration in ritual. The combination of the latter two flourished in the Mimbres area and combined to produce the familiar iconography in rock art and on ceramic bowls. Icons on earlier Mogollon ceramics suggest major stylistic stimulus from the Hohokam region that was the foundation to the eleventh century florescence (Brody 1977).

Thus the Mimbres figurative art in pottery, petroglyphs, and pictographs that seemingly display Mexican influence are reconstituted through a combination of local ideology with Hohokam and Mogollon filters. This artistry carried a symbolism that extended deep into Mimbres culture. Many of the motifs have been associated with Mexican death symbols (Brody 1977:19-21). Following either Mexican or perhaps indigenous Mogollon cultural beliefs, the figurative pottery was apparently used as burial offerings (Moulard 1984). Thus it can be inferred that in Mimbres culture of the 950/1000-1150 period a cult of the dead was developed in addition to the Warrior Society.

Other pan-Pueblo symbols of later periods are identifiable in Mimbres iconography. These include the War Gods, earth and sky deities, the horned serpent, perhaps Spider Mother, masked beings, and several deities that could represent what today are chief katsinas. Most of these symbols have counterparts in Mesoamerica (Hedrick et al. 1974:7). The chief katsinas in modern Hopi culture are allied with specific clans (Wright 1977:29), are the most powerful katsinas, and are the most important, appearing primarily in the major ceremonies. These katsinas are recognizable in the fifteenth and sixteenth century kiva murals and apparently are the oldest, and are often the simplest in appearance. Perhaps the simple round-headed or cone-headed figures in Mimbres iconography are these priestly katsinas, or inspiration for their later development.

Perhaps inspired by the religion elaborated by the Mimbres people that was made so visually and symbolically powerful, a new iconography developed during the thirteenth century that has been called Salado by archaeologists. Groups sharing elements of "Salado Culture" were involved in local production of Gila Polychrome pottery, and characteristically were aggregated settlements with compounds, which probably contained integrative structures varying by area but often with platform mounds. This Salado "system" was seemingly both economic- and ritual-based. Its influence includes geographic areas considered in chapter 3, especially the middle Rio Grande Valley and the Mogollon Rim. The Rio Grande was more affected by Casas Grandes, whereas the Mogollon Rim was more influenced by a Hohokam filter. The role of Casas Grandes in this system is probably significant, especially in the areas beyond the Hohokam heartland from modern Tucson eastward. Cultures sharing in Salado iconography are different, and not all can be considered to have developed, or later developed, the katsina cult. In fact most probably did not; however, Salado interaction with Mogollon Rim groups clearly provided some stimulus for what we define as the katsina cult. Other characteristics associated with the cult, some developing in the Mimbres culture, also appear or further develop during the 1200s, including rectangular kivas and enclosed plazas.

Four Attributes Associated with Cult Origins

In chapter 3 the geographic and temporal distribution of several attributes, in addition to katsina designs, were discussed. Four of these, the rectangular kiva, the plaza-oriented pueblo, Fourmile style pottery decoration, and Rio Grande style rock art will be considered in more detail. Because all either predate or involve katsina iconography, it will be useful to look at these four elements and trace when and where they earliest occur to assist in our search for the origin and age of the katsina cult. Rio Grande style rock art has been defined by Schaafsma (1972). The definition of Fourmile style used in this discussion includes the following icons: masked beings (katsinas), mythological beings (animal, human, or a combination), and bird/bird feather motifs. All of these icons are depicted on interior bowl bottoms and many have asymmetrical layouts.

Several maps have been developed to show the distribution of these four attributes. The maps will compare the distribution of each attribute in the greater Southwest during two time periods, 1250/1300–1400 and

1400–1540, except for the Fourmile style which uses the periods 1250–1325, 1325–1450, and 1450–1540.

Fourmile Style

For purposes of discussion the Fourmile style will be divided into an early style (similar to Carlson's [1970] Pinedale style) and a classic style (similar to Carlson's [1970] Fourmile style). The early style has a preponderance of bird, especially parrot, motifs built on symmetrical layouts (refer to Figs. 3.11 & 3.17). The classic style maintains elements of the earlier style but adds asymmetric layouts in centered designs, masked figures (katsinas), and mythological beings (Figs. 3.12 & 3.13).

The early Fourmile style ceramics include Homolovi Polychrome and Chavez Pass Polychrome types in Winslow Orange Ware, Pinto Polychrome in Roosevelt Red Ware, Kwakina Polychrome in Zuni Glaze Ware, in addition to Pinedale Polychrome. Additionally, Casas Grandes and Chihuahuan Polychrome ceramics also share attributes of this style. All of the foregoing types apparently develop about 1275–1300 and disappear by 1400. As a result, the distribution map for the period 1275–1325 shows a broad presence of this style (Fig. 5.1). After 1325 asymmetric motifs emphasizing birds can be found. This stylistic shift is recognized by archaeologists through the creation of a new series of pottery types, except among the Winslow Orange Wares. The classic Fourmile style is depicted on Fourmile Polychrome about 1325, on Chavez Pass Polychrome and Homolovi Polychrome about 1325, on Sikyatki Polychrome and Jeddito Black-on-yellow of the Jeddito Yellow Wares by 1375, and on Kechipawan Polychrome, in the Zuni Glaze Wares about 1375 (Carlson 1982; Hays 1985; Kintigh 1985; Smith 1971). The stylistically related Rio Grande Glaze Ware, Style IV dates 1475 (Snow 1982). The late date for Style IV relative to other Fourmile style ceramics will be considered below. Among Salado Polychromes, a shift to design styles more similar to Casas Grandes Polychromes also occurs by 1300. Thus, Gila and Tonto Polychrome seem to be products of dynamics between northern and southern groups, probably a result of populations and exchange from both areas.

Masked figures may first appear about 1300 but seem to increase in frequency after 1325. The mythological beings also are rare early and seem to develop about 1325 or later. The later florescence of these beings is based on their high frequency at Sikyatki, a Hopi Pueblo postdating 1400, and the occurrence of both katsinas and mythological beings at the Homol'ovi sites dating 1300–1400. The distribution of ceramics containing masks and their contexts is much more restrictive, occurring primarily on Fourmile

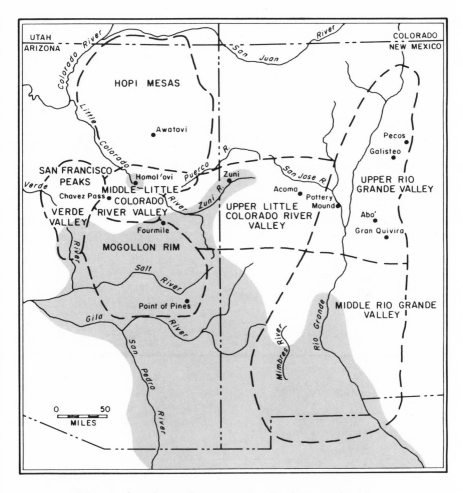

FIGURE 5.1. Major trade and manufacturing areas of early Fourmile style
ceramics, 1275–1350.
(Drawn by Ron Beckwith, Arizona State Museum)

Polychrome, Pinedale Black-on-white, Homolovi Polychrome, Chavez
Pass Polychrome, and more rarely on Sikyatki Polychrome, Jeddito Black-
on-yellow, and various Rio Grande Glazes. Figure 5.2 contrasts the distributions of the early and classic Fourmile styles between 1325 and 1450,
whereas Figure 5.3 illustrates the distribution of classic Fourmile style
ceramics depicting masked figures from 1300 to 1400. Figure 5.4 illustrates
the reduction in area of distribution of the classic Fourmile style associated with regional abandonments after 1450.

The remarkable differences between Figures 5.2 and 5.3 illustrates that a
new dynamic ritual specialization was developing with distinctive iconography by 1300, or shortly thereafter. These specialized mask icons developed out of the more generalized bird or feather-oriented iconography
elsewhere. The key to developing mask "styles" is changing conventions
of symmetry. The conventions were rarely violated, except in Fourmile
Polychrome, during the 1300s. An interesting, and so far unanswerable,
question becomes: did the ceramic iconography precede actual masking

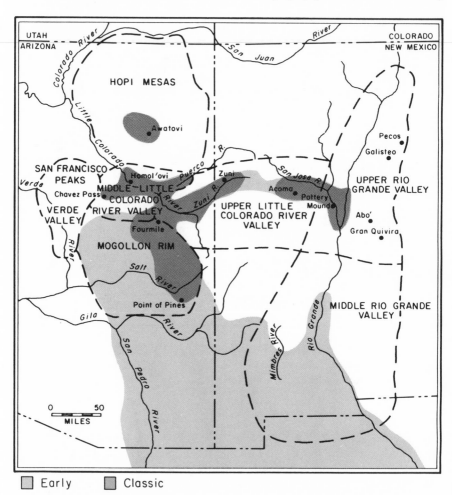

☐ Early   ■ Classic

FIGURE 5.2. Distribution of classic versus early Fourmile style on pottery
and in kivas, 1325–1450.
(Drawn by Ron Beckwith, Arizona State Museum)

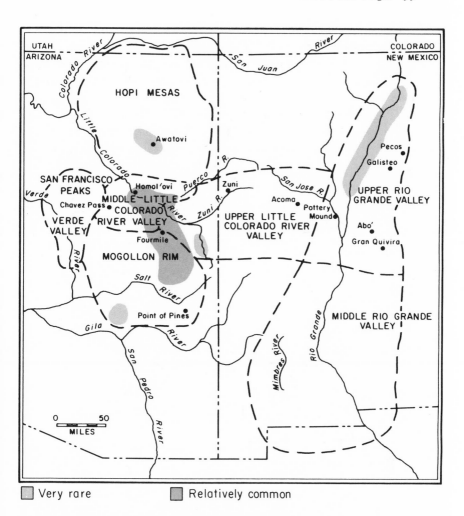

FIGURE 5.3. Distribution of classic Fourmile style ceramics depicting katsinas, 1300–1400.
(Drawn by Ron Beckwith, Arizona State Museum)

and depict mythological beings, or did it reflect developing norms in the society? This question will be returned to when the structure of society before and after the katsina cult is considered.

The broad participation of many diverse people and cultures in a brown ware, polychrome decorated pottery tradition frequently having stylized bird motifs has been a topic of much study and discussion. This so-called Salado culture, as defined by associated polychrome ceramics, is part of the early Fourmile (Pinedale) style system described above (see Fig. 5.1). The emphasis on parrots and macaws suggests that northern Mexico and especially the Casas Grandes area, which was crystallizing in the 1200s, were focal points for development of this style. Not coincidentally, it would seem, the shoe-form pot, piki stone (stone comal), and possibly rectangular ceramic vessel form appeared in the Hohokam area and here and there in areas making Salado Polychromes during the late 1200s. Developing out of this regional base were more local ceramic styles, such as

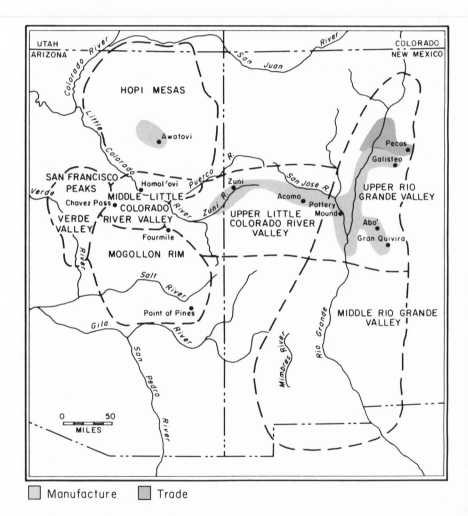

☐ Manufacture   ☐ Trade

FIGURE 5.4. Distribution of Fourmile style ceramics and murals, 1450–1540. (Drawn by Ron Beckwith, Arizona State Museum)

Escondida and Ramos Polychromes in the Casas Grandes area, Gila and Tonto Polychromes in the area between the rim and northern Mexico, and even regional variants of El Paso Polychrome along the Rio Grande. These southern influenced styles contrast with contemporary Fourmile style ceramics at Kinishba, Point of Pines, and Grasshopper.

Salado sites are large, usually having over 100 adobe rooms surrounding a plaza. As at Grasshopper, the interior plaza may have served the function equivalent to a great kiva. Haury (1985:391) has suggested this for the Forestdale area. Such a possibility is underscored by the large ceremonial structure found in the interior plaza of the Ormand Village (Hammack et al. 1966:29). The focus of ritual in plazas having platform mounds or converted to great kivas, such as at Grasshopper and Kinishba, may be northern reflections of this Salado pattern. The suggestion here, then, is that enclosed plazas were ceremonial units for Salado sites and that the parrot or bird iconography was associated with the ritual performed in the plazas. Massive parrot pens at Casas Grandes (Di Peso 1974) indicate a source area for the parrots and underscores their, or their feathers', importance to the culture. It is probably not surprising that parrot burials and parrot effigy pots have been found in excavations at most large fourteenth century pueblos from the Homol'ovi sites on the north, to Tuzigoot on the west, to the El Paso area on the east (Brook 1982; Kenaghy 1986), and to Casas Grandes on the south.

Therefore, the Fourmile style apparently represents a rapid and widespread shift in the decoration on primarily bowl interior bottoms beginning about 1300 in the upper Little Colorado River area and spreading north, south, and east over the next century. Thus, its depiction on local ceramic traditions, such as at Homol'ovi and Point of Pines, may signal local adoption of the katsina cult. Multimedia mask depictions in these same areas supports this impression. Thus, as Kenaghy (1986:561) has pointed out, these vessel designs may be iconographic intensifiers signaling the presence of symbolic information, in this case perhaps pertaining to the katsina cult.

Enclosed Plazas

The second attribute considered is the plaza. Plazalike orientation first appears in Chaco Canyon pueblos in the eleventh century and in a less formalized way at Mimbres phase sites at the same time. Earthen berms surrounding post-Chaco great houses in the Cibola area (Kintigh 1990), have plazalike characteristics and possible ritual roles. These could tie Chaco Canyon plaza architecture to true enclosed plaza-oriented sites ap-

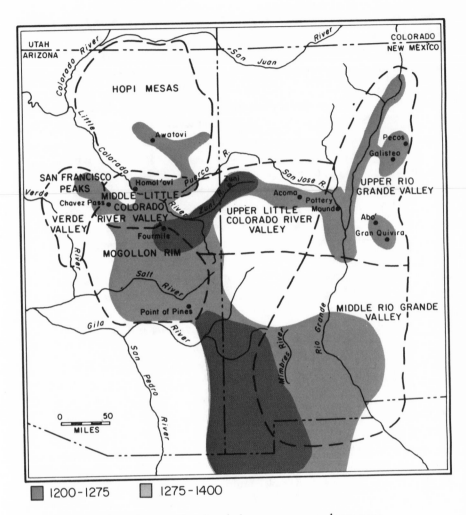

FIGURE 5.5. Distribution of enclosed plazas, 1200–1275 and 1275–1400.
(Drawn by Ron Beckwith, Arizona State Museum)

pearing a century or so later; however, most evidence points to a southern origin. By the thirteenth century enclosed plazas characterized a broad area of the southern Mogollon from Casas Grandes on the south to the headwaters of the Gila River on the north (Fig. 5.5). The pueblos associated with these plazas were all puddled (coursed or rammed earth), walled structures. Exceptions to the rule of early plaza-oriented villages predating 1275 occurring only south of the Gila River is the masonry Broken K Pueblo in the Hay Hollow Wash of the upper Little Colorado River drainage system. Additionally, several villages illustrated by Kintigh (1985) at Zuni have enclosed rectangular plaza areas and are ceramically dated by Kintigh to the 1200–1275 period. Whether pre-1275 plaza-oriented village plans north of the Mogollon Rim have a southern origin, are indigenous, or evolved out of Chaco forms is not clear and not crucial to the focus of the discussion that follows.

By 1300 the enclosed plaza style had spread north to the Hopi Mesas and occurred at the Homol'ovi sites, at Kintiel, and at Zuni. Plaza-oriented pueblos also were the rule throughout the northern Rio Grande area by 1350 (Fig. 5.5). Whether the new Rio Grande pueblos layout was inspired by western Pueblo neighbors or the Mogollon people to the south is not known for certain. However, the appearance of glaze wares on red backgrounds in the Rio Grande pueblos about 1325 in imitation of styles imported from Zuni beginning about 1300 would support west to east flow rather than a south to north flow for the enclosed plaza architecture layout.

As with the distribution of Fourmile style pottery, the distribution of plaza architecture shrinks substantially after 1400 or slightly later (Fig. 5.6). Of course the distribution parallels pueblos occupied in the fifteenth century, which is much reduced from the preceding century. A notable change in pueblo layout develops about 1400 and begins to replace the central enclosed plaza of the fourteenth century. This new layout is the "street-oriented" or open plaza style that is characteristic of many historic pueblos (see Stubbs 1950), (Fig. 5.7). Late prehistoric and protohistoric examples occur at Hopi, at Zuni (Kintigh 1985:89), and at Las Humanas (Hayes et al. 1981:13). This shift opened up the village, allowed all households to face the same direction (preferably to the south or southeast), provided more plaza areas for work and ceremony, and allowed physical separation of social groups. It is notable that at the same time the transition to the more open style plaza takes place, those adopting it are apparently socially more stable. As noted by Kintigh (1985:115), at Zuni between 1250 and 1400 over 28 pueblos with 13,000 rooms were built and abandoned. Typically these were oval or rectangular roomblocks surrounding plazas. The pueblos established about 1400, many with the open plaza layout, are the same pueblos occupied at Spanish contact and on to the Pueblo Revolt, or later. The abandonment of most pueblos during historic times was due to Spanish interference or epidemics, rather than internal friction. The architecture may in part reflect changes in the social system of the occupants that permitted this stability. This prospect will be considered later.

Rectangular Kivas

The third attribute whose distribution will be considered is the rectangular kiva. As traced briefly earlier, the rectangular kiva appears to be a

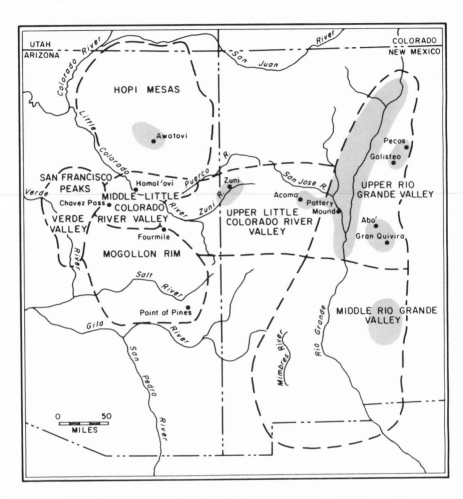

FIGURE 5.6. Distribution of enclosed plazas, 1400–1540.
(Drawn by Ron Beckwith, Arizona State Museum)

mixture of Anasazi kiva floor features and layout with traditional Mogollon (or Western Pueblo) square or rectangular pit house architecture. The classic late prehistoric (post–1300) rectangular kiva may have had its beginnings in the eleventh and twelfth centuries in the Mimbres area and farther north in west central New Mexico into the Reserve and Tularosa area where rectangular "great kivas" typify the ceremonial structures (cf. Bluhm 1957; LeBlanc 1983; Martin 1979). This tradition continued into the thirteenth century shifting northward and westward (Martin and Rinaldo 1960; Martin et al. 1961; Martin et al. 1962). Around 1250 both rectangular great kivas and small rectangular kivas with raised platforms and features similar to classic fifteenth century Hopi kivas (Smith 1972) appear together at Hooper Ranch Pueblo in the upper Little Colorado River Valley (Martin et al. 1961). These specialized features occur in the later small rectangular kivas in the area.

The development of the rectangular kiva west of this heartland in east central Arizona from Point of Pines to Forestdale is more complex. Formal, rectangular kivas in the classic western Pueblo style at Hopi were predominant in the Point of Pines area by 1300 (Smiley 1952:Table 1); however, Haury (1985:389) questions whether small rectangular kivas are present at all at Forestdale before 1275, or the Pinedale Phase. In lieu of small rectangular kivas one finds great kivas both before and after 1300 in the Forestdale area, at Kinishba, and in the Grasshopper area (Fig. 5.8). As summarized by Smiley (1952:Table 1), rectangular kivas have been tree-ring dated at Kintiel at 1276 and at Pinedale Pueblo at 1300. At Point of Pines

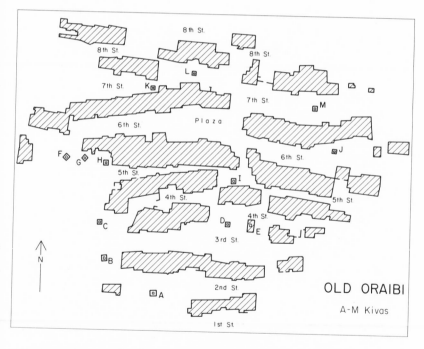

FIGURE 5.7. An example of the "street-oriented" layout of Pueblos that developed after 1400.
(Redrawn by Ron Beckwith, Arizona State Museum, from *Old Oraibi: A Study of the Hopi Indians of Third Mesa* by Mischa Titiev, Fig. 3, by permission of the Peabody Museum, Harvard University)

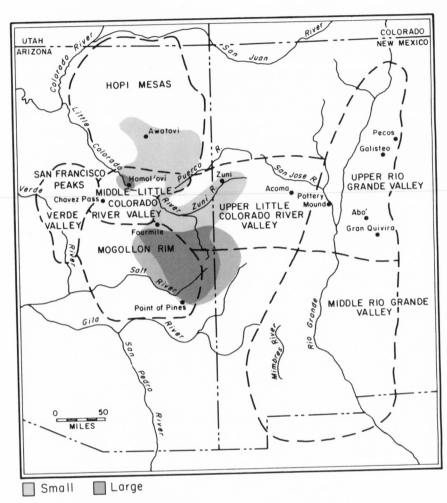

☐ Small   ☐ Large

FIGURE 5.8. Distribution of small rectangular kivas and great kivas,
1200–1400.
(Drawn by Ron Beckwith, Arizona State Museum)

one is dated 1300 on the basis of associated tree-ring dated ceramics.
Kintigh (1985) reports rectangular kivas in the Zuni area by 1300 and
Martin and Rinaldo (1960:134, 143) report rectangular kivas at Hooper
Ranch that were built probably between 1250 and 1300. Two rectangular
kivas and a rectangular great kiva are also present at Homol'ovi III by 1300
and probably by 1280 on the basis of tree-ring dated ceramics and a calibrated radiocarbon date on the closing material of one kiva, which dated

675 +/− 55 yrs: A.D. 1277–1318 (Adams 1989:225). Smith (1972) notes that the small rectangular kiva form was also at Awatovi by 1300.

This distribution indicates a broad, rapid spread of a distinctive architectural style, the rectangular kiva, that replaced circular forms or ramp-entered, rectangular great kiva forms in the north and nonkiva ceremonial forms in the south during the latter quarter or perhaps latter half of the thirteenth century. Lekson (1982) reports rectangular kivalike structures in a thirteenth century Animas Phase pueblo in the Red Rock Valley of the Gila River in west central New Mexico. Clear continuity between the 1150 rectangular pit-kivas (Martin 1979) of west-central New Mexico and the post–1275 classic rectangular kivas of east-central Arizona is presently lacking. There appears to be an almost mutually exclusive distribution of rectangular great kivas instead of small rectangular ones from the San Francisco River west to Forestdale and Grasshopper until after 1275. North of the Mogollon Rim great kivas seem to disappear altogether after 1300.

The alternative to the Mogollon origin to the rectangular kiva is to consider the McDonald Phase rectangular kivas of the Hopi Buttes (Gumerman and Skinner 1968) to be antecedent to the fourteenth century classic rectangular kivas of Point of Pines, Awatovi, Kawaika-a, Kintiel, Pinedale, and elsewhere. The Mogollon origin of the rectangular kiva is preferred over a Colorado Plateau origin for four major reasons. First, the Hopi Buttes "rectangular" kivas are different from the classic "Hopi" style rectangular form. They are square pit structures with benches appended to one side rather than rectangular pit structures having a raised platform on one end, such as the ones in the upper Little Colorado River area. Second, architectural and artifactual complexes associated with the Mogollon village also have their origins to the south. These include in particular plaza-oriented layouts, aggregation, and polychrome pottery. Third, ceramic trade types at villages having rectangular kivas are predominated by southern (White Mountain and Salado) polychromes rather than northern (Tsegi) polychromes. Finally, stylistic change on ceramics at all of the pueblos where such analyses have been summarized or illustrated is affected by early Fourmile style iconography. This style is manifest as Jeddito Black-on-orange and Polychrome at the Hopi Mesas; as Pinedale Polychrome in the White Mountains, as Homolovi Polychrome at the Homol'ovi pueblos, as Kwakina Polychrome in the Zuni area, and as Pinto Polychrome along and below the Mogollon Rim. All of these types date 1275–1325 or the same time that other changes are taking place in these areas (refer to Fig. 5.4) in terms of the development of rectangular kivas and the appearance of enclosed plazas. All have varying frequencies of stylized parrots or parrot (bird) figures (Carlson 1970; Smith et al. 1966;

Smith 1971; Young 1967). All have white decorations or outlines added to a black-on-red (orange or brown) tradition. The center of these stylistic changes is the upper Little Colorado River, not the Hopi Buttes area or points north.

Details of the transition of the rectangular kiva form may lay in the sequence of sites dug by Paul Martin and his colleagues and students in the Pine Lawn and Tularosa River Valleys of west central New Mexico, in the upper Little Colorado River Valley between Springerville and St. Johns, and in the Hay Hollow Valley region of the upper Little Colorado River. From perusing these various works the following sequence is suggested. From about 1000–1250 the dominant ceremonial structure is all of the above listed areas and probably from the Grasshopper/Forestdale area south to Point of Pines was the rectangular great kiva. Although initially built of pole roof supports and wattle-and-daub sides, it eventually became mostly a masonry structure. It was initially built several meters away from the pueblo. These kivas always had southern or eastern ramp entries. Excellent examples of the early part of the sequence occur in the Pine Lawn area in the Reserve Phase (1000–1150) Sawmill site (Bluhm 1957). Later examples of these great kivas were found at the Mineral Creek and Hooper Ranch sites along the upper Little Colorado River (Martin et al. 1961). Dating about 1225, Martin et al. (1962:219–220) note that at the Rim Valley Pueblo along the upper Little Colorado River there were no apparent kivas, but that there were ceremonial rooms within the pueblo.

Later, more formalized examples of ceremonial rooms appear, now usually with raised platforms on the south or east ends. It is logical to equate these platforms with a modification of the ramp entries of the separate great kivas. Kivas within the roomblock with platforms occur at Hooper Ranch Pueblo (Martin et al. 1962), Carter Ranch Pueblo (Martin et al. 1964; Longacre 1970), and at Broken K (Martin et al. 1967; Hill 1970). Those at Hooper Ranch date about 1200–1250. Those at Carter Ranch date about 1200–1225 and at Broken K date to between 1180–1250. Both Hooper Ranch and Carter Ranch also have isolated great kivas. Carter Ranch has a wall on the east side of the roomblock that could be considered as enclosing a plaza. Broken K does not have a great kiva but instead has an enclosed plaza. As has been suggested by Longacre (1964), the plaza may replace the great kiva.

The next stage is the elimination of the great kiva and its replacement by the enclosed plaza area as a pan-village ceremonial structure. Within the plaza are some of the small kivas with platforms formerly located in the roomblock, although some are still abutted by rooms, even in modern pueblos. This process is earliest seen at Broken K dating about 1250 (Hill

1970). In some areas below the rim from Forestdale/Grasshopper to Point of Pines/Kinishba the great kiva continued as the major ceremonial focus of society. Only in the Point of Pines area were the great kivas accompanied by the raised platform, rectangular kivas that developed on the north side of the Mogollon Rim (Fig. 5.8). After 1275 the rectangular kiva with the platform on the south or east side appears associated with villages usually having enclosed plazas over a very broad area (Fig. 5.8).

At this point, a few words need to be said about great kivas, plazas, and their place in Pueblo ritual. Today, plazas are the focus of public performances of Pueblo ritual whether it be katsina or nonkatsina. The evidence cited above indicates a transition in the late 1200s from rectangular great kivas to rectangular enclosed plazas (Longacre 1964:210). Archaeologists have long maintained that great kivas functioned to integrate larger segments of the local population. One way to make ritual more integrative is to make aspects of it more accessible, or public. As villages increased in size in the late 1200s, it became absolutely essential that the community members work together or cooperate to occasionally place their own needs or that of their families secondary to the needs of the community. To effect such changes requires activities that demand cooperation and that make the individuals feel they are an essential element to the success of the whole. Public rituals perform such needs in societies at similar cultural levels throughout the world and they used "integrative architecture" to stage such events (Adler 1989). The historic and prehistoric Pueblo people were no different. The village "sipapu" (sipaapuni) or spirit hole to the underworld is located in the plaza in modern Hopi communities, clearly suggesting a pan-village ceremonial role for the plaza. The plaza in its enclosed, rectangular form of the thirteenth and fourteenth centuries continued the pan-village ceremonial function of the great kiva. (At Kinishba, Grasshopper, and Foote Canyon Pueblo [Rinaldo 1959:181], plazas were covered and converted to great kivas.) The enclosed plaza was first a ceremonial place and was used to conduct public ritual. When not needed for ritual, the plaza was available for secular activities, much like modern Pueblo kivas, as well as plazas.

The rectangular kiva, what has been termed the Hopi-style clan kiva, spread to the east along the Rio Grande after 1350 and most likely not until about 1400 (Fig. 5.9). The Rio Grande rectangular kivas, however, are quite specialized in having murals, some of which display the classic Fourmile (or Sikyatki) style of designs associated with masked figures. These murals are not painted on the indigenous circular kivas that were also in use. At the same time, the occupation of the large pueblos in the upper Little Colorado River Valley, the upper Salt River region below the Mo-

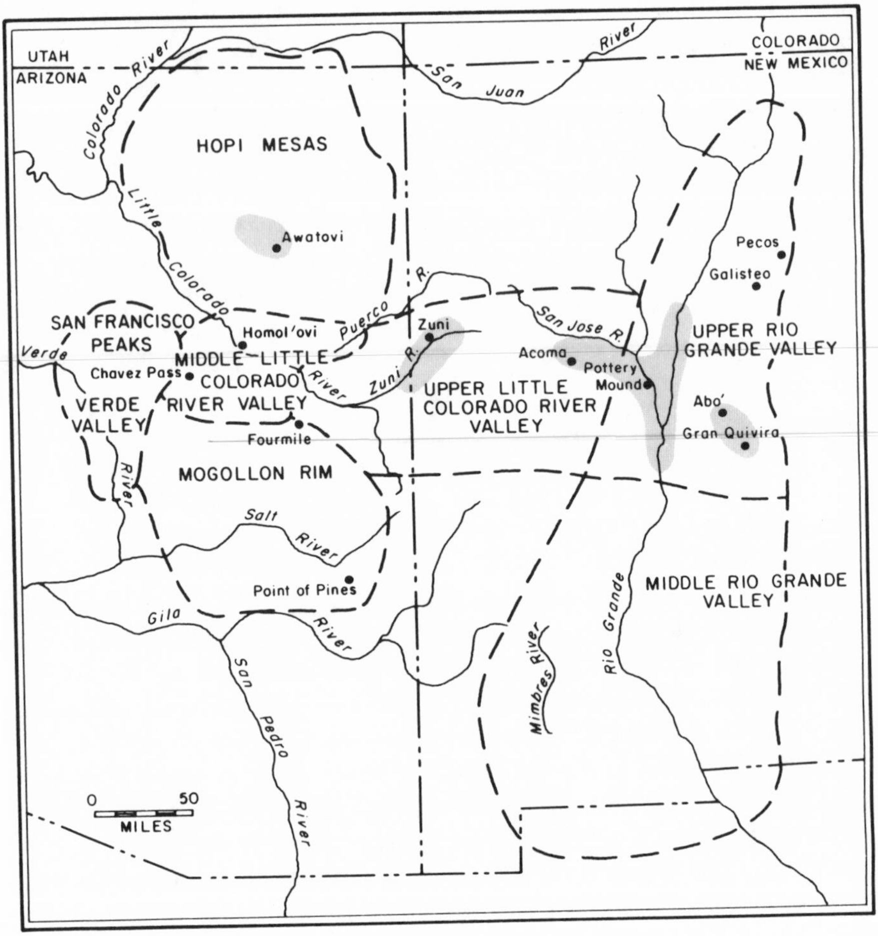

FIGURE 5.9. Distribution of rectangular kivas, 1400–1540.
(Drawn by Ron Beckwith, Arizona State Museum)

gollon Rim, and the central Little Colorado River Valley ceased. Therefore, after 1400–1450 the rectangular kiva form with the platform is
restricted to the Hopi villages, Zuni, Acoma, and various villages in the
upper Rio Grande Valley (Fig. 5.9).

Rio Grande Style

The fourth and final attribute to be analyzed with respect to its distribution is the Rio Grande rock art style (Schaafsma 1972). First, it is necessary

to distinguish the distribution of the Jornada style from the Rio Grande style. Although Schaafsma (1972:97) limits the northern extent of the Jornada style to just north of Carrizozo, it seems that the style in the Abó district near Las Humanas is an extension of that tradition with its flat-headed figures bearing striped chins. Schaafsma (1972:131) notes this similarity. For this reason Figure 5.10 does not include the Gran Quivira area as part of the Rio Grande style rock art tradition.

As outlined in earlier sections on distribution of katsina cult attributes through selected areas, it was noted that the Rio Grande style extended into the Cibola or Zuni area (Young and Bartman 1981), the Homol'ovi area (Pilles 1975) and Petrified Forest area (Cole 1989b; Jennings 1980) of the central Little Colorado River Valley, and in the vicinity of the Hopi Mesas (Turner 1963) (Fig. 5.10). Figure 5.11 illustrates the same pattern of change from the pre–1400 period to the post–1400 prehistoric period noted in the other attributes discussed in this chapter. That is, the distribution of Rio Grande style rock art co-occurs with the location of the historic pueblos.

Schaafsma (1972:129–130) defines the Rio Grande style as having depictions of masks, often as the predominant element. She notes that anthropomorphs also occur, as do shield-bearers. Other style characteristics are the Kokopelli, bird motifs, occasional serpents, the spiral and concentric circle, shields, hand prints, crosses or stars, and terraces. The mask, being a hallmark, is not ubiquitous in its distribution or frequency within the area Schaafsma considers the Rio Grande style area. The modern Tewa Pueblo region north of Santa Fe rarely has masks (1972:146). Figure 5.12 depicts the distribution of the Rio Grande style with mask motifs. In the eastern region of our study area they occur in the Galisteo Basin, the Pecos Pueblo area, and along the Rio Grande from Santa Fe south to San Marcial. In the west they are known in the Zuni area, the Homol'ovi sites area, the Petrified Forest area, and near the Hopi Mesas. Isolated elements are also known along the lower Little Colorado River and rarely in southeastern Utah in drainages heading south into the San Juan and Colorado Rivers (Turner 1963).

Two major problems with the Figures 5.10 to 5.12 maps are those dogging most regional studies of rock art: incomplete coverage to allow evaluation of distributional maps and difficulty in dating rock art panels. Although major gaps in the location of the Rio Grande style are apparent in the western section from Hopi to Zuni, lack of systematic survey and documentation cannot rule out the presence of the style in these areas. With katsinas and masks depicted on Fourmile Polychrome in the upper Little Colorado River region, one would expect comparable rock art; however,

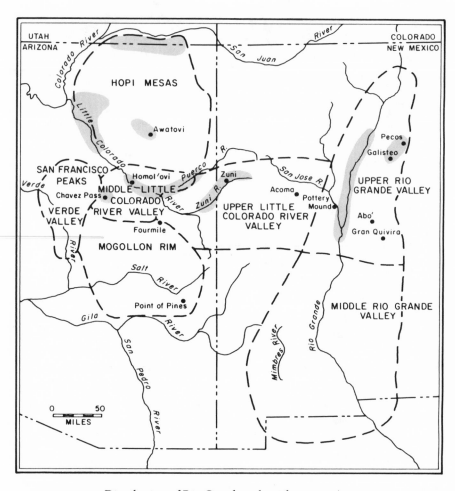

FIGURE 5.10. Distribution of Rio Grande style rock art, 1325/1350–1400.
(Drawn by Ron Beckwith, Arizona State Museum)

such a relationship is not always predictable; for example, the rarity of
katsina masks on ceramics is belied by their relative frequency on rock art
in the Hopi Mesas area. The Rio Grande style was virtually unknown in
1972 in the Zuni area when Schaafsma published her study of rock art in
New Mexico, but the motif was found to be quite common once a systematic survey was conducted (Young and Bartman 1981). Thus the presence
or absence of rock art cannot be inferred, but can only be evaluated after
better data are compiled.

    The spatial distribution of the style is an important element in deter-
mining its origin. If the style is concentrated in a broad area and spotty

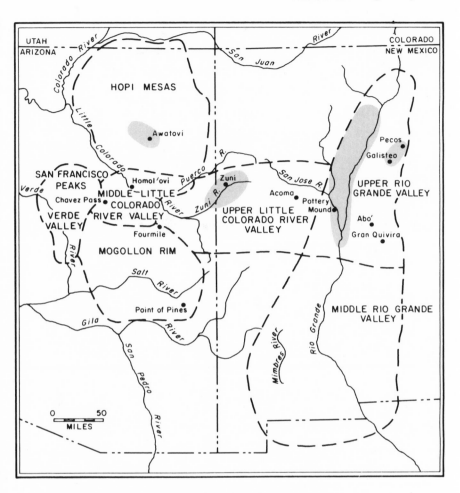

FIGURE 5.11. Distribution of Rio Grande style rock art, 1400–1540.
(Drawn by Ron Beckwith, Arizona State Museum)

elsewhere, this would suggest the area of concentration is the likely place
of origin. Its broad distribution in the upper Rio Grande Valley and
overlap and superficial similarity to the Jornada style, apparently depicted
at the same time in the middle Rio Grande Valley, led Schaafsma (1972) to
conclude that the Rio Grande style developed out of the Jornada style
(1972:16). In fact Schaafsma concludes that the style represents the appearance of the katsina cult in the Rio Grande Valley.

There is no question that the Rio Grande style and the Jornada style
comingled in the southern sections of the northern Rio Grande Valley,
especially in the Galisteo Basin and the San Marcial areas. It is also

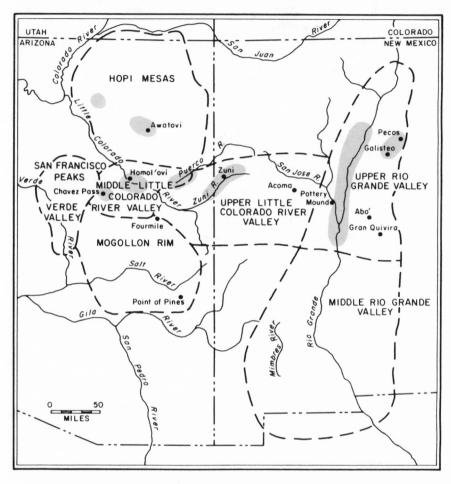

FIGURE 5.12. Distribution of Rio Grande style rock art with masked motifs
as common elements.
(Drawn by Ron Beckwith, Arizona State Museum)

noteworthy that the Jornada style elements do not occur in the western
distribution of the Rio Grande style, that is outside the Rio Grande
Valley. This would suggest one of two possibilities: (1) that the origin of
the Rio Grande style was not in the Rio Grande Valley area but to the
west outside the influence of the Jornada style; or (2) that the two styles
are not the same age. There are no systematic instances of one style
superimposed over the other. Thus although the data are not extensive,
they do not suggest that either style was older than the other.

The kiva mural evidence is noteworthy in dating the Jornada style.

Schaafsma (1972:160) describes the strong similarity between the Jornada style and the Kuaua murals, which have been dated to the fifteenth century. The Jornada style is also popular in the rock art at Abó, which is stylistically quite similar to Kuaua and thus probably dates fifteenth through seventeenth century (Brody 1988:18). It would seem that the Jornada style in the Albuquerque area and south to the Abó area may date fifteenth century and later, rather than the 1350 or earlier that it would need to be to influence the Rio Grande style as dated by Schaafsma (1972:158). In fact with the exception of a sherd of Talpa Black-on-white from the Taos district dated 1250–1400, there is no clearcut evidence cited by Schaafsma for placing her beginning date of the Rio Grande style at 1350 rather than at 1400. In fact the influence of the Zuni area in the form of glaze decorated pottery and possibly village layout on the Rio Grande area about 1325 could be used to argue for early fourteenth century influence from the west rather than the south.

In the final analysis there are no really reliable dates for the Rio Grande style rock art. Perhaps the strongest date and association comes from Homol'ovi II. Extensive Rio Grande style rock art panels occur around Homol'ovi II. Excavation in five rooms by the Arizona State Museum in 1984 recovered a Paayu Polychrome (early Sikyatki Polychrome style) bowl with a Sun Forehead katsina mask design (Hays 1985), (Fig. 5.13). Two radiocarbon dates from features of two rooms contiguous to the room from which the katsina mask bowl was found and having identical ceramic assemblages date 600 +/−75 years (calibrated to A.D. 1340–1397; mean = 1350) and 610 +/−85 years (calibrated to A.D. 1337–1373; mean = 1352) (Hays and Adams 1985:Appendix E). It is reasonable to conclude that the related Rio Grande style rock art was being manufactured by the latter half of the fourteenth century. A possible 1350 date is identical to the one proposed by Schaafsma (1972), but revised to 1325 (Schaafsma and Schaafsma 1974). The 1325 date is generally tied to the beginning of the Classic Period in Rio Grande archaeology which, as in the west, is associated with aggregation and the development of enclosed plaza-oriented villages. As discussed in the earlier part of this section, however, enclosed plaza-oriented villages developed in the west 25–50 years before first evidence of katsina cult iconography (masks on Fourmile Polychrome bowls).

With much broader evidence of fourteenth century katsina cult iconography on ceramics in the west and association of Rio Grande rock art at Homol'ovi II with a 1350 date, it is tempting to claim a beginning date for the Rio Grande style in the west as early as in the east. Realistically, however, any absolute dates for the beginning of the Rio Grande style

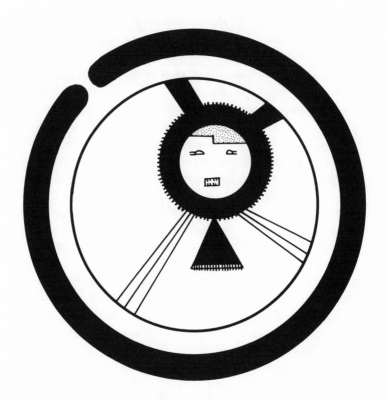

FIGURE 5.13. Asymmetric katsina mask on a Paayu Polychrome bowl from
Homol'ovi II.
(Arizona State Museum collections; drawn by Kelley A. Hays,
Arizona State Museum)

must be taken with a grain of salt. It is probably safe to say that the style
first appears in the fourteenth century in the west. It is also possible that
the style is fourteenth century in the Rio Grande Valley; however, the
evidence is all circumstantial. Problems with all of the standard explana-
tions developed by Schaafsma (1972) for placing the beginning date of the
Rio Grande style at 1350 have been detailed in this discussion, including
the Jornada ties. A relationship between the two styles is undeniable, for
both appear in the Pottery Mound murals (Crotty 1987), but the relationship does not appear to be evolutionary.

It seems appropriate at this point to consider the Jornada style iconography of the middle Rio Grande Valley and its possible relationship
to what has been identified here and earlier by Schaafsma (1972) and

Schaafsma and Schaafsma (1974) as the katsina cult exemplified in rock art as the Rio Grande style. Briefly, the Jornada style seems related to a complex of characteristics that include El Paso Polychrome. El Paso Polychrome is on sites apparently associated with the Jornada style rock art from the Hueco Tanks near El Paso on the south to the San Marcial area of the Rio Grande Valley on the north to Lincoln Phase sites on the northeast, although El Paso Polychrome occurs only as trade pieces in its northern and northeastern distribution. The distribution of the Jornada rock art style extends much farther north than that of El Paso Polychrome (Hawley 1936). Sites with El Paso Polychrome are more aggregated, some having enclosed plazas, than previous time periods in the region; however, no kivas are known for the region of manufacture, only for regions of trade, implying different ritual roots to the style in contrast to the Rio Grande style. Additionally, katsina masks or masked figures apparently were never depicted on El Paso Polychrome. Characteristics of the Jornada style iconography include masks with flat-topped heads, striped or decorated chins, terraced headdresses, oval or lenticular eyes, a nose, and simple mouths. Figures in this style occur mixed with the Rio Grande style north to Santa Fe. Elements associated with the Jornada style, such as shields, also are broadly distributed in the Rio Grande Valley area, but not to the west of the Valley. Figures in the Jornada style also characterize the fifteenth century Kuaua kiva murals and one panel of the fifteenth century Pottery Mound murals. Figures in the Jornada style do not appear west of the Rio Grande Valley until the historic period when they are seen at Zuni. The Jornada style in rock art is clearly exemplified in pictographs and petroglyphs in the Abó region, pretty much to the exclusion of the Rio Grande style. The Abó rock art could date anywhere from 1300 to 1672, but if associated with the early kiva murals at Las Humanas that bear shields and iconography related to the Jornada style, a date of fifteenth century would seem most reasonable. Brody's (1988) analysis also suggests a fifteenth century beginning date for the Abó rock art. The shields at Pueblo del Encierro in the Cochiti area are also remindful of Jornada iconography and were dated by Schaafsma (1965) to about 1500.

It seems evident that the Jornada style extends in a broad area from the El Paso vicinity to Santa Fe, pretty much confined to the Rio Grande Valley corridor, spilling east onto the plains in the Abó area and north to the Galisteo Basin. Although the Jornada styles associated with El Paso Polychrome indicate a thirteenth to fourteenth century date for the style in the lower sections of the middle Rio Grande Valley, its appearance in the northern Rio Grande seems concentrated in the fifteenth century.

Inference for this date comes principally from the kiva murals having Jornada iconography. The Jornada rock art style could easily postdate the Rio Grande style where they overlap in the Rio Grande Valley. The mixture of the two styles in the Rio Grande Valley north of San Marcial with the Jornada style dwindling in intensity as one proceeds northward clearly mimics a style separate from the Rio Grande style. If the Rio Grande style were derived from the Jornada style, the distribution of other Jornada style elements would be unrelated to distance from the Jornada heartland to the south. As noted earlier, the Jornada style elements seen in the Rio Grande Valley would also be expected where the Rio Grande style is found farther west. It is not.

The frequent association of the Jornada style with shields both in rock art and in murals suggests that warfare may be a more important element of the Jornada style cult than with the western katsina cult. The Kuaua murals strongly emphasize this association. Among the Tewa, interestingly, the most universal societies are the Scalp and the associated Women's Societies, which are linked to war. Masked Whipper Katsinas are associated with the Tewa Scalp Society and are a universal factor among Pueblos in associating warriors and masked dancers. Initial development of a warrior society has been speculated in the Mimbres iconography. This could prove to be the ultimate origin of some aspects of the Jornada style, in particular those associated with warfare. The relationship between the Jornada style and the Mimbres style was first observed by Schaafsma (1972). The Kuaua murals and the rock art of the northern Rio Grande Valley area of the fifteenth century undeniably indicate the presence of the katsina cult. The mixture of the western cult with the Jornada style cult probably gave a unique flavor not only to the iconography of the northern Rio Grande Valley area, but also to the ritual drama.

Summary

Figure 5.14 is a composite map plotting the overlap of the four attributes considered in this section. Ironically, the Rio Grande rock art style does not overlap with the Fourmile style in ceramics. Most likely the explanation for this unexpected, almost mutually exclusive pattern is the lack of research on the rock art of the upper Little Colorado River Valley, although the styles could fill similar roles in signaling the presence of the cult and would be simply different systems for accomplishing the same goal (Cole 1989b; Kenaghy 1986). Nevertheless, the best alternative at this point is to consider the overlap of three of the four attributes. The

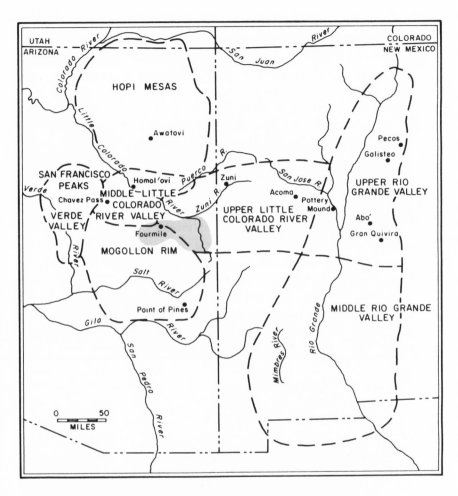

FIGURE 5.14. Overlap area of the distribution of small rectangular kivas,
enclosed plazas, and Fourmile style iconography, 1250–1350.
(Drawn by Ron Beckwith, Arizona State Museum)

Fourmile style was selected over the Rio Grande style because it is better
dated, because it is earlier, and because its overlap with the other two
attributes is more clearcut and earlier than with the Rio Grande rock art
style.

The earliest co-occurrence of the attributes is plotted on Figure 5.14.
Although the period 1250–1350 is offered as a conservative estimate, the
enclosed plaza, rectangular kiva, and distinctive Pinedale style (early Fourmile style) iconography all appear seemingly simultaneously about 1275.

Katsinas and katsina masks appear on classic Fourmile style (Fourmile Polychrome) probably as early as 1325. The convergence of enclosed plazas, classic rectangular kivas (having south- or east-facing raised platforms), and Fourmile style iconography overlap in a relatively small area in the upper Little Colorado River Valley bounded on the west by the Silver Creek drainage, on the north and east by the Little Colorado River, and on the south by the Mogollon Rim (Fig. 5.14). A more specific definition for the south boundary can be described as slightly north of the crest of the Rim where the pinyon-juniper forest replaces ponderosa pine as the dominant tree species. The Showlow ruin lies along the southern limit of this area. It is noteworthy that Fewkes (1904:144–145) recorded Hopi and Zuni accounts of katsina beings originating near Fourmile ruin in the upper Little Colorado River area. Both groups still made pilgrimages to sacred lakes in the area at the turn of the century.

On the basis of arguments developed earlier about the relationship of the four attributes to the katsina cult, the conclusion to be drawn is that the katsina cult developed in the area described above between 1275 and 1325. The figures for the four attributes illustrating later time periods depict the spread of the cult from its initial development. From the upper Little Colorado River area the initial spread of the cult seems to have been northward into the Petrified Forest and Homol'ovi areas and quickly into the Hopi Mesas and probably into the Zuni area (as exemplified in Kechipawan Polychrome). This early spread predates 1400 and is associated with several ceramic types with depictions of katsinas (see Ferg 1982; Hays 1989) and the development of the Rio Grande rock art style. All of these areas already had rectangular kivas and plazas, and this association seems critical in the spread of the katsina cult. Although the cult may have been present in the Rio Grande Valley by 1350 or so in the form of the Rio Grande rock art style, it is not until after 1400 that there is the best evidence for the cult spreading rapidly into the Rio Grande area, and it also seems to be transformed in the Zuni villages.

The post–1400 katsina cult that spreads to Zuni and into the Rio Grande area is peculiarly Hopi. The refinement of the cult at Hopi possibly resulted from the unique environmental situation of the people. Of all the Pueblo groups of this time, the Hopi had the most precarious dry-farming existence. The katsina cult offered a pantheon of deities and ancestors who could be approached and closely worked with to derive more rain. The cult's early association with precipitation is easily perceived in every modern Pueblo village's association of the katsina with spring or lake water or well-watered mountains and the attribution of these wet places with katsina homes.

The well-integrated cult of the dead and of rain and associated ceramic and kiva mural iconography of the Hopi then spread back to the south and east to contemporary villages dating 1400–1450. Thus in the Rio Grande Valley there is Pottery Mound and at Zuni there is Matsaki Polychrome. At Pottery Mound there is possible site intrusion of Hopi (Hibben 1955), but Matsaki Polychrome is clearly a copy of Sikyatki Polychrome and related types (Woodbury and Woodbury 1966:326). At Pottery Mound and other sites in the region, rectangular kivas first appear (Hibben 1960; Judge 1975:44), whereas at Zuni, although not the first, rectangular kivas become the only form by this time (Smith et al. 1966). It may have been this secondary spread that Dutton (1963) saw as katsina cult in the Kuaua murals, although the Jornada style to the murals suggests a southern tie instead or in addition to a Hopi tie.

The weaker status of the katsina cult among the modern Tewa and Tiwa may be due to: (1) the earlier existence (or later substitution for the katsina cult) of a moiety system as the social mechanism for integrating a large population into a village based on the segmentary lineages; (2) the better water situation in the Rio Grande Valley making a rain-associated cult less significant; (3) the extensive alteration of eastern Pueblo ceremonialism by Spanish-introduced Catholicism; or (4) substitution of a less mask-oriented Jornada style cult for the Hopi style cult more popular to the south in the Pottery Mound area. Of course a combination of the above is most likely. It may be that with better understanding of the Tiwa and Tewa, aspects of these early cults may become apparent. For instance, the Oxua, or deities, of the Tewa, although not katsina, are comparable in their male-only impersonations, association with Made People in that the latter can become Oxua, and the translation of Oxua as "cloud beings" (Ortiz 1969:91–97). In a real sense the Oxua are a cult of the dead, but evidently restricted to Made People. The animals and plants impersonated, their method of impersonation, and the ancestor worship aspects all indicate the Tewa Oxua cult may be more closely related to the Jornada "cult," as interpreted from Jornada style rock art, with headdresses and with few masks.

6

Archaeological Patterns Related to the Cult

At this point it seems appropriate to summarize what can be perceived by an archaeologist as components of the cult from stylistic, architectural, and artifactual grounds. The integration of these attributes with the location of their appearance and dissemination through time should bring us up to date.

Some discussion on the Mimbres culture has been introduced from time to time. The significance of Mimbres culture as to the katsina cult is indirect at best, although Carlson (1982a) would disagree. Brody (1977) has detailed the dissimilarity in the Mimbres iconography from the later Fourmile Polychrome, Sikyatki Polychrome, and kiva mural iconography that have been linked to the katsina cult here. Brody (1977) and Moulard (1984) have linked numerous Mimbres icons to a cult of the dead. Brody extends this concept to Mexican ties and the concept of Tlaloc, suggested earlier by Schaafsma and Schaafsma (1974). Although some iconographic themes, such as terraced designs and parrots, are common to both the Mimbres style and the later Jornada style, the more substantial differences suggest another source for the Jornada style.

The Jornada style develops or appears at the same time El Paso Polychrome expands into southeastern New Mexico. Stallings (1931) comments that El Paso Polychrome is centered in the El Paso/Hueco Tanks area and extends considerably into Chihuahua. The Hueco Tanks Jornada style rock art also appears to be at the center for this style. Their association with Animas Phase sites that are aggregated, made of adobe architecture, and have enclosed plazas probably ties the style to the development of the Casas Grandes trading center only 200 km southwest of El Paso. But these characteristics can also be found in a broad band of settlements extending west to the Tonto Basin that have been grouped rather generically as Salado. In fact Salado Polychromes are characteristic of Animas Phase sites in southwestern New Mexico. El Paso Polychrome, although stylistically possibly related to Gila Polychrome, seems more clearly derived from Chihuahuan Polychromes. The influence of Casas Grandes as seen through Cliff Phase and El Paso Phase sites extended only into the southern reaches of the middle Rio Grande Valley to the vicinity of El Paso. These are the very areas where El Paso Polychrome was being manufactured. Nevertheless, it is quite possible that the diffusion not only of technology and style, but of ideas from Casas Grandes had an impact on the people of the middle Rio Grande Valley from El Paso to the San Marcial area during the late thirteenth and fourteenth centuries, lasting until 1400 or a little later.

On the basis of arguments presented in the last chapter, however, it seems unlikely that the Jornada style associated "cult" had any major influence on the Pueblo people of the upper Rio Grande Valley until the fifteenth century. What was the nature of the Jornada cult? Mexican iconography, such as the plumed serpent and masking, is clearly present. Masking has a long history in Mexican ritual. Arguments presented in the previous chapter and expanded in chapter 7 suggest the Jornada style "masked cult" mixed with the western Pueblo katsina cult in the Rio Grande Valley during the fifteenth century, perhaps having a more dominant role with respect to the katsina cult in some villages than in others. Probably the key element of acceptance of the katsina cult over the Jornada cult in most villages was its integration into existing Pueblo ritual based in the kiva. There is no evidence that the Jornada cult had any basis in the kiva until entering the Pueblo area in the Salinas region. The fourteenth century enclosed-plaza villages of the Cliff and El Paso Phases may have been used for public ritual performances, as they were for the western katsina cult and for the modern cult. This could have facilitated their absorption into the Rio Grande villages, especially those organized into moieties (suggested by the presence of large, circular kivas), in contrast to villages having the small, rectangular kiva-based katsina cult.

The origin, development, and spread of the katsina cult, as it is manifested in Pueblo villages today, is the central concern of this document to this point. Much detail has been presented in tracing various elements presently associated with the cult or seemingly bearing icons of masks or masked figures. To understand the origins of the cult it was necessary to identify the elements associated with the cult and trace their distribution through much of the southern Colorado Plateau and northern Mogollon Rim. Principal material elements of the cult are its iconography and its setting, that is, the surroundings needed for performance of the katsina cult. In order to find and trace the cult, the significant elements derived from studies of modern katsina religion were determined to be the mask or masked figure icons, the kiva, and the village layout. Masked figures appear in rock art (termed the Rio Grande style), on pottery (termed the classic Fourmile style), and in kiva murals (also the classic Fourmile style). Tracing katsina cult masks and masked figures on these three media revealed a broad distribution from the Frijoles Canyon/Santa Fe region of the Rio Grande Valley on the northeast, to the Gran Quivira region on the southeast, to the upper Little Colorado River Valley on the southwest, and to the Hopi Mesas on the northwest. Masks or masked figures appear on pottery perhaps by 1325, on rock art by 1350, and in kiva murals by 1375–1400. Katsina icons in general were more concentrated in the western area and were probably a little earlier than in the east.

A notable association of kiva murals having masked personages with rectangular kivas suggested that the origins of the cult or its early development were probably associated with the rectangular kiva. An absolutely critical element to the effectiveness of the katsina cult in Pueblo ceremony is its public aspects, that is, performances that can be attended and observed by all village members. Invariably, public katsina dance ceremonies occur in the plazas of the Pueblo villages, as do nearly all public aspects of Pueblo ceremonialism. The archaeological literature from the Point of Pines area in the Salt River drainage of east central Arizona through the upper Little Colorado River to the Hopi Mesas indicates that rectangular kivas, enclosed plazas, and aggregated villages all appear together about 1275. It does not seem purely coincidental that katsina iconography developed in some of the same areas where these other major changes in prehistoric Pueblo village patterns were also occurring.

The task then was to trace the development of the rectangular kiva form, the enclosed plaza, and katsina cult iconography. The enclosed plaza form has a very wide distribution from northern Mexico to the Hopi Mesas. Its appearance seems almost simultaneous from north to south dating perhaps as early as 1200 in Animas Phase sites in the upper Gila River (Lekson 1982) and south into Chihuahua. Adobe compound walls, a variant of the distinctive northern enclosed plaza, are associated with both classic Hohokam architecture and Salado architecture of the thirteenth and fourteenth centuries. Perhaps not coincidentally, coursed adobe architecture (and some adobe bricks) occurs during the late thirteenth and fourteenth centuries in areas formerly dominated by masonry architecture from the Acoma area on the east to the Homol'ovi and Hopi Mesas areas on the west (Dittert 1959; Fewkes 1904; Smith 1952). Salado Polychromes (Gila and Pinto Polychromes) are also prominent in many assemblages from Acoma to the Homol'ovi pueblos (Crown et al. 1985; Dittert 1959; Martin and Rinaldo 1960), indicating the architectural influence came from groups well below the rim where adobe architecture and Salado Polychromes were predominant. Cremations at Hawikuh together with Salado Polychrome led Smith et al. (1966) to speculate that Salado people actually settled in the Zuni area in the 1300s. Irrespective of actual migration of people, regional exchange of material culture and ideas were clearly the case. Shared perceptions of public architecture, a category into which the enclosed-plaza form is classified, developed during the thirteenth century. This public area, according to architectural layout, was the focus of aggregated communities throughout the sedentary settlements of the northern Southwest (northern Mexico and the American Southwest). The continuous distribution of the enclosed-plaza form points to the idea for the layout in the later prehistoric Pueblo area as being introduced from outside.

Careful consideration of the distribution of settlements dating to the 1275–1350 period and of the reconstruction of the dated spread of the enclosed-plaza concept suggests that the idea spread to the north via Salado contacts through two routes. The appearance and spread of enclosed plazas predating 1300 is concentrated in two distinct areas: the western Pueblo area from the upper Little Colorado River to the Hopi Mesas and the eastern Pueblo area along the Rio Grande extending onto the Pajarito Plateau from the Albuquerque area to Taos (Wendorf and Reed 1955).

Unlike the enclosed-plaza, which clearly has a thirteenth century southern origin, the rectangular kiva developed out of the northern Mogollon region. Its origin has been traced from rectangular great kiva forms of the eleventh and twelfth centuries in the Pine Lawn and Tularosa Valley of west central New Mexico to small rectangular kivas with southern or eastern platforms in the late thirteenth century in the upper Little Colorado River Valley. The diffusion of the enclosed-plaza village plan into the area where rectangular great kivas were public architecture and rectangular ceremonial rooms within the roomblock were probably nonpublic ritual staging areas forever altered Pueblo public architecture and ceremonialism. Between 1250 and 1300 on the north side of the Mogollon Rim, the rectangular great kivas were replaced by rectangular plazas, and the rectangular ceremonial rooms had become rectangular kivas within the plazas. Ceremonies were planned and performed in the kivas in private and performed in the plazas in public. The private ceremonies allowed ritual knowledge to be controlled by the religious leaders whereas the public ceremonies could be used to involve all segments of the village population facilitating cooperation and integration of the village populace.

The integrative aspects of public ritual were becoming more and more important. Carlson (1970) observes that Pinedale Polychrome design is similar to that of the northern polychromes. To Carlson this suggests immigration into the Mogollon Rim area beginning about 1275 by people from the Anasazi region to the north. The immigration followed abandonment of the Four Corners area due to environmental change of catastrophic proportions. Haury (1958) documents a migration of Kayenta Anasazi from north of the Hopi Mesas into the Point of Pines area in the late 1200s, and another is suggested by Reid and Whittlesey (1982) into Grasshopper Pueblo. Di Peso (1958) believes there was a Kayenta Anasazi enclave in the San Pedro River Valley in the southeastern corner of Arizona and that the Kayenta were a stimulus to the creation of Tucson Polychrome. A major influx of immigrants into the region seems evident. The expanding population was concentrated into larger and larger villages. To allow even short-term success in integrating the divergent populations required new integrative systems by the village leaders. The development of the enclosed-plaza-oriented village layout about 1275 seems to be a response to the need to find innovative ways to form cooperative units within the populace. The burning of an immigrant Kayenta village at Point of Pines, presumably by local inhabitants (Haury 1958), indicates the importance of integrating the immigrants with the local populace rather than maintaining separate settlements.

The form of the kiva, or ceremonial structure, in which the preparation of a katsina ceremony took place in and of itself would not appear significant. Nevertheless, the murals having katsina figures or katsina masks depicted on them that have been documented occur with but one exception, kiva 10 at Pottery Mound (Hibben 1975), on rectangular kivas. From a sample of over 30 kivas this is a rather startling association. It would seem most likely that the association of the rectangular (or square) kiva with kiva murals tied to the katsina cult has a historical or evolutionary explanation. Religious institutions are slowest to change in human society and Pueblo culture is, if anything, exceptional in the maintenance of its traditional values, in particular those related to ritual (Bunzel 1932; Parsons 1939). Employing perhaps circular reasoning, the answer to why the katsina cult is associated only with rectangular kivas is most likely because the cult originated and developed in villages where the rectangular kiva was the preferred form. The archaeological data certainly confirm this prediction. Earliest recognizable icons of masked beings or katsina masks occur on Fourmile Polychrome pottery. The center of production for this distinctive pottery type and the location of the ruin and wash that bear its name is the upper Little Colorado River Valley. This is also the location of the development of rectangular kivas with raised platforms that are located outside the roomblock. This is the style of kiva on which the murals are depicted. This distinctive style of kiva had developed between 1250 and 1275. Katsina cult iconography develops, perhaps as early as 1325, on Fourmile Polychrome ceramics. Its development obviously took place in villages having not only rectangular kivas with raised platforms, but also having enclosed plazas.

The archaeological evidence indicates that the rectangular kiva form was an integral part of katsina ritual. This association was so strong and deemed so important that eastern Pueblo groups accepting the katsina cult built small, rectangular kivas in which to perform the katsina ritual, often next to their traditional large, circular kivas. In contrast the enclosed plaza, although essential to public performances of katsina cult ritual, was also integral to other Pueblo ceremonies having public performances. Along with the katsina cult, these other Pueblo rituals served to integrate the village populace.

Katsina cult iconography was considered in two general forms in the attribute discussion of the last chapter. What has been termed the Fourmile style was applied to ceramic design and to kiva mural decorations. The most important aspect to the depiction of the icons on ceramics is their asymmetrical layout (Smith 1971). Abstract birds are particularly interesting because they occur regularly both in the kiva murals and on ceramics, especially Fourmile Polychrome, Homolovi Polychrome, Sikyatki Polychrome, Kechipawan Polychrome, and Matsaki Polychrome. These styles appear earliest on Fourmile at about 1325, on Homolovi Polychrome between 1325–1350, on Sikyatki and on Kechipawan about 1375–1400, and on Matsaki Polychrome at 1400 or later. The imitation of Sikyatki Polychrome in color, form, and design on Matsaki Polychrome clearly shows that Matsaki Polychrome is a copy of Sikyatki Polychrome and therefore must be later.

The spread of the cult after being developed in the upper Little Colorado River Valley in the early 1300s will be discussed later. At this point it is important to look at the iconographic roots of the cult. Near the end of the discussion of Fourmile style, the concepts of early Fourmile style, also known as Pinedale style, and classic Fourmile style were introduced. This convention was established to allow consideration of the broader manifestation of the Salado culture and to consider its relation to the katsina cult.

Polychrome pottery decoration had two general roots on the southern

Colorado Plateau: in the upper Little Colorado River Valley about 1175 with the type Wingate Polychrome (Carlson 1970), and in the Tuba City/ Cameron area on the southwest edge of the Plateau in the forms of Citadel Polychrome and Cameron Polychrome by 1100 (Colton and Hargrave 1937), (Fig. 6.1). The White Mountain Red Wares, of which Wingate Polychrome, St. Johns Polychrome, Pinedale Polychrome, and Fourmile Polychrome are all members, use white decorations as outlines of black designs on a red (or dark orange) slipped background (Figs. 3.11 and 3.13). The Tsegi Orange Wares, of which Citadel Polychrome, Cameron Polychrome, and Tusayan Polychrome are members, is characterized by red or orange and black designs on a light orange background (Fig. 6.2). White outlines of black designs are introduced to the Tsegi Orange Wares after 1200, presumably from the White Mountain area (Fig. 6.2). About 1250 the traditions merge on the Hopi Mesas and the result is Jeddito Polychrome (Fig. 6.2).

Beginning about 1275 a major transformation in ceramic decoration occurs in both layout and color scheme. At this time the "northern polychromes" of the Tsegi Orange Ware tradition disappear with the depopulation of the region. The apparent migration of at least some of these people into the upper and middle Little Colorado River Valley and below the Mogollon Rim brought a transformation in the local White Mountain Red Ware ceramics in the form of the Pinedale style typified on Pinedale Polychrome (Carlson 1970, 1982b). The changes wrought by this merger of stylistic traditions are felt by many archaeologists to have influenced polychrome traditions even farther south below the Mogollon Rim (Haury 1958) and south into Tucson and the San Pedro River Valley (Di Peso 1958). Although Di Peso makes a strong case for Kayenta Anasazi immigration into the southeastern part of Arizona, by the 1300s Casas Grandes was also established in northwest Chihuahua, and trade with this polychrome-pottery-producing center was certainly being felt in the southern sections of the "American" Southwest.

Also by 1300 the Salado culture blossomed. Is it coincidental that the earliest of the Salado Polychromes, Pinto Polychrome, developed in the northern distribution of the Salado culture, possibly even in the upper Little Colorado River Valley (Doyel and Haury 1976:134)? It is proposed here as a working model that Pinto Polychrome was a derivative of White Mountain Red Ware following what has been termed the northern model by the 1976 Salado conference (1976:134). (See Doyel [1972] for a different model.) With expansion of Anasazi into the upper Little Colorado River, indigenous populations of upper Little Colorado River people and Ana-

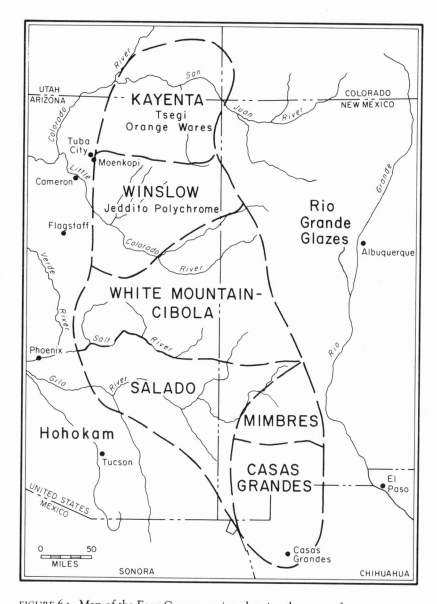

FIGURE 6.1. Map of the Four Corners region showing the areas of
production of Tsegi Orange Ware, Jeddito Polychrome, and White
Mountain Red Ware.
(Redrafted by Ron Beckwith, Arizona State Museum, from The
Polychrome Complexes by Roy L. Carlson, Fig. 1., in *Southwestern
Ceramics: A Comparative Review*, by permission of the Arizona
Archaeological Council, Phoenix)

FIGURE 6.2. Tsegi Orange Ware showing the distinctive stylistic tradition of the northern polychromes: (*a,c*) Tusayan Polychrome Style B; (*b*) Kiet Siel Polychrome; (*d,e*) Kayenta Polychrome.
(Arizona State Museum collections; photograph by Helga Teiwes, Arizona State Museum)

sazi from northern Arizona, especially producing the northern polychromes, both participated in the move below the Mogollon Rim documented by Haury and Di Peso. Their stylistic ideas, expressed in Pinedale
Polychrome, also influenced Gila Polychrome, a type produced after 1300.
These expanding populations filled the broken range country south of the
rim from the Tonto Basin on the southwest to the Safford area on the
southeast and into the San Pedro River Valley on the south. Of course the
ethnic composition of each group made their archaeological manifestation
unique; however, they were all united into the "Salado culture" by their
manufacture or exchange of polychrome pottery (cf. Crown et al. 1985).
On its southern fringes the developing Salado culture came into contact
with the polychrome ceramics of the Casas Grandes regional system (apparently economically and stylistically) including Escondida Polychrome
and Ramos Polychrome. Both El Paso Polychrome on the east and Gila
Polychrome were influenced by Casas Grandes stylistic (and probably
ritualistic) traditions. The Salado Polychromes (Gila and Tonto Polychrome) thus evolved stylistically from both the northern Mogollon/
Anasazi and the southern influences described above. The Salado regional
system, apparently connected through economic and symbolic means, had
extensive contact with the Hohokam on the southwest, this influence
being most substantial in the Tonto Basin and lower Verde Valley. On
the southeast, contact with the Casas Grandes regional system was
substantial.

The attributes that appear earliest in the upper Little Colorado River
Valley area, such as enclosed plazas, coursed adobe walls, and piki stones
are all present in the Hohokam region between 1200 and 1300 and would
suggest the Hohokam culture as the source. The later appearance of the
shoe pot and abstract parrot motifs, probably after 1300, may point to
a different source area, probably northern Chihuahua. The Salado interaction sphere, which was developing during the late thirteenth and
fourteenth centuries, probably provided the means for spread of these
concepts.

The other icons of katsina masks and mythical beings are apparently
indigenous to the southern Colorado Plateau from the upper Little Colorado River area to the Hopi Mesas. Although indirect contact through
long-distance regional exchange with the Casas Grandes people is undeniable, there is not clear indication that the trade was anything other than
down-the-line. Items in the exchange network from Casas Grandes, such
as macaws and copper bells, reveal a predictable distance-decay line. Thus
the farther a group was from the source, the fewer of these luxury, or

status, goods one finds. The effect of the Casas Grandes people on the belief system of the western Pueblo ancestors is difficult to measure. The nature of the trade suggested above and the relatively minor impact on the post-1300 iconography of the area thus suggest the influence from Casas Grandes was relatively minor. However, the importance of the macaw in cult iconography and the frequency of macaw burials in late prehistoric sites of the western Pueblo region imply that Mexican beliefs, however filtered through Casas Grandes, did contribute to what eventually evolved into the katsina cult. As mentioned, influence into the middle Rio Grande Valley from Casas Grandes was probably more substantial than into the upper Little Colorado River Valley. Differences between the later Jornada cult from the western katsina cult in the northern Rio Grande Valley could be due to more direct influence from northern Mexico.

Therefore, the early Fourmile style is shared throughout the prehistoric world of 1275–1325 from the Casas Grandes area on the south to the upper Little Colorado River Valley on the north with the Salado culture intermediate. The style is symmetrical and although mostly geometric, contains abstract birds as motifs or elements of design (Carlson 1970, 1982b; Crown 1981; Young 1967). The sudden shift to asymmetric layout is very rare in Chihuahuan Polychromes at Casas Grandes and in Salado Polychromes, leading to the conclusion that it is an innovation unique to Fourmile Polychrome and its derivative types. This symmetry shift marks the appearance of classic Fourmile style and the beginning of the katsina cult, a phenomenon unique to the southern Colorado Plateau.

When the Rio Grande rock art style was last discussed its evolution out of the Jornada style in the Rio Grande Valley as proposed by Schaafsma (1972) was challenged. Instead, it was proposed that the style may in fact be earlier in the western Pueblo area than in the east where it was first defined. Its presence in the Zuni area, the Hopi area, and around the Homol'ovi sites, and its apparent absence south of the Mogollon Rim would suggest it developed above the Mogollon Rim during the fourteenth century among the people participating in or in fact creating the katsina cult. Similarity in details of masked figures in the Rio Grande rock art style to figures on Fourmile Polychromes and to later kiva murals on Antelope Mesa at Hopi are remarkable and are not found in the Jornada style of the middle Rio Grande Valley. Especially prominent are the round-head form, round eyes, lack of nose, and rectangular toothed mouth. The conclusion drawn here is that the so-called Rio Grande style is indeed associated with the katsina cult as suggested by Schaafsma (1972) and Schaafsma and Schaafsma (1974); however, the style originated where the cult did, in the upper Little Colorado Valley about 1325.

The spread of the Rio Grande style eastward into the Rio Grande Valley corresponds with other changes in the aggregated pueblos that were developing at the time. About 1325 (Wendorf and Reed 1955; Bower et al. 1986) glaze paint on red-slipped vessels appeared in the Albuquerque area of the Rio Grande Valley, shortly after enclosed-plaza areas developed. These traits, especially the ceramics, reflect a west-to-east movement of influence. The appearance of the Rio Grande style is dated by its association with Glaze I (Schaafsma 1972). If the ceramic influence came from the Zuni area in the early fourteenth century, then it is more likely that the Rio Grande rock art style present at Zuni and associated with the early plazas there could also have a western origin and have been exported eastward. Extent of this early influence, if the katsina cult is broadened further with inclusion of the occasional depiction of katsina masks on pottery sherds, could include the Rio Grande Valley northward to the vicinity of Taos where a katsina mask depicted on a sherd of Talpa Black-on-white was recovered from Pot Creek Pueblo (Ferg 1982; Schaafsma 1972).

Thus a cult originating in the western Pueblo area centered in the upper Little Colorado Valley area would be expected to be diffused in a similar form and in similar media as its place of origin. The eastward flow of ideas in the early 1300s, as exemplified in the red-slipped glaze wares, would be predicted to include katsina cult icons in rock art and on ceramics as it was depicted in the heartland. Dittert (1959) in his Kowina Phase observes a flow into the Acoma area of ideas from the west and southwest beginning about 1300. Further analysis of the fourteenth century rock art of the Acoma area will undoubtedly reveal Rio Grande rock art style. Other changes in the Acoma area occur in the late thirteenth and fourteenth centuries that would be predicted from this analysis, including enclosed-plaza layouts in aggregated villages, coursed adobe technology, rectangular kivas, piki stones, and the appearance of polychrome pottery (1959:553–562).

It has now been established that the foundation to the katsina cult was established before 1300 in the upper Little Colorado Valley and that iconography recognized as katsina cult, that is, having katsina masks and katsina figures, appears about 1325 in the same area. The eastward spread of the cult after 1325 into Zuni, possibly into Acoma, and finally into villages in the Rio Grande Valley from Albuquerque to San Marcial has been outlined in the discussion of the Rio Grande rock art style. There is no indication, however, of kiva murals bearing katsina cult iconography in the Rio Grande Valley at this time. Dates established for the katsina cult murals in the Rio Grande area suggest their appearance is no earlier than 1400. This date will have a bearing on the discussion to follow.

What about the spread of the katsina cult northward from the upper Little Colorado area into the Homol'ovi area and the Hopi Mesas? As elsewhere, dating of the events is dependent on a few tree-ring or radiocarbon dates and abundant tree-ring dated pottery types (cf. Breternitz 1966). Fortunately, research in both areas has been relatively productive in terms of katsina cult iconography. In the Homol'ovi area Pilles (1975) and Cole (1989b) have studied the rock art. Cole in particular has researched the Rio Grande style iconography. Pond (1966) excavated a kiva with murals and 24 restorable vessels of which all but one were yellow ware pottery probably manufactured on the Hopi Mesas. Fewkes (1898, 1904) and Hays and Adams (1985) both illustrate ceramics from Homol'ovi I, Homol'ovi II, or Chevelon Ruin depicting katsinas or katsina masks. Type identifications by the author and by Peter J. Pilles, Jr., Coconino National Forest archaeologist, of the ceramics collected by Fewkes housed at the National Museum of Natural History indicate that the ceramics with katsina motifs are depicted on both Hopi yellow wares and Fourmile Polychromes traded to the Homol'ovi sites and on local Winslow Orange Wares.

The kiva excavated by Pond at Homol'ovi II is rectangular. Homol'ovi I, Homol'ovi II, and Chevelon, the three fourteenth century pueblos, all have large enclosed plazas bounded on all sides by rooms. In the cases of Homol'ovi I and Chevelon, theses are only one-or-two-rooms wide and are appended to aggregated roomblocks of contiguous rooms. All three fourteenth century sites are large and aggregated, ranging from minimally 250 rooms at Homol'ovi I to over 700 rooms at Homol'ovi II. Dating these pueblos is difficult. Excavations at Homol'ovi II in 1984 produced two calibrated radiocarbon dates of A.D. 1340–1397 and A.D. 1337–1373, which were derived from two hearths (Hays and Adams 1985:Appendix E). Two calibrated radiocarbon dates from Homol'ovi III, one from pre-yellow ware deposits (A.D. 1277–1318) and one associated with yellow wares (A.D. 1331–1345), reinforce fourteenth century occupation dates (Adams 1989). Associated with the Homol'ovi II dated rooms was a predominant yellow ware assemblage in the ceramics, including one bowl with a katsina mask design (Hays 1985:Fig. 3.6). The evidence thus suggests that the katsina cult was present at the Homol'ovi sites by about 1350. The presence of Sikyatki Polychrome with asymmetrical bird motifs in the kiva excavated by Pond (1966) and their absence in the five rooms excavated by the Arizona State Museum in 1984 suggests the kiva is later than the excavated rooms. A post–1375 date for the kiva murals is suggested, using currently accepted dates for Sikyatki Polychrome (Colton and Hargrave 1937; Breternitz 1966), but the evidence is circumstantial.

The Hopi Mesas area has already been treated in considerable detail. Turner (1963) has discussed the Rio Grande style rock art, Smith (1952, 1972, 1980) has done an exhaustive study of the kiva murals and of the rectangular kivas at Awatovi and Kawaika-a. Although no adequate study has been done of the post–1375/1400 ceramic assemblage at a Hopi site, Fewkes (1919) has done a study of prehistoric Hopi pottery designs, and Wade and McChesney (1981) illustrate some of the late ceramics from Awatovi. If anything, dating of Hopi assemblages is more problematical than elsewhere. Both Smith (1952:315–319) and Crotty (1987) have worked out a chronology of the kiva murals that they date with reference to ceramic assemblages, site location, stratigraphy, and occasional tree-ring dates. For the most part, however, the latter are either not cutting dates or occur in the fill of the structure. Smith (1952:316–318) defines four layout groups and ceramic complexes and traces the evolution of the styles represented in these groups through the ceramic complexes. The earliest groups appear before 1350 but do not bear any katsina masks or masked figures. The earliest masked figures date to the intermediate ceramic complex, which would date late fourteenth century (Smith 1971:318; 1972:18). Masked figures appear in greater and greater frequency on the Awatovi murals, climaxing in the latest ones dating to the protohistoric period (1540–1630). Smith (1952, 1980) compares numerous murals to historic katsinas. Enclosed plazas, aggregated villages, and rectangular kivas all characterize Hopi sites beginning about 1275 (Ferdon 1955; Smiley 1952).

Given the above, what are the relationships to the hypothesized origin of the cult in the upper Little Colorado Valley? The presence of rectangular kivas occurs at both Awatovi in the western mound (Smith 1972) and at Homol'ovi III (Adams 1989) before 1300. The presence of enclosed plazas is probably also early in both areas, but no dates can realistically be assigned except a pre-1350 date for Homol'ovi II. A rectangular great kiva at Homol'ovi III ceramically dated to 1275–1300 would suggest that enclosed plazas were either not yet present or had not completely replaced great kivas. Village aggregation was occurring by 1275 at Hopi and by 1300 at Homol'ovi. It seems likely the aggregation process climaxed at Homol'ovi by 1350 or slightly later, but did not culminate at the Hopi villages until after 1400 (Adams, Stark, and Dosh 1990). Hays (1985) argues that Winslow Orange Wares were not produced after about 1350. The presence of katsina masks on Winslow Orange Wares therefore would indicate a pre–1350 date for the presence of katsina cult iconography at Homol'ovi. Kiva murals and Sikyatki Polychrome are the best indicators of the cult at Awatovi and Kawaika-a. Both seem to develop between 1375 and 1400; however, the presence of a katsina face on a Paayu Polychrome (early Sikyatki Polychrome) at Homol'ovi II radiocarbon dated to 1350 suggests that katsina cult iconography may have been present on the Hopi Mesas by 1350.

Assuming these dates are relatively close, it would seem that from its development about 1325 in the upper Little Colorado that by 1350 the cult iconography had spread eastward to the Rio Grande Valley and north-ward to the Hopi Mesas and to all aggregated pueblos in between. The evolution of the katsina cult, however, does not end here. The development of katsina cult iconography in kiva murals appears to postdate 1375 with probably their earliest occurrence on the Hopi Mesas, perhaps at Awatovi. The circumstantial, but multidimensional, dating of the Ante-lope Mesa kivas at Awatovi and Kawaika-a suggests such an early date. More importantly, irrespective of the date, the Hopi katsina cult appears to have been exported to at least three areas or villages.

The first, and closest, is Homol'ovi II. Kiva murals appear in a rectan-gular kiva filled with over 20 yellow ware pottery vessels manufactured on the Hopi Mesas, including Sikyatki Polychrome having asymmetric bird motifs (Pond 1966). The second, and farthest, is Pottery Mound (Hibben 1955). Seventeen Kivas, 16 rectangular, are decorated with kiva murals almost identical in style to those at Awatovi (Hibben 1975; Smith 1952). Jeddito Yellow Ware is a common intrusive ceramic. Additionally, be-tween 1400 and 1475 yellow-slipped glaze wares developed at Pottery Mound and in the Galisteo Basin. Fourmile style designs, evidently copy-ing contemporary Sikyatki Polychromes, develop on Style III and charac-terize Style IV Glaze Wares dating 1450/1475–1515. Thus kiva murals and ceramics indicate strong influence from the Hopi area at Pottery Mound and extending into nearby areas during the fifteenth century (Snow 1982:253–254).

The third is an area, rather than one village. This area is the six Zuni villages occupied after 1400 (Fig. 6.3). About 1400 (Kintigh 1985) all of these villages began to manufacture or use almost exclusively the pottery type called Matsaki Polychrome (Woodbury and Woodbury 1966). This type is a clear copy of Hopi pottery in surface color, form, and decoration. The best explanation for the adoption of a totally different style of pot-tery, in this perspective, is the perception by the manufacturers of its necessity in activities in which they participate. The presence of Hopi

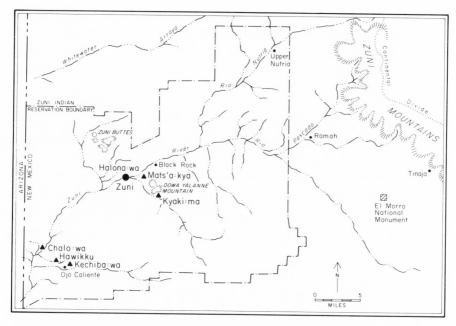

FIGURE 6.3. Location of historic Zuni pueblos.
(Adapted by Ron Beckwith, Arizona State Museum, from *Settlement, Subsistence, and Society in Late Zuni Prehistory* by Keith W. Kintigh, Figs. 1.1 & 4.1)

manufactured yellow pottery at both Homol'ovi II and at Pottery Mound associated with kiva murals suggests that the Hopi version of the katsina cult was being exported. This version included kiva murals and the practioners' use of Hopi pottery. Limited access to Hopi pottery at Zuni, although it is a common intrusive of the fourteenth and fifteenth centuries (Smith et al. 1966; Kintigh 1985), and the perceived need for yellow ware pottery in katsina cult ritual are hypothesized as explanation for the sudden development of Matsaki Polychrome about 1400. Such limited access may also explain the related development at Pottery Mound of yellow-slipped glaze wares about 1400 and their spread with Fourmile designs after 1450. It is highly probably, if preservation is sufficient, that Hopi style kiva murals will be found in kivas within fifteenth century Zuni villages.

The spread of the Hopi version of the katsina cult apparently occurred very close to 1400 and did not reenter the upper Little Colorado Valley sites either because they were the stronghold of the original cult, or they were in the final throes of abandonment. It did supplement or replace the original version of the cult, which had spread 50 years earlier throughout the occupied Pueblo world, but in more restricted areas (Fig. 6.4). The Hopi katsina cult seems to have influenced the entire western Pueblo area north of the Mogollon Rim and the southern and eastern sections of the eastern Pueblos, possibly including in addition to Pottery Mound, the Gran Quivira area north to the Galisteo Basin and along the Rio Grande from Albuquerque southward to San Marcial (Fig. 6.5). At contact these villages were occupied by Tanoan, Keres, Tompiro, Piro, and southern Tiwa-speaking peoples.

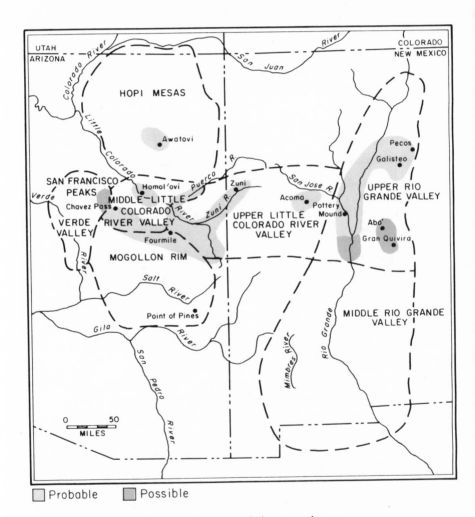

☐ Probable   ▨ Possible

FIGURE 6.4. Distribution of the Fourmile katsina cult, 1350.
(Drawn by Ron Beckwith, Arizona State Museum)

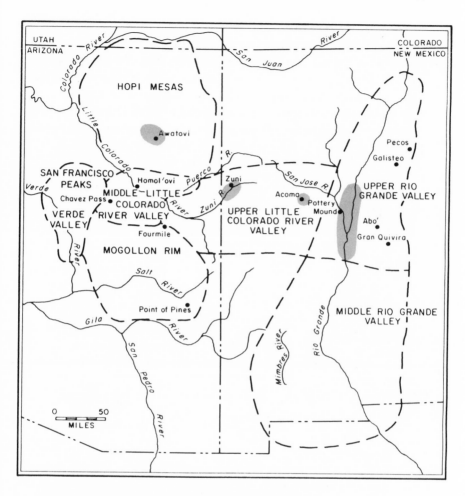

FIGURE 6.5. Distribution of the Hopi katsina cult, 1400–1450.
(Drawn by Ron Beckwith, Arizona State Museum)

Sometime after 1450, but before 1500, the Jornada style penetrated into
what would become the protohistoric Pueblo world affecting the Abó
area of Salinas (Tompiro speakers), the Rio Grande area north to the
Santa Fe area (Piro, Tiwa, and Keres), and into Pecos (Towa), and the
Galisteo Basin (Tano) (Fig. 6.6). Mixture with the Hopi cult occurred at
Pottery Mound, probably in the Galisteo Basin area, and possibly in the
Abó area. This would best account for the simultaneous development of
Sikyatki Polychrome style designs on ceramics produced in the Galisteo
Basin and the appearance of Jornada style rock art and figures on the

ceramics which date post–1475. It would also explain the depiction of Jornada style murals at Kuaua on rectangular kivas. Perhaps at this time or sometime during the sixteenth century the Jornada style expanded westward to Zuni. The striped chins and tablitas of many katsinas (and some unmasked dances) are probably related to the Jornada influence.

In summary, the katsina cult was established in the upper Little Colorado River Valley about 1325 on a pattern developed during the late 1200s, but in place by 1300. This pattern included rectangular kivas, enclosed

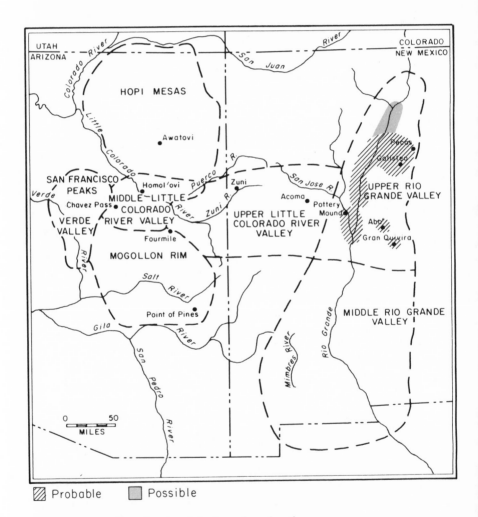

Probable   Possible

FIGURE 6.6. Distribution of the Jornada style cult, 1450–1500.
(Drawn by Ron Beckwith, Arizona State Museum)

plazas, and aggregated villages. Also part of this pattern after 1275 was a shared iconography, possibly reflecting a shared belief system, with people to the south whom archaeologists call Salado. An important reason for the shared iconography was the similarity in origins of many of the people manufacturing it. Most archaeologists agree that Pinto Polychrome developed in the region within the upper Little Colorado River Valley on the northeast and the Tonto Basin on the southwest (Carlson 1970; Doyel 1972; Doyel and Haury 1976). Although most archaeologists suggest an early thirteenth century date for its origin (cf. Doyel 1972), Carlson (1982b:223) argues cogently for a 1275 beginning date to Pinto Polychrome, and this date is accepted here. If 1275 is the approximate development date of the Salado Polychromes, then much of the spread of these types is probably associated with movement of Anasazi who were quickly absorbed into the Hohokam-influenced Mogollon in the Tonto Basin and other areas extending east and south toward the Casas Grandes regional system. For example, Carlson (1982b:Table 4) views Tonto Polychrome as derived from Kayenta Anasazi polychromes. From this perspective the upper Little Colorado River people participated in a broad, multiregional system in the late thirteenth century that fostered change or shared traits through a diffusion of ideas on iconography, village layout, and new ideas such as the piki stone. Mixed with local ideas on kiva (and great kiva) forms and given the new populations of Anasazi moving into the area, the katsina cult was born.

The more traditional approach suggests that the flow of ideas into the Tonto Basin came from the Little Colorado River Anasazi, Mogollon, and Hohokam after 1100 (Doyel 1972). The birth of the Salado Polychromes in this area after 1200 was spread by trade and diffusion. These ideas may have included piki stones and the enclosed plaza. Irrespective of the initial direction of flow, the upper Little Colorado people were in considerable contact with people in the Tonto Basin who may have served as intermediaries with people farther to the south in the Salt and Gila River valleys and into northern Chihuahua. The list of items borrowed from these areas appearing in the upper Little Colorado area is extensive and significant, including, perhaps most importantly, the enclosed-plaza village layout.

The katsina cult was expressed in icons depicted in rock art and on ceramics, planned in rectangular kivas, and performed in enclosed plazas. The purpose of this cult was probably to develop cooperation among the constituents of the villages into which it was introduced. For this reason it proved popular in villages throughout the Pueblo area from the Rio Grande on the east, to the Hopi and Homol'ovi areas on the west, and possibly to Point of Pines and Kinishba on the south (Cummings 1940; Di Peso 1950).

Upon reaching the Hopi area, about 1350 or earlier, the cult was elaborated and transformed. Mural art, already a tradition at Hopi (Smith 1952) and other areas (Vivian 1964), became the centerpiece for visual expression of the cult. Ceramics continued to be an extension of this expression, elaborating even further on the Fourmile style in both style and design, although basic elements of asymmetric bird forms continued to predominate. The emphasis of the Hopi katsina cult also may have shifted to a stronger emphasis on the rainmaker role for which the katsina cult of today is most widely known. The shift from the relatively moist Mogollon Rim country of the cult's origin to the semiarid Hopi Mesas region where precipitation averages about 250 mm/year (10 inches) would account for the changes in emphasis.

This rain cult spread during the fifteenth century. Its spread would not necessarily coincide with droughts, but the figures are revealing. There was a drought on the Hopi Mesas during the 1370s, and in Hopi, Cibola, Santa Fe, and the Jemez Mountains along the Rio Grande Valley during the 1410s (cf. Rose, Dean, and Robinson 1981). Subsequent droughts struck Hopi in the 1430s, 1440s, and from 1455–1465. In Zuni (or Cibola) there were also droughts in the 1440s, 1450s, and 1470s. In the Jemez Mountains and Santa Fe there were droughts in the 1410s, 1450s, 1460s, and 1470s (Dean and Robinson 1978). Could the acceptance of the rain cult in the Zuni and the Rio Grande area be a result of a prolonged drought from 1415–1424 during which every year was below normal? Matsaki Polychrome is dated as appearing about 1400. Could the spread to Pottery Mound have occurred during the severe drought of 1418–1424 or a lesser drought from 1390–1409 (Dean and Robinson 1978)? Could the adoption of Fourmile style designs and layout on Rio Grande Glaze Wares between 1450–1475 be associated with the droughts of the 1450s–1470s?

The early fifteenth century dates correspond to the guesstimated date of the appearance of kiva murals at Pottery Mound, Matsaki Polychrome at Zuni, and kiva murals at Homol'ovi. However, the spread beyond the Pottery Mound area seems more closely dated to 1450/1475, associated with late Style III and Style IV Glaze Wares. The spread of the Hopi version of the cult was apparently less extensive than the earlier upper Little Colorado Valley cult for a couple of reasons. First, a cult emphasizing rain would be less attractive to agriculturalists practicing irrigation along the Rio Grande, as were many fifteenth century villages. It is interesting that the areas having the most indication of influence from the Hopi cult

(Salinas, Acoma, Zuni, and possibly the Galisteo Basin) have the least reliable water supplies and were the most reliant on rainfall for successful crops. Second, shifts in settlement, village layout, and village structure also occurred about 1400. The early fifteenth century settlements were still occupied at Spanish contact indicating a stable social structure had been achieved. This stability occurs about the time of hypothesized Hopi katsina cult introduction at Pottery Mound. It may also benefit from the integrative tools introduced through the Fourmile katsina cult. The association of rock art with katsina masks near many of these settlements supports the latter possibility. It is also possible that the dual organization (moiety) system had already stabilized these groups and that the changes offered by the Hopi katsina cult were not as attractive to a stable social order as to one in flux. The important role of katsina ritual to all Pueblo groups, with the possible exception of northern Tiwa-speakers, indicates that the moiety system alone may not have been adequate for integrating the village populace.

Finally, the Jornada style cult, derived from the middle Rio Grande Valley in the mid- to late 1400s, seems to have spread to some of the same villages as the Hopi cult in conjunction with Glaze Style IV but also affected different areas and people. The Jornada cult, according to the icons and those who have studied them (Brody 1977; Dutton 1963; Schaafsma 1972, 1980), had both rain and warrior overtones. Its acceptance in formerly nonreceptive areas of the Rio Grande from Albuquerque to Santa Fe could relate to the severe drought of the 1450s to 1470s throughout the region. The warrior ties at Kuaua and in the rock art could relate to Dutton's (1963) hypothesis that the village was attacked and burned about 1400 and only reoccupied about 1475, when the kiva iconography began to be painted. Schaafsma (1980:298) relates warrior overtones to the possibility of Aztecs assuming control in the Valley of Mexico in 1428 and the spread of the Huitzilopochtli cult.

Use of rectangular kivas to depict the Jornada style murals at Kuaua may merely reflect the persistent use of this form for mural decoration throughout the Pueblo world after 1325 or the tie of a rain cult to a religious architectural form associated with an earlier rain cult from Hopi. The association of the Jornada style iconography with the Hopi style kiva may also be further proof that in many villages, perhaps most, the Jornada cult was combined with the Hopi cult after 1450, and they spread into many areas together. The fact that the same droughts (1440s to 1470s) affected Zuni makes the appearance of Jornada style katsinas, such as the Sa'lako (a powerful rainmaker), less due to chance or warfare and more likely due to drought. The use of structures other than kivas by the Sa'lakos may be another Jornada style tie where kivas are not part of the society's ritual. Nonkiva ceremonial structures also appear at Acoma in the 1300s (Dittert 1959) and at Las Humanas after 1500 (Hayes et al. 1981; Peckham 1981). The latter contain katsina-like murals, but apparently not in the Jornada style (cf. Crotty 1987; Peckham 1981).

The hypothesized development and evolution of the katsina cult presented above has now brought us to the Spanish contact period, which forever changed the Pueblo world. Although alluded to in this chapter, the meaning of the katsina cult to its prehistoric practitioners has only been mentioned in passing. The next chapter will look at the structure of the katsina cult, its role in prehistoric Pueblo society, how this role changed through the evolution of the cult, and what ramifications these interpretations will have on archaeological interpretations of the late prehistoric period of the Pueblo Southwest.

7

Synthesis and Structure of the Katsina Cult in Prehistoric Pueblo Culture
Consideration of the Hypothesis

In chapter 3 a hypothesis on the katsina cult was presented stating simply that if the katsina cult were present in a prehistoric group, significant and recognizable changes would be identifiable. Implications of the hypothesis were that the cult would play a major role in integrating aggregated or aggregating communities; that public ritual areas would be present, such as great kivas or enclosed plazas; that symbolic aspects should be present; that rest areas should be present; and that other material correlates should be present, such as rectangular kivas, piki stones, and the like.

In chapter 5, four attributes associated with the cult were evaluated: the enclosed plaza, the rectangular kiva, Fourmile style ceramics and murals, and Rio Grande style rock art. It was determined that cult iconography, enclosed plazas, and rectangular kivas were all linked and developed in the upper Little Colorado River Valley between 1275 and 1325. The development of the cult coincides perfectly with the massive dislocation of people out of the Four Corners region of the Colorado Plateau and their resettlement into the upper Little Colorado Valley with indigenous Mogollon or western Pueblo people. Therefore, it was concluded in the last chapter that the initial development of the cult was integrative, involving aggregates of widely disparate backgrounds. The immigrants may have chosen to locate within existing settlements for protection or due to prior relations established through trade or kinship. Those accepting the populations may have seen the immigrants as potential labor. Irrespective, it is probable that the immigrants settled in an area already partitioned by the occupants, and negotiation for land was necessary. The immigrants would be accepted into the settlements and given land in exchange for labor, cooperation with the indigenous occupants, and acceptance of the natives in leadership positions. With the arrival of these immigrant groups, existing intergroup systems may have become inadequate. Thus in a positive feedback loop, the aggregation of people, as a cooperative attempt to deal with settlement change and population dislocation, spawned the development of the katsina cult, which in turn stabilized the aggregated community allowing it to grow further.

Presence of the katsina cult outside the core area can be easily recognized, supporting the hypothesis. The presence of cult iconography, rectangular kivas, and enclosed plazas from the Rio Grande Valley on the east, to the Hopi Mesas on the northwest, to Point of Pines on the south indicates that all probably had variants of this early cult. Point of Pines and Kinishba Polychrome have Fourmile style iconography on local ceramics, slabs with painted katsina masks have been found in both areas, rectangular kivas occur at Point of Pines, and both areas have enclosed plazas at aggregated villages. The date for this constellation of attributes is probably 1350. According to the hypothesis, the early cult is present in both communities.

Similar arguments have been made for the Homol'ovi site group and the Hopi Mesas, both of which apparently had enclosed plazas, rectangular kivas, and cult iconography by 1350. Kintigh (1985) has noted the presence of enclosed plazas and rectangular kivas at Zuni by 1275; however, datable katsina cult iconography in the form of Fourmile style ceramics does not appear until 1375 on Kechipawan Polychrome, although Rio Grande style rock art and Fourmile Polychrome with katsina motifs may appear in the area earlier. Nevertheless, a date of 1375 for the arrival of the katsina cult at Zuni is still the most reliable date supported by extensive archaeological evidence.

Data for recognizing and dating the spread of the katsina cult in the Rio Grande Valley is still problematical. Arguments for western origin of the cult about 1325 have been forcefully made in this paper. Less forcefully made was the movement of this cult from west to east early in the fourteenth century. A tie between movement of red-slipped glaze wares and of the katsina cult from the Zuni and White Mountain area into the Rio Grande area in the vicinity of modern Albuquerque was preferred (cf. Bower et al. 1986; Carlson 1982b; Snow 1982). However, with no clear indication of Zuni participation in the cult until 1375, either the cult flowed directly from the heartland of the upper Little Colorado area and the production center of Fourmile Polychrome, which is suggested as a possibility by Carlson (1982b), or the cult did not enter the Rio Grande area until after 1375. Either scenario is possible and, except for dating the Rio Grande style, is not significantly important to our arguments here. The Rio Grande style has been associated with Glaze 1 (or A) Rio Grande ceramics, which is used as the basis for dating it. Glaze 1 was the only style until 1400 (Snow 1982:Tables 5 & 6). Thus an arrival date for the katsina cult in the area of 1325 or 1375 would not affect the existing data. The Cieneguilla Glaze-on-yellow sherd with the katsina figure depicted on it from Pueblo del Encierro is a type that was manufactured from 1300 to 1450 (Snow 1976, 1982). The Talpa Black-on-white sherd with a katsina face from Pot Creek was manufactured from 1250 to 1400 (Ferg 1982; Schaafsma 1972).

The iconographic base of the katsina cult in the Rio Grande area focuses on rock art rather than ceramics and rock art. This was discussed earlier as possibly a result of differing ways of signaling that the katsina cult was present in a village, or area (Kenaghy 1986). The best evidence for presence of the katsina cult in the Rio Grande drainage around 1400 is at Pottery Mound (Hibben 1955). Kiva murals, the presence of traded Hopi yellow wares, and a shift to a white or yellow-based glaze ware point to Hopi and possibly Zuni influence in establishing the cult. Fourmile style ceramic change in the Rio Grande area (probably copying Sikyatki Polychrome or Matsaki Polychrome) did not occur until Glaze III (C), after 1450 and seems most clearly associated with the spread of the Hopi or a Hopi/Jornada version of the cult. Thus the early katsina cult in the Rio Grande Valley is recognized by the presence of rectangular kivas, enclosed plazas, and Rio Grande style rock art in the Galisteo Basin and south of Santa Fe (Fig. 6.4). By the fourteenth century most of the Rio Grande Valley villages had one or two large kivas, suggesting that an integrative system different from western Pueblo groups, possibly the moiety system, may have been in place. The relationship of the katsina cult as an integrative social system to the moiety system was probably quite variable, based on modern ethnographic information. Apparently, during the fourteenth and fifteenth centuries each area or even village developed integrative social structures based on layers of moiety divisions or on combinations of moiety divisions and kiva- or moiety-based katsina organizations.

Visibility of the katsina cult changed markedly after 1400 when the Hopi style of the cult was exported widely. Explanation of this shift will be deferred until the next section. The key differentiating ingredients to the Hopi version of the cult from the Fourmile style are the addition of kiva murals with katsina themes and associated Hopi yellow ware pottery or local ceramics influenced by the Hopi yellow wares, such as Matsaki Polychrome. The Hopi style cult was apparently focused in the western Pueblos and in the Pottery Mound area, based on available data. Further differentiation of the katsina cult occurred after 1450, as characterized by Kuaua and the development of Glaze IV style ceramics. This version of the cult was strongly influenced by a Jornada belief system. This overlay of

Fourmile style ceramics, Jornada style rock art, and kiva murals signals an expansion of the cult into areas north of Santa Fe for the first time after 1450 and into areas already penetrated by the initial Fourmile cult (Fig. 6.6).

Thus by 1500, based on archaeological evidence, the katsina cult in its broadest sense, using iconography from rock art, murals, and ceramics was present in all of the western Pueblos of Hopi, Zuni, and probably Acoma, and in the eastern Pueblos south and east of Santa Fe. The cult was also probably present in the Tewa villages, although the archaeological data suggest this only in the El Rito de Los Frijoles and nearby regions of the Pajarito Plateau occupied to 1400 or so by ancestral Tewa (Schaafsma 1972:146–149). The archaeological data closely parallel the strength and distribution of the cult as represented in historic Pueblos. The prehistoric equivalents to Humanas, Salinas, Keresan, Tano, Towa, southern Tiwa, Tewa, and Piro-speaking people all have indications of some variation of the katsina cult. The Hopi katsina cult is apparent at Zuni and in the Piro area at Pottery Mound (Fig. 6.5). The Hopi-Jornada style is most evident in the southern Tiwa area, Galisteo Basin, in the Abó area of the Salinas, and probably in the Humanas area (Fig. 6.6). The original Fourmile cult was probably in place in the other Salinas (Tompiro) Pueblos, and in the Galisteo Basin. It was probably replaced by the Jornada version at the Towa-speaking villages of Pecos and Jemez, in the eastern Keresan villages, in the Galisteo Basin, and possibly in the southern Tiwa villages (Figs. 6.4 & 6.6).

In conclusion, the hypothesis presented in chapter 3 predicting that presence of the cult will be recognizable using several criteria has been supported. The complexity of changes in the cult, especially in the Rio Grande Valley in order to explain the archaeological record should not detract from the basic, generic archaeological evidence. Wherever cult iconography appeared on fixed media, such as rock art or kiva murals, the cult apparently was present. Wherever cult icons were a common theme on ceramics, the cult was present. The distribution of such cult iconography is virtually identical with the presence of the katsina cult in historic or protohistoric pueblos. Intensity of the cult, or its significance in the ritual of the people can best be measured by distribution of the Hopi and Jornada katsina cults. The best indicator is the ritual drama depicted on the kiva murals on Antelope Mesa and at Pottery Mound, but the effect can be seen at the Homol'ovi sites and at the Zuni pueblos. The Jornada cult was equally intense at Abó, Gran Quivira, and Kuaua. It is not accidental that the historic strength of the cult was greatest at the Tompiro villages of Salinas and Las Humanas, in the western Keresan villages, at

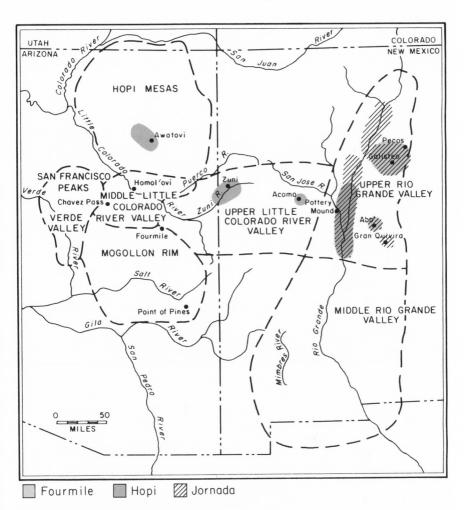

FIGURE 7.1. Composite map of cults, 1500.
   (Drawn by Ron Beckwith, Arizona State Museum)

Zuni, and at Hopi. The historic distribution is identical to the prehistoric
record (Fig. 7.1).

Structure of the Katsina Cult in Prehistoric Pueblo Culture

The hypothesis and implications suggest the structural role of the katsina
cult in prehistoric Pueblo culture. The elements considered in evaluating
the origin, development, and spread of the katsina cult are all bound by

the common theme, inherent even in modern Pueblo society, of maintaining equilibrium. Success is ultimately measured in the culture's ability to survive. Highly successful cultural patterns not only thrive, but expand. The Roman empire, the American "empire," and Navajo culture are examples of the latter. In contrast, Pueblo culture has endured. Pueblo culture has survived not only because it found a cultural niche and stuck to it, but also because it was adaptive. Unlike the more successful cultural systems, Pueblo culture has changed in order to "remain the same." A central theme for historic Pueblo culture in maintaining equilibrium through adaptive change is cooperative behavior. Translation of the word *Hopi* is "well behaved." One who does not rock the boat, who does not deviate from narrow patterns of expected behavior, who works within the social framework of the village, and who adheres to the ritual principles of one's culture is well behaved. The contention of the following arguments is to support the concept that such cultural values led to the establishment and expansion of the katsina cult. A corollary to such a model is that although cooperation is an essential ingredient in integrative behavior, so too is conflict or retribution. There has to be a means of supporting proper behavior and punishing improper behavior. The second corollary is that archaeological data can be garnered to support such a thesis.

The proposition stated in model form would be:

I. Pueblo society is based on obtaining consensus in decision making at the leadership level.

II. Pueblo society ideally seeks an equilibrium state within and between the people and their surroundings.

    A. Equilibrium is maintained through two opposite forces: cooperation and controlled conflict or retribution.

        1. Cooperation seeks to have all elements of the village work together for the benefit of all concerned.

        2. Controlled conflict is used to punish transgressors, those who deviate and endanger the cooperative efforts of others.

III. The integration of Pueblo society is achieved through management of rewards and punishments of society members by leadership consensus in order to maintain equilibrium.

All "elements" of Pueblo society—social, political, ritual, economic, or whatever divisions are selected—are orchestrated to achieve or maintain equilibrium. Adjustments can be made to gradual external or internal change in the culture. However, when major stress or change threatens the cultural equilibrium, exceptional adjustments must be made to restore equilibrium, realizing that restoration of equilibrium may be more analogous to a pendulum swinging back and forth moving slowing back to an equilibrium state.

The katsina cult developed or at least crystallized as a result of attempts to respond to one such disequilibrium. In fact cultural change, as manifest in the archaeological record of the late thirteenth and fourteenth centuries in the upper Little Colorado Valley, was a record of attempts to regain the balance disrupted by resettlement of Anasazi groups in the upper Little Colorado region and to changing precipitation patterns (Dean and Robinson 1982:Figs. 8.3–8.5). The source of the new populations is at least in part the people of the Kayenta, Tusayan, or nearby areas. Carlson (1970, 1982b) believes Pinedale Polychrome is a derivative of Kayenta Anasazi contact and that other populations settled in the Wide Ruin area, at Point of Pines, in the upper San Pedro River Valley, and in such a way as to influence Tucson Basin decorated ceramics. The possible settlement decisions stemming from a large-scale immigration into an area where resources are dwindling due to moderate drought and where populations have grown to near-carrying capacity are basically two: join the indigenous population in new or existent settlements, or build and maintain separate settlements. Following the model outlined above, one would predict that the course groups sought was one that reduced stress and emphasized cooperative behavior rather than conflictive behavior. But which option would best fit the model outlined above? The archaeological data clearly point to the aggregation option as the one selected. But why was this the case?

The first problem was probably land ownership or control. Most likely all of the best areas for agriculture in the late 1200s were already owned or controlled by indigenous inhabitants. Pueblo oral histories are very specific on land ownership and control and immigrants' being granted permission to use available parcels of land. The latest arrivals got the farthest and usually the worst land for growing corn. A second concern of the indigenous occupants was probably safety. By including immigrants in one's village, one reduces the likelihood of conflict because spacing between villages is farther and bonds can be developed between members of the same village, whereas distrust can develop between separate villages of immigrants and indigenous people. Third, in all likelihood marriage was exogamous. It is in all modern western Pueblo societies with respect to lineage, clan, and phratry, where the latter exists. Immigrants would add to the marriage pool. Exogamous marriage rules are also an excellent means to expand ties to other groups within the village and to nearby villages. With each village (probably) sharing males from other nearby villages, the likelihood of an attack on a neighboring village is reduced.

The fourth reason for aggregation is efficiency. Pueblo groups throughout the Southwest had begun to aggregate in the twelfth century with the process accelerating in the thirteenth century. In the upper Little Colorado Valley area Broken K Pueblo (Hill 1970), dating 1150–1280, and Carter Ranch Pueblo (Longacre 1970), dating 1100–1225, are typical examples of incipient aggregation that anticipates the enormous growth of pueblos after 1275. This early aggregation was facilitated at most villages by great kivas that served as integrative structures. Although the means is generally understood from an archaeological standpoint, the reason is not nearly so clear. Prior to aggregation into single structures, people evidently lived in clusters of sites with one having the great kiva, for example the Sawmill site in the Pine Lawn Valley area of west central New Mexico (Bluhm 1957). Actually the nature of interaction between the clustered groups and the aggregated groups probably differed little. Within the Pine Lawn area each hamlet or household probably farmed nearby land, married into neighboring groups, and participated in intergroup ritual in the great kiva. These same activities would have taken place in an aggregated settlement, such as Broken K. The differences between the two organizational structures were the development of leadership and the establishment of hereditary status differences (cf. Lightfoot 1984; Lightfoot and Feinman 1982). The villages established by these leaders were more efficient in use of land and better able to use land resources through cooperative means. Although reciprocity through exchange of marriage partners led to cooperative relationships between or among several of the hamlets, within the context of a larger village reciprocity could be controlled by people in leadership positions to better ensure the welfare of all. For example in an area such as the Hay Hollow Valley in the upper Little Colorado River area, numerous small villages could each farm enough land to support their families or small kin groups. However, as often happens in the Southwest, precipitation can be spotty, or some fields may be better advantaged for runoff from localized showers. In an area where resources are plentiful, this might cause temporary hardship that can be overcome through reciprocal ties with neighbors. In areas near carrying capacity, local exchange may be inadequate and moving to a more favorable area no longer feasible. Aggregation provides a solution to the dilemma. With an increased population, a broader land base can be maintained through an enlarged labor force. Farmable areas in diverse landforms, some producing differently from others in variable precipitation regimes, would allow a more dependable village-wide food supply to be grown. Such a minimization of loss and maximization of gain (a minimax strategy) was employed by Hopi villages in the historic period. Additionally, a larger labor force would make construction and maintenance of agriculture-intensifying systems more feasible. Thus in nearly all areas where aggregation occurs, it is accompanied by intensified land use. Occasional production of food surpluses could also be used to barter with nearby groups for exotic products or be banked to smooth over future shortages. To accomplish this aggregation requires leadership and the maintenance or elaboration of cooperative devices that could bind a society together through stressful and nonstressful periods.

For these reasons the aggregation option was selected in the late 1200s. It was a process that was ongoing and the principles were understood by both immigrants and local inhabitants. The key, therefore, lay in creating social constructs that would bind the diverse groups. The great kiva was a group-integrating structure already in place for perhaps 200 years in Mogollon and local pueblo groups, perhaps some involved in the Chaco system, throughout the region. The great kiva, it is proposed, was the stage for public ritual performances to which all (or at least initiates) were invited and probably expected to attend. Pan-village ritual was an important part of the matrix that bound the people together. With larger populations a larger stage for presentation of public ritual was needed. The enclosed plaza, a more-or-less pan-southwestern layout appearing about 1200 (Ferdon 1955), was the ideal solution. The enclosed plaza, in effect, became a greater kiva, with the nonpublic aspects of ritual maintained in ritual rooms that moved into the enclosed plaza and became kivas.

The change to enclosed plazas is synchronous with the disappearance of the great kiva, the appearance of rectangular kivas in the plaza, and enormous growth in village size. These events all occur after 1275 and before 1325. In many cases the changes are apparently in place by 1280. Pueblo leadership was able to integrate the immigrants into new villages utilizing new cooperative systems. The general efficacy of these cooperative ventures can be measured in the relative longevity of occupation of these sites (about 25 to over 50 years) and the virtual absence of indications of conflict. When one considers the task that the leadership of the upper Little Colorado Valley communities faced with immigrants moving en masse into their region vying for land that was probably at a premium due to already large population and reduced resources, the success of the new pattern is truly remarkable.

The crystallization of this new village layout and the cooperative system it fostered was the fertile soil in which the katsina cult sprouted. The exact sources of the ideas that crystallized as the cult are not perfectly clear. The broad interaction sphere in which the pueblos of the upper Little Colorado area participated are a likely source for at least some of these ideas. Broadly shared iconography with Salado, Pueblo people below the Mogollon Rim, and even with makers of Chihuahua Polychrome from Casas Grandes and elsewhere in what today is northern Mexico points to influence from points south. Significant icons on ceramics include frequent abstract bird forms, occasional bird (mostly parrot) motifs, and occasional asymmetric layouts. Addition of piki stones and shoe-form ceramic vessels, the adoption of the enclosed plaza, and the widespread occurrence of coursed adobe architecture (all characteristic of groups below the Mogollon Rim) in late thirteenth century cultural assemblages from Homol'ovi to Acoma substantiate their participation in a regional interaction sphere including the classic Hohokam and northern Mexico. It is suspected that elements in the katsina cult had their origins to the south. It is also clear from the evidence already reviewed that the distinctive iconography of the katsina cult developed in the upper Little Colorado Valley and not farther south. So the cult, although uniquely Puebloan, has elements from non-Puebloan sources.

The crystallization of the elements in early Fourmile iconography, as the regional stylistic pattern extending to the south has been termed, into the classic Fourmile style in an area going through the transformations that were documented in the upper Little Colorado Valley is entirely expected. The leaders of the newly constituted aggregated villages developed a device to symbolize their cooperative venture, the mask. The concept of masking is quite old in Mexico and apparently in the Southwest, if Archaic and Basketmaker rock art depictions of individuals in or carrying masks are to be taken literally (Schaafsma 1981:25). Whether masking was already a part of the religious repertoire or introduced from the south is not essential to the argument. What is significant is its association with aggregated villages utilizing new cooperative systems to integrate members of each village. The enclosed plazas as centers of public ritual would be ideal stages for the new katsina ritual, probably already present in masked form, if early icons are to be taken literally. In this vein such public devices as rock art and even pottery could be used to "announce" or inform individuals that were not members of the village that katsina ritual was practiced in the village.

The cult served to integrate all segments of Pueblo society and to enhance the secret religious knowledge of the leadership, which was a major
basis to their authority. The cult was probably integrated into the existing
ceremonial structure of the Pueblo groups of the upper Little Colorado
area. It developed out of the socio-religious tradition of great kiva ceremonies, which were performed in public for all to see. Its success in
gaining popularity and acceptance by the populace was due to its colorful
iconography, highly symbolic of its ritual role, and the opportunity for
every member, or at least all males, of the village to join the katsina cult.
This katsina society, therefore, crosscut the social system in place in the
late 1200s and 1300s. It served to integrate both the immigrant and the
indigenous segments within the society, involving them in a common
ritual purpose rather than individual or kin-only goals. Perhaps as importantly, to convince people to join a group, sanctions must have been
created for transgressors. For example, the universal presence of the
Whipper Katsina in Pueblo culture as an enforcer of social mores is a
sanction that, from rock art evidence, could be prehistoric. These sanctions were probably merely outgrowths of an already existent structure of
punishments designed to deter deviance and to convince all to work in
harmony together for the better of the whole. These sanctions probably
did not differ markedly from those in place in Pueblo society today. As
noted, the Pueblo ideal is encapsulated in the word *Hopi*, meaning well
behaved. People not behaving in an acceptable manner can be publicly
humiliated, ostracized, or even killed in modern Pueblo society (Ellis 1951).
Such was probably the case prehistorically as well. Thus, not to accept the
katsina, not to participate in katsina ceremony with one's fellow citizens
was to endanger the success of the ceremony and to bring hardship to all.
Modern public ceremonies are conducted with this expectation, and so
would have been their prehistoric counterparts.

What were the themes of this early cult? Several have been discussed
both in the context of the modern cult and in evaluating the archaeological
evidence of cultlike phenomena. To modern Pueblo practitioners, the
katsina cult is involved in ancestor worship and in the concept of afterlife
(Anderson 1951:197–217; Titiev 1944). When initiated Hopi die, their spirit
or breath is transported to the underworld, and when the katsina season
comes, they climb a ladder to the top of the San Francisco Peaks and
return to the Hopi Mesas as katsinas or cloud people. Thus a second
central theme to katsina ritual is the bringing of rain to the fields. Tied
into ritual improvement of crop production is fertility. Fertility is as
significant as rain in katsina ritual at Zuni (Bunzel 1932; Wright 1985) and
most eastern Pueblos (Parsons 1939).

A poorly understood aspect of katsina ritual is its role in warfare. As outlined by Ellis (1951), all Pueblos seem to have a structure, generally termed the Warrior Society, that operates during times of conflict or warfare. Unfortunately, none of the Pueblo warrior societies was still functioning when ethnographic work began. Among the western Pueblos, where the katsina cult is most visible and has been systematically studied, the relationship between the katsina cult and the Warrior Society is variable, but patterned. All of the western Pueblos have as leaders a priesthood consisting of clan leaders at Hopi and of kiva societies and society heads at Zuni and Acoma. Among the leadership of each village are one or more "offices" termed the War Captain or War Chief. These individuals are charged with protecting the village from both internal and external threats. Membership in the Warrior Society is kept strictly separate from the katsina society, as is the leadership.

Viewed from within, there are many katsinas that are considered warriors. There are even oral histories of Pueblos at war with katsinas (White 1932; Wright 1985). Certain Hopi katsinas bear warrior marks (Colton 1975) and there are stories about battles in which they participated. The key to understanding the modern katsina cult is to realize that its structure parallels that of Pueblo society. Just as there are warriors in Pueblo society, there are katsina warriors in katsina society. Thus the role of the katsina cult in war is to sanctify its existence and even to commemorate significant battles, an example of which is the Hopi Hee'e'e katsina, or Warrior Maiden.

The abundance of early war-related iconography in kiva murals at Hopi, Kuaua, and Pottery Mound in the form of shields or sun shields is never integrated with the katsina cult icons. For instance at Kuaua the Warrior and Rain Priesthoods are indicated as being integrated, whereas the katsina society remains separate. Although in relating stories of creation or history of the village people, katsinas are frequently depicted as warriors, their direct involvement in war is not supported. The preponderance of warrior katsinas, if their function has remained the same to the present, in early katsina murals and rock art may not signify that the katsina cult was war related. Rather it may parallel the role of such warrior katsinas in modern Pueblo societies as protectors of the village or the people and as punishers of transgressors or those who misbehave, for example the Whipper Katsina.

In the first chapter the varied roles of the katsina in western Pueblo society, in particular, and in many eastern Pueblos were presented. Katsina ritual involves the many clans of Pueblo society either directly as an autonomous society in the west or through intermediate Medicine or Curing Societies in the east. This integrative role has been repeatedly emphasized. But Pueblo katsinas also redistribute food and, to a less degree, wealth within the village during their public ceremonies. These public plaza dances at Hopi occur almost weekly beginning at the end of March or in early April. Major katsina ceremonies occur at Zuni, Acoma, and most eastern Pueblos also in late winter or early spring. The timing of these events corresponds with the period of greatest potential food stress in Pueblo society. If the previous season's crops have been poor, some families could be facing starvation. Stores given to the village chief for redistribution could be called upon at this time (cf. Ortiz 1969). On the other hand, those in the village who had better stores could be called upon by the katsinas to share with those less fortunate. Twice during each day of a plaza dance, which lasts one or two days, food is given to the performers, and these gifts are earmarked by the katsinas or by the donators for specific families. Because western Pueblo societies are matrilineal and matrilocal, the food is brought by the women and given to the women, young children, and the very old. In this role the katsinas redistribute food to ensure the survival of as many members of the village as possible.

Continuity of the village is always highest priority. In times of severe stress, however, villages will slough off excess population, with people seeking temporary shelter among relatives and friends in neighboring villages or tribes. The depopulation of the village is planned with those of the "first" clans, those having higher status (often concentrated within a single lineage of the clan), remaining behind. These social groups control the ritual cycle of the village and remain to keep this cycle intact. Pueblo ceremony is a daily obligation marked by periodic public ceremonies. The daily obligations must be maintained, or any chance at regaining the favor of the deities who control the weather is lost. Of course maintenance of the katsina society is a key ingredient to retaining the structure of Pueblo society.

A constellation of activities led by or involving the katsinas is used to bind the village. It includes policing and controlling deviant behavior through the Whipper Katsinas, or their close relatives. These beings and related disciplinarians have many roles. They discipline children during planned elements of some ceremonies, such as Powamuya at Hopi, or can be called upon when needed. Whippers control access to some katsinas, who are considered too dangerous for mere humans to touch.

Katsinas are also used by the religious leaders to organize and supervise work parties, such as cleaning springs or ditches, or repairing dams and cisterns (Stephen 1936; Titiev 1944; Wright 1977:44). Therefore, katsinas regulate and organize work parties for maintenance and perhaps construction of public facilities built for the benefit of the community. The religious leaders are responsible for organizing such projects. As noted earlier, these religious elite are provided personal and community stores by the village people. These elite are also the ones most involved in the transfer and exchange of religious knowledge within their community and with outside trade groups. What is suggested, then, is that as in modern Pueblo society, the religious elite were the political leaders responsible for construction and maintenance of public works, distribution of community food stores, and trade involving ritual knowledge with other villages. The authority of these traditional leaders would have been considerably enhanced and enforced through the addition of the katsina cult in the fourteenth century.

A common theme running through all of these activities is the exercise of political authority whose primary goal is to ensure the continuity of the village. This is accomplished through cooperation, that is, through getting all segments of the village to work together in harmony. Cooperation is obtained through several mechanisms, not the least of which is the katsina society. Pueblo society is constantly mediated through deviance-reducing devices. The katsina cult uses many methods to reduce deviation, including criticism by the clowns during public ceremonies, discipline of children and adults by specific katsinas, and others. On the other side of the coin, proper behavior is amply rewarded.

These themes are all reminiscent of patterns predicted for prehistoric Pueblo society in the late 1200s and 1300s. To integrate people of divergent backgrounds and varied beliefs, mechanisms of social control were elaborated, in particular the katsina cult. The cult was developed to institutionalize a broader basis in Pueblo society to reduce deviation and increase cooperation, two elements prevalent in the modern katsina cult.

Food redistribution at the village level was probably also a key element of katsina cult at its inception. As noted throughout the Pueblo world of the late thirteenth and fourteenth centuries, trade increased substantially among the inhabitants of the large aggregated pueblos. Upham (1982), Lightfoot (1984), and Reid and Shimado (1982) all project that food was at least a component of the trade network and would have offered an additional buffer to localized food shortages suffered by one segment of the network. Katsina performances by members of one village in another is a common occurrence in Pueblo culture. In addition to the ceremonial aspects of the visit, the visitors usually engage in bartering in products they want or need in exchange for products brought with them (Stephen 1936). Therefore, rituals, and katsina rituals in particular, are mechanisms of exchange within Pueblo culture. In fact the rapid spread of the katsina cult in the fourteenth century could be accounted for by invoking just such a mechanism. The frequent co-occurrence at villages having the katsina cult of White Mountain Red Ware or Jeddito Yellow Ware distant from the manufacturing sources of these types could be the result of just the processes described above.

On a related note, the public performances of rituals at Hopi (Stephen 1936) was always attended by visitors from neighboring villages and tribes. Before, during, and after the ceremony, Navajos, Utes, and others would trade with the inhabitants for a wide range of commodities, including corn, textiles, basketry, and pottery. In exchange for these locally produced items, the Hopi would receive meat, wood, basketry, and sometimes shell. In effect the katsina rituals result in informal markets. Craft specialization may have resulted from these informal affairs. Prehistoric specialization seems to be at the level of the village or village cluster, rather than at the level of the individual (cf. Bishop et al. 1988). The organization of the exchange of these specialist-produced items is as yet unclear. Whether specialization was organized and directed by a leadership core or was more entrepreneurial needs better formulation. The best example of such a network is the specialization in crafts by most Pueblos today. Most villages have distinctive ceramic styles. At Hopi the First Mesa villages specialize in pottery, Second Mesa villages specialize in coiled baskets, and Third Mesa villages specialize in wicker baskets. Although modern market conditions have significantly altered Pueblo arts and crafts production, it is still noteworthy that all of the above are crafts manufactured by women. The men's crafts, such as doll carving and weaving, are performed in all of the villages. Maintenance of these craft distinctions appears to result from the organization of Hopi society. Matrilocal residence ensures that female-produced crafts are retained in the village or village cluster, whereas male-produced crafts are frequently taken to other villages or village clusters due to exogamous marriage rules. Therefore, craft specialization, if manufactured by the group maintained in the village or village cluster by residence rules, could be the result of decentralized modes of production rather than by a centralized leadership core.

In any case, control of local resources encouraged specialized production and trade in the fourteenth century between Pueblo groups. People in the Hopi Mesa pueblos produced yellow ware pottery, people in the Homol'ovi site cluster apparently specialized in cotton production, and the Chavez Pass/Anderson Mesa cluster probably controlled the Government Mountain obsidian source (Harry 1989). At the Homol'ovi sites, for instance, yellow ware pottery does not occur in thirteenth century deposits, and obsidian is rare, occurring primarily in finished-tool form. Both are common to abundant after 1300 (Adams 1989:227). Elaboration of the trade networks and specialization in production or control of local resources clearly are associated with the aggregation of people into very large pueblos beginning after 1275. A critical element in successful aggregation was the katsina cult.

Summary

This chapter began by restating the hypothesis that the katsina cult is archaeologically recognizable. This recognition has been documented throughout this discussion. More significantly, recognition of the katsina cult in a prehistoric context allows the researcher to infer much more about the nature of the society embracing the cult. The katsina cult presently serves Pueblo society in many ways. In a society existing in an environment marginal to successful agriculture, as is the Colorado Plateau, it is incumbent to have all elements of the village working cooperatively in food production enterprises. During the late thirteenth century, environmental change and population immigration led to the development of the katsina cult, probably out of elements already in the upper Little Colorado cultural pattern infused with elements from farther south. Environmental transformations rendered much of the Four Corners region unsuitable for continued occupation by horticulturally based populations. The migration of these people to already populated areas on the Hopi Mesas and along the middle and upper Little Colorado River Valley created a stressful situation of imbalance between local resources and population. Resolution of this problem could have taken one of two courses: warfare or development of cooperative institutions. The history of the Pueblo people prior to 1275 is characterized by very little conflict. This "value system" probably was influential in choosing the latter solution (cf. Gumerman and Dean 1989). The benefits of aggregation were the reduction in conflict resulting from the mere size of the pueblo populations, an increased labor pool suitable to intensifying agricultural needs, and the ability to improve access to a greater diversity of resources through control of land and increased trade. The resulting aggregated pueblos, however, were unstable. Similar solutions of aggregation had been chosen in the A.D. 800s associated with a similar environmental degradation episode (Dean et al. 1985; Euler et al. 1979). The critical differ-ence this time was the development of the katsina cult, an institution designed to crosscut groups with divergent backgrounds and interests. The aggregation process, instead of ending with the stabilization or im-provement of environmental conditions in the sixteenth century, was maintained. The integrative institutions of the moiety, various cross-kinship societies, and the katsina cult were successful in holding the kin groups together. The appearance of "nomadic" groups in both the east (Athabascans) and the west (Utes) may also have played significant roles in keeping the pueblos aggregated.

The development and scheduling of elaborate ritual systems in modern Pueblos is controlled by the religious priesthood, or leadership core. De-velopment of the katsina cult would have enhanced the power of this religious elite by controlling access to religious knowledge. Additionally, katsina cult iconography provides a powerful symbolic tool. By depicting visual reminders of the cult in public media, such as rock art and on pot-tery, the populace is constantly made aware of the presence and impor-tance of the cult. These icons, however, serve only to remind; they do not convey sacred ritual knowledge, which is depicted in private arenas, such as murals in the kiva.

The cult allows people to dichotomize, those involved in the cult and those (outsiders) not involved. This us versus them attitude is critical to maintaining group cohesiveness. But even within a group of people, say a village, the cult symbolizes a dichotomy between those who have access to or control the secret aspects of the cult and those who do not. This is manifest in the striking lack of detail in the public symbols (ceramics and rock art) and the contrast to the private imagery in the kivas. Sanctions against access to knowledge controlled by another group are very power-ful and usually involve death to the transgressor. Control of knowledge is vital to maintenance of power in Pueblo society. Ritual knowledge, how-ever, is diffuse. In particular in the katsina cult, leaders of all of the principal clans are required to participate in planning and performance of the major ceremonies at Hopi and, to a less degree, elsewhere. All initiates can enter the sacred domain of the kiva and view the sacred murals. As a result, leadership is centralized and institutionalized but yet diffuse. In terms of village policy, only by consensus can decisions be carried out. Nevertheless, leadership has responsibilities for the well being of all of the people and through ritual, especially through the katsinas, public works projects can be implemented, exchange can be culminated, and individual behavior controlled. Elements of exchange and public works, such as development of springs, terraced gardens, and irrigation systems, are elaborated in the fourteenth century as part of the aggregation process.

The katsina cult reflects the social fabric of the village. In other words, the katsina cult provides the standard against which Pueblo society can be measured or compared. Individual katsinas represent the theocracy of the village. Katsina groups within the katsina pantheon are structured after families in the village society. Benevolent and malevolent beings are depicted. Katsinas can act as disciplinarians or benefactors. It is this flexibility that makes the katsina cult both a powerful and a particularist tool in Pueblo society. In the above sense it could be said that the cult symbolizes Pueblo ideals or cultural values. Its icons in the kiva, in the pueblo, or on the outskirts of the pueblo symbolize to all members of the society their individual roles in ensuring that the community function properly. By virtue of such proper behavior, all will prosper and be rewarded by the gods through their messengers, the katsinas. At the same time, public representations or icons of the cult only symbolize its presence and do not convey the secret, sacred, ritual knowledge conveyed only in private gatherings of the initiated.

Thus the katsina cult achieves its integrative role through two mechanisms: (1) its ability to crosscut existing social organization, and (2) its flexibility, allowing political leaders to control and maintain the village population. The changes in prehistoric Pueblo culture from 1275 to 1500, as indicated through archaeological remains, reflect the maturing of these roles for the katsina cult.

8

A Case Study
The Homol'ovi Site Group

The Homol'ovi site group consists of six pueblos. These pueblos were first recognized and studied by J. Walter Fewkes of the Smithsonian Institution in 1896 (Fewkes 1898, 1904). Fewkes learned of the existence and approximate location of the pueblos from Hopi informants who considered them ancestral homes to several clans, particularly on First Mesa. A major focus of Fewkes's excavations in the Homol'ovi sites was to document Hopi ancestry. Fewkes concentrated his excavations at Homol'ovi I and Chevelon; he also tested at Homol'ovi II and Homol'ovi III and was clearly interested in amassing large collections for the Smithsonian Institution. Thus he focused his attention on the burial areas. Several of the ceramic vessels and a rock slab recovered by Fewkes depicted katsina masks or figures.

Since 1896 very little research has been conducted in the Homol'ovi area. Pond (1966) reported on the murals found in a kiva in the west plaza of Homol'ovi II. Pilles (1975) documented several rock art panels. Both of these studies suggested the presence of the cult through iconography. Initiated in 1980, several unpublished studies of the six pueblos have been done by several institutions. The purposes of these investigations were to assess the archaeological remains and significance of the individual sites. This was necessary due to extensive vandalism to the pueblos that began with the establishment of the Mormon communities of Brigham City and Sunset in 1876 (Fewkes 1904). Fewkes's work probably focused attention on the burial remains of the sites and accelerated the "pot-hunting." The alarming proportions that this vandalism had reached by the late 1970s prompted a concerted cooperative effort on the part of the Bureau of Land Management, State of Arizona, City of Winslow, and private individuals to protect and preserve the pueblos. The assessments were to determine what remained. In 1986 the six pueblos were incorporated into

an 11,000-acre area that was designated as the Homolovi Ruins State Park.
In 1984 the Arizona State Museum, University of Arizona, launched a
long-term research program to study the Homol'ovi sites area. Both intensive survey and excavation are part of the research program that is designed to provide an interpretive framework for the Homolovi Ruins
State Park and to investigate several research problems. A major focus of
the research project is the study of aggregation. As this essay has endea-
vored to demonstrate, the development of the katsina cult is intimately
tied to aggregation. The ongoing research in the Homol'ovi study area,
combined with clear indications that the katsina cult was present there,
make it an ideal area to evaluate the effect the cult had on a local
population.

The Model

Given the discussion in chapter 6, the assumption that the Homol'ovi site
group had the katsina cult seems quite supportable. The model to be
tested here is designed to evaluate the effect that the katsina cult had on
the culture of the Homol'ovi people and to predict not only the archaeological manifestations of these effects, but also to explain why they
occurred.

   Archaeological survey indicates the 30 square mile study area was occupied by at least four groups living in small hamlets of pit houses during the
twelfth and thirteenth centuries, on the basis of tree-ring dated ceramics.
These hamlets of perhaps 30 people each preceded the establishment and
expansion of the Homol'ovi pueblos. The model of late thirteenth and
fourteenth century culture change in the Homol'ovi study area, on the
basis of arguments presented in chapters 6 and 7, are expected to develop
as follows:

   I. Shortly after 1275 immigrant populations should begin settling in the
      area as a result of major population movements prompted by envi-
      ronmentally caused (or augmented) processes.
      A. This expansion in populations should be the result of the
         Homol'ovi areas being more attractive for settlement than other
         surrounding areas due either to its being more desirable because
         of temporary environmental changes caused by the late thirteenth
         century environmental transformation or due to the stability of
         the area because it was relatively less affected by the changes.
      B. Immigration should be archaeologically demonstrable.

II. Village aggregation should take place with or soon after the arrival of the immigrants.
   A. The aggregated villages should have enclosed plazas.
      I. Enclosed plazas are elaborate ritual spaces, critical to integrating aggregating populaces from diverse backgrounds.
   B. The aggregated villages should have rectangular kivas.
      I. Rectangular kivas develop as the enclosed plaza becomes formalized and ritually oriented.
II. Katsina cult iconography should appear soon after the aggregation process begins.
   A. Initially, these icons should be publicly placed to inform outsiders and remind insiders of the cult's presence.
      I. Public icons will signal or imply the presence of the cult, not impart information about it.
   B. At the same time, or possibly later, private iconography will develop in much more elaborate form.
      I. Elaboration of private iconography will occur because only knowledgeable initiates will view it.
   C. Indications of redistribution within the village should be demonstrable.
IV. The aggregation process should continue because it can be maintained by the integrative mechanisms brought by or fostered by the katsina cult.
   A. Expanded trade should develop.
   B. Changing land use should occur.
      I. Intensification of agriculture.
         a. Development of village and kin-group boundary markers.
      2. Extension of agriculture.
   C. Specialization in production should develop.

Implications of the Model for the Homol'ovi Area

About 1275 the central Little Colorado River became a desirable area in which to live. The reasons for this attraction will be explicated later. Following the model, it is expected that the Homol'ovi study area will sustain a population increase in the late thirteenth century as a result of population movements apparently related to the degradation episode occurring in lowland areas elsewhere on the Colorado Plateau. The increased population will be due to immigration into the area and will be recognizable, using archaeological data, in terms of new architectural traditions, ceramic styles, and the like.

The immigrants into the area should be absorbed into existing villages or coalesced into nearby villages as they arrive, or within a short time of their arrival. All of the aggregated villages should have enclosed plaza areas and rectangular kivas, and these should be in place by the late thirteenth or early fourteenth century.

Soon after the development of the aggregated pueblos with the enclosed-plaza layout, katsina cult iconography should appear in local rock art and on local ceramics. It would be expected that in addition to the local ceramics, that some Fourmile Polychrome, imported from the upper Little Colorado Valley should be present. It is also predictable that Fourmile Polychrome will have the asymmetric Fourmile style and some vessels may even have katsina figures. The cult will act in its dual roles by being visible in public places as reminders of proper behavior for all community members, and in private areas where ritual secrets are maintained in kivas and associated initiation rooms. Distribution of cult iconography will not be random. Icons will be controlled by those in authority to protect the secret aspects of the cult. At the same time, utilizing the symbolic meaning of the cult icons, the leaders will be able to galvanize the members of the community into cooperative enterprises.

As noted by Johnson (1989), Pueblo society is composed of lineages, is inherently unstable, and will remain together in large groups only for a short time unless leadership (or a crosscutting social institution) can coalesce the group. Moiety divisions; various curing, warrior, or clown societies; and the katsina cult all crosscut lineages and are capable of coalescing kinship-focused groups. Thus to maintain aggregated pueblos, the katsina cult was instituted at the fourteenth century Homol'ovi sites.

Developing out of these aggregated villages will be expanded trade, increased land use through both extensive and intensive means, and specialization. Although very difficult to detect archaeologically, redistribution within the pueblo will be instituted. These are benefits of maintaining aggregated settlements, and the cult is integral in fostering and maintaining all of these developments.

Although the structure was seemingly in place, status differentiation, which would have been enhanced by the katsina cult, did not develop into a stratified society. The available structure was in the form of a core leadership or priesthood. The tool to augment and centralize the authority and power of this priesthood was available in the katsina cult. Using the modern Pueblo katsina cult as a model, the cult can be used to control labor, to act as "enforcer" (almost a militia), to redistribute food (or wealth), and to conduct or control trade. However, a key element to transferring status differentials, inherent in all human societies either ascribed or earned, into institutionalized status positions and finally into social stratification is the ability to accumulate wealth. The Colorado Plateau is simply too marginally productive, especially for domesticated crops, to consistently produce the surplus necessary to restructure the Pueblo social system. In fact the more structured societies of the eastern Pueblo groups (cf. Ortiz 1969) may be a direct result of the Rio Grande having the potential for broad agricultural intensification, such as canals and irrigation ditches, in an area with an adequate growing season.

The Homol'ovi Research Program

The Homol'ovi Research Program is working on a lengthy schedule of research among the Homol'ovi site group, which is defined as Homol'ovi I, Homol'ovi II, Homol'ovi III, Homol'ovi IV, Cottonwood Creek Ruin, and Chevelon Ruin, including study of the surrounding area (Fig. 8.1). One year of excavation has been completed at Homol'ovi II, the largest of the pueblos with nearly 700 ground-floor rooms and three plazas, two enclosed (Hays and Adams 1985), (Fig. 8.2). Excavation covering a five-year period has been completed at Homol'ovi III, the smallest Pueblo, having about 40 rooms, including several pit structures (Adams 1989). One year of excavations has been conducted at Homol'ovi IV, a pueblo of 150–200 rooms. Previous researchers have mapped, surface collected, and in some cases augered each of the six main pueblos (Adams (1980; Andrews 1982; Hantman 1982; Weaver et al. 1982).

An intensive survey of the surrounding area has been conducted in conjunction with the excavations, with coverage emphasizing the east side of the Little Colorado River between Homol'ovi I and Homol'ovi II. Pedestrian survey of 30 square miles has identified 360 sites. The survey has concentrated on locating, identifying, collecting, and mapping the sites to enable the program to place them in a time-space-use framework (Lange 1989).

Based on tree-ring dated ceramics, three general periods of occupation of the study area have been recognized. The earliest is the Basketmaker III–Pueblo I period according to the Pecos Classification. This occupation would probably date about A.D. 600–850. The area was apparently only slightly used until reoccupied again about A.D. 1100, lasting until about 1275, or during the Pueblo III period. The final occupation corresponds

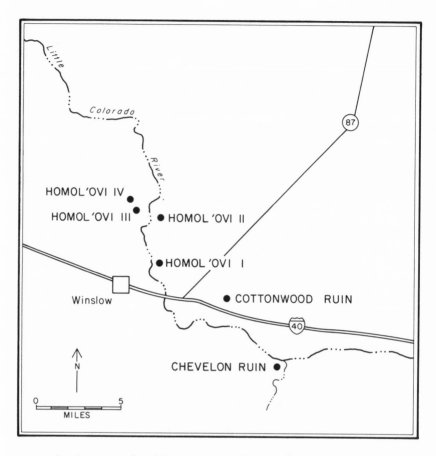

FIGURE 8.1. Location of pueblos comprising the Homol'ovi site group. (Drawn by Ron Beckwith, Arizona State Museum)

with the establishment of the pueblo sites, about 1275, lasting until 1400, or slightly longer (termed the Pueblo IV period), when the area was abandoned, at least according to archaeological evidence, until Mormon settlement in 1876.

Permanent settlements of pit house villages characterized the first two occupations (Young 1989). These hamlets consisted of several houses each with associated surface features and structures. The twelfth and thirteenth century hamlets apparently used large, shallow, unroofed, pit structures as settlement or community integrative structures akin to kivas, given the settlement size (Young 1989). Both the A.D. 600–850 and A.D. 1100–1275 occupations used the gravel terraces along the east side of the river for their settlements. Although a mixed economy of domestic crops and wild plants and animals characterized both early assemblages, relative differences in their subsistence mix is suggested by their exploitation of local resources, in particular their strategy for growing domesticated crops. The Basketmaker people apparently only dry-farmed, using stabilized sand dunes within a kilometer of their hamlet. The Pueblo III inhabitants continued to use the local sand dunes, but shifted their agricultural emphasis to nearby side drainages where flood water (akchin) farming techniques could be used effectively (Lange 1989:207–210). Concentrations of Pueblo III agricultural sites in the lower sections of the large side drainages may even suggest that they were taking advantage of seasonal flooding of the Little Colorado River to diversify their agricultural strategy.

In either subsistence mix, the nonagriculture–dominated Basketmaker III or agriculture–dominated Pueblo III strategy, population was uniformly low. Even assuming that all structures in each hamlet were occupied concurrently, a very unlikely event, population in the 30 square mile study area would have been 120 people (4 sites × 6 pit structures × 5 occupants/pit structure). More than likely, population was less than 100

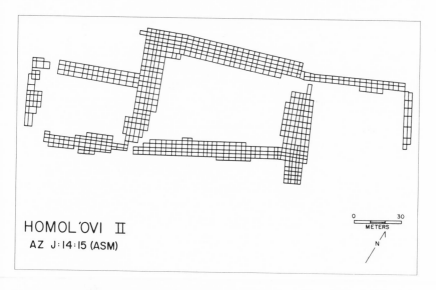

HOMOL 'OVI II

AZ J:14:15 (ASM)

0   30
METERS

N

FIGURE 8.2. Site plan of Homol'ovi II.
(Redrawn by Ron Beckwith, Arizona State Museum, from *An Archaeological Assessment of Homolovi II Ruin* by Donald E. Weaver, Jr., Steven G. Dosh, and Keith E. Miller, Fig. 3, by permission of the Museum of Northern Arizona, Flagstaff)

in either case. For comparative purposes, the 1,000 rooms of Homol'ovi I and Homol'ovi II that were built and used in the 1300s could have housed 1,000 or more people, and certainly several times the population of the earlier occupations.

The changes in the cultural pattern predicted by the katsina cult model for the area beginning about 1275, or in conjunction with the environmental transformation of the 1275–1300 period on the Colorado Plateau, occur quite dramatically. In consultation with the Quaternary Studies program, Northern Arizona University, a model of changes in the Little Colorado River floodplain and its impact on the occupants of the region can now be proposed (Kolbe 1990). As related by a member of the expedition (Peterson 1973), Mormon settlers on the floodplain within a kilometer of Homol'ovi I in the 1870s tried to dam the river and irrigate crops along the broad flat floodplain. They were continually flooded out and their dams destroyed, along with the irrigation ditches and crops. By 1884 both the Sunset and the Brigham City Mormon settlements had been abandoned. In historical terms, entrenchment of the Little Colorado River was initiated about 1888 (Hack 1942a; Hereford 1984; Kolbe 1990). Between 1888 and 1905 the river cut a wider and wider channel, restricted from growing deeper by bedrock. Another alluvial period associated with high water discharge occurred from about 1905 to 1927, followed by a brief erosional period from 1928 to 1937. Since 1938, with brief interludes, the river has deposited alluvium, in some cases up to 1.5 m. Although the threat of flooding along the river is still real, the energy and destructiveness of these floods is much reduced from the Mormon period, due to levees and other devices constructed in the area during the last 20 years. The point of this discussion is that the Little Colorado River can change rapidly and significantly in character.

The implications for the late 1200s are clear. First, the channel was probably cut rather quickly, in a matter of five years or less. Second, and quite significantly, the floodplain became farmable with entrenchment of the river. Both the pueblos of Homol'ovi III and Homol'ovi IV, and possibly Homol'ovi I, were established within or along the edge of the floodplain, an impossibility, particularly for Homol'ovi III, when the floodplain was aggraded. Therefore, as proposed by the model, the late thirteenth century environmental transformation allowed expanded settlement along the central Little Colorado River Valley, where the Homol'ovi sites are located today. Rather than stability in the area versus surrounding areas, quite specific changes in the arable land status of the area after 1275 versus before 1275 caused the major immigration into the area. Alluvial deposits and modern flooding in the study area suggest that as many as 5,000 hectares of floodplain became accessible to farming after 1275 that were not available before 1275, due to entrenchment of the river. It is as yet unclear whether irrigation or management of seasonal floods was used to water floodplain crops. However, management of the permanent stream in Moenkopi Wash by Hopi prior to Mormon settlement in 1875 utilized simple diversion dams rather than the elaborate ditches developed by the Mormons (Godfrey 1988:24–25).

Because the floodplain was a new agricultural resource, it may not have been owned by indigenous Pueblo farmers. This would have been especially true on the west side of the river where no pre–1275 habitation sites have been located but where both Homol'ovi III and Homol'ovi IV were built within one kilometer of each other.

The katsina cult model for the Homol'ovi study area predicts that new immigrants will be archaeologically demonstrable and distinguishable from the indigenous inhabitants. As noted above, the pre–1275 occupants of the study area lived in small, hamlet-sized, pit house villages with small, nonmasonry surface rooms of only two or three contiguous rooms. Integrative structures appear to be large, shallow, earthen-walled, unroofed, pit structures, rather than "typical" kivas (cf. Gumerman and Skinner 1968). Pit houses are also earthen walled. Local Little Colorado (sherd-tempered) Gray and White Ware pottery characterize the ceramic assemblage. The Homol'ovi III and Homol'ovi IV sites represent radical departures from this pattern and from each other.

Homol'ovi IV is built of 150–200 small, masonry rooms crammed stair-like along the talus of a small butte (Fig. 8.3). Homol'ovi IV kivas are masonry and rectangular. Initially, ceramics are dominated by Jeddito Orange Ware (later, with the use of local clays, these became Winslow Orange Wares) with abundant Tusayan Gray and White Wares. None of these ceramics was made locally and together with the architecture and village style suggest the occupants migrated from the vicinity of the Hopi Mesas 80 km or more north. There is virtually no yellow pottery at Homol'ovi IV, suggesting it was abandoned by 1300 and never reoccupied.

Homol'ovi III, on the other hand, was built of large rectangular rooms, originally of sandstone, but later of coursed adobe. Layout of the 40 surface rooms is linear. The surface rooms open to an unbounded plaza area having two rectangular kivas (one, half masonry and one earthen) and a rectangular, masonry great kiva (Fig. 8.4). The presence of a great kiva at Homol'ovi III indicates that the traditional western pueblo (upper Little Colorado River) integrative structure of the thirteenth century

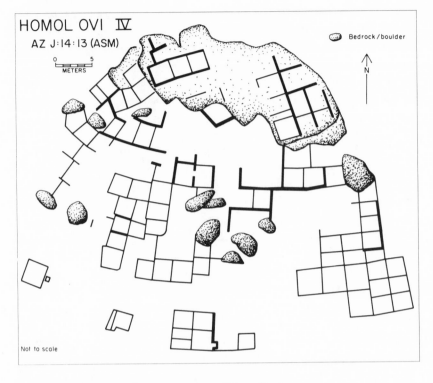

FIGURE 8.3. Conjectural reconstruction of Homol'ovi IV.
(Drawn by Ron Beckwith, Arizona State Museum)

was transferred to the Homol'ovi area. Although it is probable the great kiva was used for intravillage ritual activities, it is possible that through intermarriage or other mechanisms the great kiva involved membership from several nearby settlements. A single radiocarbon date from the roof matting of a kiva built later than the great kiva dated 1277–1318 (U of A) supports the ceramics-derived date of construction of the great kiva to 1275–1300 (Adams 1989).

The contrast in size, construction, and layout of Homol'ovi III to Homol'ovi IV is striking, as are both to the indigenous hamlets. The contrast is especially striking because the two sites are a kilometer apart. The Homol'ovi III ceramics are initially dominated by White Mountain Red Ware, Cibola White Ware, and Cibola Gray Ware all manufactured in a fairly narrow area 50–80 km southeast of Homol'ovi III. Room size, kiva shape, presence of a great kiva, settlement plan, and the ceramic assemblage all point to the occupants immigrating to the Homol'ovi area. There were two major uses of the Homol'ovi III site prehistorically. The first, devoid of yellow ware, was a year-round habitation hamlet that, like Homol'ovi IV, was built after 1275 and abandoned about 1300. The second occupation has yellow ware ceramics that eventually come to dominate the decorated ceramic assemblage. The yellow wares are imported Jeddito (Hopi) Yellow Ware suggesting a 1325–1400 occupation, or seasonal reuse, by inhabitants, probably from Homol'ovi II, 3.2 km east. Therefore, major immigration into the study area is archaeologically demonstrable and came not from one but from at least two areas between 1275 and 1300 (Adams 1989).

The model predicts that village aggregation should take place soon after immigrants move into the area. Unlike the upper Little Colorado Valley area where immigrants may have been absorbed directly into the indigenous villages, at least in part this was not the case in the Homol'ovi study

FIGURE 8.4. Plan view map of Homol'ovi III.
(Drawn by Ron Beckwith, Arizona State Museum)

area. This is probably because the Homol'ovi area was made productive by the erosional cycle of the late 1200s rather than a refuge area of stable soils or relatively higher precipitation. In the latter case most arable land was probably already owned and cultivated. In the Homol'ovi area, on the other hand, land in the floodplain may not have been owned or may have been something that could be given, or given up, to immigrants perhaps because it had not been used for agriculture. Nevertheless, in the upper Little Colorado and the Homol'ovi areas aggregation is predicted and does occur.

Also as predicted by the model, all of the fourteenth century habitation sites in the central Little Colorado River study area have both rectangular kivas and enclosed plazas, although the shape of all the kivas has not yet been determined. These suggest influence from the upper Little Colorado area and that the stage is being set for the arrival, or development, of the katsina cult. The katsina cult model predicts that development of aggregated sites and enclosed plazas are both responses to reduce conflict between indigenous and nonindigenous groups. What evidence in the Homol'ovi study area supports this conflict-reducing model?

The most significant indicators are the abandonment of the small pueblos of Homol'ovi III, Homol'ovi IV, and probably Cottonwood Creek Ruin, and the relocation of these people into the large pueblos of Homol'ovi II, Homol'ovi I, and Chevelon Ruin. Abandonment of the small pueblos occurs about 1300, and it is at this time that the large pueblos witness substantial growth. Abandonment of Homol'ovi III was accompanied by the disuse of the great kiva which was later partly filled with trash and burned. Clearly, the great kiva did not satisfy the ritual or integrative needs of fourteenth century Pueblo society. Thus, the aggregated pueblos were comprised of populations from at least three different backgrounds. Population growth resulted in construction of roomblocks that encircled and formalized open space developing into large enclosed plazas at each of the aggregated pueblos, with two at Homol'ovi II, the largest site.

The pattern of growth at the three villages is different. The enclosed plazas at Homol'ovi II are apparently part of the growth of the pueblo. At Homol'ovi I and Chevelon the enclosed plazas are attached to a large, clustered roomblock and give the appearance of being later additions to each pueblo. The pattern at Homol'ovi I and Chevelon, however, may also be due to the topography of the areas in which they were built. Both of the pueblos are built on small knolls and simply did not have space for a large, enclosed plaza. The attached appearance of the Homol'ovi I and Chevelon plazas also more closely follows the segregated appearance of the rectangular great kivas they replaced, and may have in fact been intentional in imitation of this pattern.

Given the different appearance of the aggregated pueblos, it may not be coincidental that only the rock art at Homol'ovi II has abundant katsina motifs both as figures and as masks. Early construction of enclosed plazas for public ceremonies and the most prominent display of katsina motifs supports the hypothesis that in the western Pueblo area, the two are interrelated. The fact that Homol'ovi II is greater in size than Homol'ovi I and Chevelon combined would also indicate that the katsina cult not only played a central role in developing institution-fostering, cooperative behavior, but also that the cult was successful at this enterprise. The presence of murals, probably of katsinas dancing, in a rectangular kiva in the western plaza of Homol'ovi II strongly supports the hypothesis that the planning and staging of katsina dances occurred in the enclosed plazas (Pond 1966).

Dating the appearance of the katsina cult at the Homol'ovi sites has been suggested as early utilizing the rock art. The best evidence, however, is through the ceramics recovered by Fewkes (1898, 1904). As noted in chapters 2 and 7, the rooms excavated by the Arizona State Museum at Homol'ovi II radiocarbon dated to about 1350 (Hays and Adams 1985). The restorable vessel assemblage from these excavations revealed that 22 of the 23 vessels were Hopi yellow ware (21 of 22 decorated) and only one was locally manufactured Winslow Orange Ware. One of these vessels, a bowl, had a Sun Forehead katsina painted on the interior bottom (Fig. 5.13). Whether the Winslow Orange Ware was manufactured or an heirloom piece, the pattern clearly demonstrates that the Homol'ovi people either were not or were rarely manufacturing their own decorated pottery by the mid–1300s. A paucity of firewood in the Homol'ovi area is cited as an explanation for the need and desire to import most ceramics from the Hopi area. Excavations at Homol'ovi II and Homol'ovi III indicate that after 1275 cotton became an important commodity grown in the area and that this was the principal item used to barter for the Hopi pottery (Adams 1989; Miksicek 1985).

As a result, Winslow Orange Wares, the decorated locally manufactured ceramics, were apparently manufactured only between about 1275 and 1350, with the end date perhaps closer to 1325. Date of the local ceramics is highly significant because several have katsina masks depicted on them (Fewkes Collection: National Museum of Natural History; Wattron Collection: Field Museum of Natural History). This suggests that the katsina cult was present in the Homol'ovi area by the first half of the fourteenth century.

Apparently, the cult was present or forming at the same time the pueblos, in particular Homol'ovi II, were experiencing phenomenal growth, primarily from immigrants, and were constructing enclosed plazas. The date of these developments, based on a predominance of Winslow Orange Ware, was between 1275 and 1350.

In terms of explanation, the data suggest that as immigrants were attracted to or added to existing Homol'ovi villages, enclosed plazas were built to house the public ceremonies used by the village religious leaders to integrate the differing factions. Members of all factions may have been encouraged to present ceremonies or participate with others in ceremonies. Rituals involving divergent factions, organized through societies, were the most important and the most successful in integrating the village and encouraging cooperative behavior. The katsina cult was one of the cross-kinship societies that was being developed.

The cause for the aggregation in most areas was: (1) environmental change apparently causing the reduction in local carrying capacity that resulted in emigration of indigenous people from their homelands; (2) incorporation of immigrant groups into existing settlements in refuge areas, that is areas having adequate water and land resources; and (3) incorporation mitigated conflict, ensured maintenance or broadened the control of local land resources, and enhanced the labor pool. By controlling local resources and agreeing to share outlying areas with new immigrants, potential conflict was reduced, which would pose a threat to the local leadership. Once under local control, the benefits promised would have to be met. These benefits would be a chance at survival, enhanced by large settlement size, and feeling part of existing social groups through participation in integrative rituals. Both of these would be met by the katsina cult. Participation in village ritual, both planning and performance, and the redistribution function of the cult would ensure both interaction with local social groups and increased security about survival.

At the Homol'ovi sites aggregation was facilitated by environmental change in a two-stage process. First, the immigrants were attracted to the area by the degradation of the river valley that began in the 1270s and opened up new areas for farming, areas that may not have been used or owned by the indigenous occupants of the area. Tree-ring records and water-discharge reconstruction for the Little Colorado River suggest that beginning at 1300 and lasting to the 1330s another precipitation pattern settled over most of the Colorado Plateau and into the Little Colorado River basin in particular (Dean and Robinson 1978; Kolbe 1990). This wetter pattern would have resulted in alluviation in the Little Colorado

River floodplain, making it more flood-prone. Both Homol'ovi III and Homol'ovi IV were probably abandoned as a result of this change in precipitation pattern. The occupants moved to Homol'ovi II, or possibly to Homol'ovi I. The choices facing the Homol'ovi III and Homol'ovi IV occupants when contemplating abandonment were four: (1) They could try to survive on land that carried a big risk of flooding. (2) They could move to the east side of the river, where arable land was already owned by Homol'ovi I and Homol'ovi II inhabitants, and hope to be allowed either to use the land, which by modern Pueblo standards would be unlikely, or take the land and fight the owners. (3) They could move completely out of the area and try to find land suitable to support them. (4) They could move in with the Homol'ovi I or Homol'ovi II inhabitants and be partitioned a section of arable land for their use. Hopi oral histories repeatedly refer to the fourth process as the mechanism used to integrate new immigrants to an area (Courlander 1971; Nequatewa 1936). Note that in traditional Pueblo society the land continues to be owned by the village "chief" and can be retaken from the group given permission to use it, if use lapses. It seems highly likely that the fourth option was taken.

Although their specific meanings are not known, markers (actually shrines) dividing land into ownership units are clearly visible around agricultural areas used by the Homol'ovi I and the Homol'ovi II people. As is the case in historic Pueblo villages, land ownership and its division were probably vested in the authority of the leadership groups of the large villages, and these shrines, as is the case today, probably marked lines of ownership based on the leaders' decisions. It is noteworthy that at Homol'ovi II some of these markers are accompanied by rock art depicting katsinas and katsina masks. It is conceivable that the village leadership at Homol'ovi utilized the cult to sanctify its land distribution decisions. Each group's katsina totem could have symbolized whose land it was to all of the village's members. In modern Hopi society each clan has one or more symbols that frequently are carved into rock (Cole 1989a; Colton and Colton 1931; Michaelis 1981).

The apparent division and ownership of arable land near Homol'ovi I and Homol'ovi II may be the harbinger of the formal land division one finds associated with modern Pueblos. Both Ortiz (1969) and Nagata (1970:99) describe four land use categories. For the Hopi these can be termed village site land, community land, clan and society land, and outland. Village site land is the location of the village. Clan and society land is used for farming and is controlled by those social units. Clan lands extend 1 to 2.5 km from historic (pre–1900) Hopi villages (Forde 1931; Page

1940). Communal land is just outside the pueblo where vegetable gardens are grown around springs or seeps. Outlands are used for hunting of large game, quarries, firewood, and shrines, and lie beyond clan land. Use of these resources, however, is controlled by the village and by clans. Incidentally, both Hopi and Zuni seasonal farming villages are located on either outland or communal property lands. The seasonal occupation of Homol'ovi III could parallel such historic seasonal farming villages and therefore would be located on either outland or communal property lands. Field houses located on many of the lands nearer Homol'ovi I and Homol'ovi II could have been the local equivalent to clan and society lands.

Thus at the Homol'ovi sites, aggregation apparently accelerated soon after 1300 when groups from different areas began sharing the same villages. Attempts to integrate these groups began with construction of enclosed plazas as areas for massive public rituals. Within 50 years after these initial integrative attempts, the katsina cult was introduced into Homol'ovi society. The cult was probably introduced from the upper Little Colorado River area. It provided both symbolic and functional purpose to the Homol'ovi people. First, and foremost, the cult served the leadership of the aggregated villages. It was in the leaders' best interests to retain large villages, for they added to their prestige and authority. Thus the structure of the cult, mimicking the village hierarchy, served this purpose. But aggregated villages also benefit individuals. With greater spacing between villages, intervillage competition could be mitigated resulting in fewer tensions between villages, although there were more within the village. However, the cult was designed to mollify internal tensions. Aggregated villages also provided more potential wealth to the village and to most individuals. Increased trade and specialization are just two reasons.

Once the cult had established a foothold at Homol'ovi, certainly at least at Homol'ovi II, the aggregation process became successful. Perhaps the added-on look of the plazas at Homol'ovi I and Chevelon resulted from their copying the successful Homol'ovi II village layout. (A similar process is described by Renfrew [1986] as competitive emulation.) On the other hand, each aggregated village may have merely adopted a different look resulting from the same influences. In any event, all three have cult icons on pottery and painted slabs (Fewkes 1898). Given the probable function of katsina icons on ceramics and rock art as symbolic messaging of the presence of the cult (Kenaghy 1986), perhaps the absence of nearby suitable rock outcrops at Homol'ovi I and Chevelon promoted an increase in depictions of katsinas on ceramics to compensate. Along this line Cole (1989b) notes the predominance of rock art in the Homol'ovi area and elsewhere in visible locations consistent with their use as iconographic intensifiers, that is, as indicators of the presence of the cult and no more (Fig. 8.5).

Homol'ovi I, Homol'ovi II, and Chevelon also experienced outgrowths of the aggregation process allowed by the cult and predicted by the model. Three traits mentioned in the model as outgrowths of aggregation are expanded trade, changing land use, and specialization. Let us examine each of these developments utilizing the Homol'ovi data.

The first consideration is changing land use. The development of the Homol'ovi sites after 1300 resulted in a more diversified land use. As a matter of fact, the characterization that the Homol'ovi sites used the floodplain and upper side drainages, as well as lower side drainages and sand dunes is actually a simplification. After 1300 land used actually went through a two-stage process. The degradation of the Little Colorado River opened up the formerly marginal floodplain to agriculture, and this niche was exploited by new immigrants to the area who founded Homol'ovi III and Homol'ovi IV. Archaeobotanical remains from Homol'ovi III indicate that several varieties of corn, beans, and squash were being grown, as well as cotton (Miksicek 1989). The wet period from 1300 to the 1330s eliminated part or all of this floodplain from dependable agricultural production and the occupants of Homol'ovi III and Homol'ovi IV moved to Homol'ovi II or Homol'ovi I. During the early 1300s the agricultural land on the east side of the river in the vicinity of Homol'ovi I and Homol'ovi II was stretched into ever more marginal areas to upper sections of side drainages. Artifact scatters and field houses dominated by Winslow Orange Wares signal the beginning of these changes in land use with yellow wares marking the greatest extent of their distribution later. Land use was characterized by fields having temporary shades or more lasting semisubterranean, jacal field structures with stone and earthen walls (Lange et al. 1986; Lange et al. 1987; Young 1990).

Reversal to a drier weather pattern by the 1330s probably prompted the greatest expansion in Homol'ovi culture. The floodplain once again became available for agricultural practices allowing further population expansion. However, the floodplain not only grew maize, it also grew extensive quantities of cotton (Miksicek 1985, 1989). In fact cotton remains are so extensive in plant samples from both Homol'ovi II and Homol'ovi III, that it is safe to conclude the Homol'ovi people were specializing in the production of cotton. The central Little Colorado River Valley has

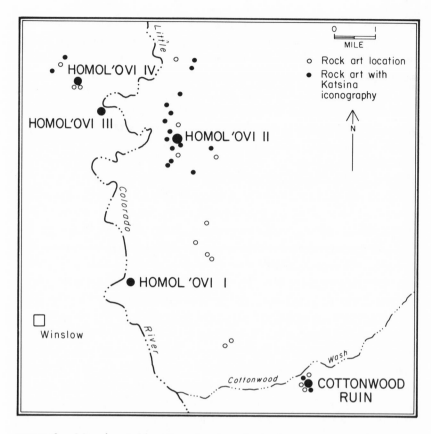

FIGURE 8.5. Map showing location of rock art having katsina iconography
in the vicinity of the Homol'ovi pueblos.
(Redrawn by Ron Beckwith, Arizona State Museum, from original
drawings by Sally J. Cole; originally published in *Rock Art Evidence for
the Presence and Significance of the Katsina Cult at 13th–14th Century
Homol'ovi in the Central Little Colorado River Valley, Northeastern
Arizona*, Master's thesis by Sarah J. Cole, Fig. 2, used with permission)

relatively ideal conditions for growing cotton on the Colorado Plateau.
Elevation is 1478 m (4850 ft) with a growing season of about 180 days
(Adams 1980), more than long enough for the hardy, indigenous cotton.
The alkaline soils of the floodplain and the ready source of water from the
Little Colorado River, either through periodic flooding, as done by nineteenth century Maricopa Indians; through diversion dams, as done by
nineteenth century Hopi at Moenkopi (Godfrey 1988); or through diversion using canals and irrigation ditches make the area well suited to cotton
production (Kent 1957:470).

Through much of antiquity in the Southwest, cotton has been grown and widely traded. The Hohokam seem to have first supplied the Colorado Plateau populations with cotton by A.D. 700 with the Verde Valley a later production area. By A.D. 1100 there were pockets of production on the Colorado Plateau (Kent 1957:467). As many of these production areas were abandoned by 1300, supplies must have been critically short, with the people below the Mogollon Rim again supplying not only cotton, but also textiles (cf. Kent 1983). Samples from both Homol'ovi III and Homol'ovi II deposits are characterized by cotton seeds second only in frequency of domestic plants to maize.

Therefore, with additional aggregation of the Homol'ovi pueblos through the mid-1300s came expansion of land use and specialization in production of cotton. The relative paucity of spindle whorls suggests that weaving was not a dominant industry at Homol'ovi and that the raw fiber may have been traded, although weaving tools could have been made entirely of perishable materials (as they are today at Hopi) and be underrepresented in the archaeological record (Adams, J. 1980). At Spanish contact in the sixteenth century, the Hopi were well known for their production and trade of cotton textiles and of raw cotton (Kent 1957:469). The Hopi relied on the Moenkopi area, a name translated by Kent (1957:469) as "cotton fields," for much of their cotton. The Moenkopi area has identical resources to that of the Homol'ovi area with an elevation of 1,463 m (4,800 ft) providing a similar growing season and a perennial stream providing needed water. A Hopi village, old Moenkopi, was established in the vicinity of modern Moenkopi by the 1400s and may have replaced the Homol'ovi area as a production center for cotton provided to the pueblos on the Hopi Mesas (Colton 1974; Mindeleff 1891).

Associated with specialized cotton production was a shift in land use. Before 1300 each small settlement (probably 20–50 rooms) had its own farming area. After 1300, to support aggregation, the pueblo inhabitants were forced into a more sophisticated approach to land use. As a prologue it should be mentioned that historic Pueblos use seasonal farming villages (Ellis 1978) and have at least three- to four-part land statuses (Forde 1931; Nagata 1970; Ortiz 1969; Page 1940). With expansion of land holdings by the aggregated Homol'ovi villages to support the growing populations, came the development of seasonal sites. Homol'ovi III and probably Cottonwood Creek Ruin both functioned as seasonal farming villages when the floodplain became available again for farming by the 1330s. Homol'ovi III is 3.2 km from the nearest aggregated village, Homol'ovi II. Cottonwood is 8 km from Homol'ovi I and Chevelon. Both of these distances exceed that for clan-held farmland among the Hopi (Forde 1931;

Page 1940) and would occur in outland areas. This same land status is also the location of historic farming villages.

Historic villages, such as Moenkopi, are founded for one of two reasons: to expand production of food when arable land around the aggregated village is inadequate, or to utilize resources unavailable to the aggregated village, such as springs or a permanent water flow. For example, Moenkopi village was reestablished in the 1870s to supplement food production and to provide resources that could not be grown or could be grown less effectively near the Hopi Mesas. This would suggest that Homol'ovi III was reestablished in the floodplain either to expand production of food for Homol'ovi II or to grow a crop, such as cotton, that could not be produced nearer the village. Without knowing in some detail the nature of the floodplain in the midfourteenth century, it is difficult to choose between the two options. Plant samples studied from the seasonal use of Homol'ovi III suggest that both cotton and corn were grown locally but that cotton was a commodity of equal importance to maize (Miksicek 1989).

Clearly, the Homol'ovi III people were specializing in cotton production. Major changes occurred in land use between 1300 and the 1320s or so. Before 1300 land use was controlled by small, local pueblos. By the mid–1300s there is kinship-held land near the aggregated village that was demarcated by boundaries of shrines, some marked by rock art, including katsinas. This land was probably devoted to corn, beans, and squash and characterized by field houses and temporary "shades" that archaeologists recognize as artifact scatters having pottery, chipped stone, ground stone, and stone hoes (Lange et al. 1986; Lange 1989). The floodplain was devoted to both maize and cotton.

Beyond the view of the aggregated villages or just in particularly good resource areas, seasonal sites were established by reusing existing pueblo structures. The people reoccupying Homol'ovi III may have been original inhabitants of the hamlet, either land-poor individuals needing an additional area to support their needs or cotton-producing specialists. Unique resources, such as springs, are considered communal property by modern Pueblo land use practices (Nagata 1970), and until better data can be developed, the assumption is that Homol'ovi III and local cotton and corn production were not controlled by one group or by the village leadership. If such control could be gained and exercised, as suggested by some researchers (Upham 1982), then the basis for hereditary status could be expanded into a stratified society. Control over a valuable commodity, such as cotton, should result in wealth accumulation, architectural differentiation, and other status differences. None of these is yet apparent in the archaeological record at Homol'ovi, although Upham (1982) argues that elite individuals did indeed accumulate wealth at Nuvakwewtaka (Chavez Pass), 50 km southwest of the Homol'ovi area.

With production of a valued commodity, such as cotton, the Homol'ovi people expanded trade relations with nearby aggregated villages. In exchange for cotton and other riparian resources, such as birds and turtles, the Homol'ovi people received pottery from the Hopi Mesas, obsidian from Chavez Pass or the Anderson Mesa pueblos, and ceramics from upper Little Colorado River villages and Salado people (Bishop et al. 1988; Harry 1989). It is likely that the traded vessels contained other perishable and nonperishable artifacts that are not preserved or recognized in the archaeological record.

The trade artifacts suggest that the Hopi Mesas were the principal trade partners. By 1350 all, or nearly all, the decorated pottery was manufactured on the Hopi Mesas (Bishop et al. 1988; Hays 1985). The Hopi pottery filled a void in the Homol'ovi product needs. Although satisfactory clays and tempering materials were locally abundant in the Homol'ovi area, fuelwood was not. With demands on wood far outstripping supply, savings in energy expense would have been welcome and was provided by Hopi yellow ware. In turn, the Hopi used and needed cotton, from the Homol'ovi people. Although yellow pottery is found at other aggregated villages above and below the Mogollon Rim, it never approaches the quantity at the Homol'ovi sites. Homol'ovi probably acted as an intermediary in some of the transfer of the Hopi yellow ware to Chavez Pass and into the Verde Valley. With the vast quantity of yellow ware at the aggregated Homol'ovi sites and its presence throughout the spatial extent of each village, the yellow ware and exchange in general do not seem to be controlled by the village leadership. Private entrepreneurs, trade parties, and ceremonies were all common mechanisms of trade in historic Pueblos. Exchange of ceremonial knowledge, including katsina ceremonies, may have acted as devices promoting cooperation between villages, in particular between settlement clusters, and could have been controlled by the village leadership.

Summary

As predicted by the katsina-cult-based model of culture change at Homol'ovi, the cult allowed the aggregated villages to stabilize and further increase their populations to the carrying capacity of the area. Aggregation led to changing land use (both in extension and intensification), specialization in cotton production and probably other riparian resources, and much expanded trade, especially to the Hopi Mesas. Involvement of the katsina cult in the late thirteenth and fourteenth centuries development in the Homol'ovi pueblos has proven to be predictable and significant. As soon as aggregation is rapid and involves divergent populations, mechanisms develop to integrate the populace. The enclosed-plaza community ritual center is the first development followed closely by the katsina cult. The success of these integrative mechanisms resulted in continuity of the aggregated villages and continued expansion. Distribution of cult iconography in public media, such as rock art and ceramics, indicates the cult was used by the leadership in involving all segments of the populace in the ceremonies. Such community integration would allow the leadership to organize community labor to make the land productive. Land productivity would be enhanced through maintenance of diversion dams, irrigation ditches, and the like. Redistribution of food would be another by-product of a leadership utilizing katsina ritual.

Land use in the Homol'ovi area was modified, probably resulting in patterns similar to modern Pueblo land use patterns. An important result of the expanded land use and the diversity of arable land types first available to aggregated settlements by the 1320s or 1330s was production of surplus and specialization in cotton production, much of which went for trade. The katsina cult was the cement holding the aggregated villages at Homol'ovi together. Gradual loss of the land base through erosion of surface soils is suggested in the survey data around the Homol'ovi pueblos and contributed to, if it did not cause, eventual abandonment about 1400.

9

Conclusions

The katsina cult was a major influence on Pueblo culture above the Mogollon Rim after 1300 or so. Its impact can still be measured in the modern descendants of these prehistoric people. Although the cult developed in the upper Little Colorado River Valley, apparently in the early 1300s, its roots can be traced to a number of divergent sources, most notably Mogollon or Salado groups below the rim that introduced architecture, an artifactual assemblage, distinctive characteristics of iconography, and probably ritual from northern Mexico. Shared icons on ceramics ranged from the polychromes produced at Casas Grandes, to the Salado Polychromes, to the White Mountain Red Wares.

Although arguments have been made for an early introduction of the katsina cult from Mexico into the upper Rio Grande Valley by 1325 or 1350 using rock art (Schaafsma and Schaafsma 1974; Schaafsma 1972), an alternative explanation of the origin of the cult in the upper Little Colorado Valley and its spread eastward is postulated here. The early cult was embraced by most early fourteenth century aggregated communities in the Pueblo world. Its popularity stemmed from the social, political, and economic roles the cult played in the structure of each village. First of all, the cult was accepted because the village leadership recognized in it a tool to enhance their power through restricting access to ritual knowledge and as a means to integrate their village membership. Alternative cross-kinship social units to the cult, such as societies or moieties, also served this integrative function. The fact that katsina society membership is based on moiety affiliation in most moiety-based societies in the Rio Grande area indicates that the moiety system was probably operating in aggregated communities in the Rio Grande Valley when the cult arrived in the fourteenth or fifteenth century.

The early cult functioned to ritually bind the members of a community, many of whom were immigrants from divergent social and political backgrounds. Its usefulness to leaders and the ease with which it could be symbolized made the cult appealing to Pueblo communities. The cult was apparently transformed at Hopi in the late 1300s into a more dynamic, visual, rain-oriented cult. Kiva murals and elaborated nonkatsina decorations on pottery are icons related to the later katsina cult. Its influence is most visible at Homol'ovi II, at the Zuni pueblos, and at Pottery Mound. Thus katsina iconography was utilized in its public form to communicate its presence and to suggest an underlying depth to its symbolism that could not be known to the uninitiated. The elaborate portrayal of cult symbolism in the privacy of kivas accessible only to the initiated reinforces this perspective.

Jornada style iconography then appears in the upper Rio Grande Valley after 1450 in kiva murals at Kuaua and Las Humanas and in rock art through much of the area. The Jornada style cult seems to complement the Hopi katsina cult, which is best manifest in the continued depiction of murals in rectangular kivas and the associated manufacture and trade of Fourmile style Glaze IV ceramics based in the Galisteo Basin.

There is no need to list katsina cult material culture here. Two noteworthy associations are the enclosed plaza and the rectangular kiva, both integral to the preparation and presentation of the cult. The enclosed plaza allowed the public portrayal of the cult. This facilitated the integration of those initiated to the symbolism of the cult and emphasized the difference between those initiated and those not initiated. The rectangular kiva complemented the plaza as the focus for the private aspect of katsina ritual.

The most significant aspect to the cult from an archaeological standpoint is its role in considering prehistoric social development among Pueblo people. The cult is the clearest manifestation of the changes occurring in Pueblo society after 1275 and before 1400. The cult allowed aggregation by encouraging cooperative networks to form in the village social units. Without the integration made possible through the cult, it is possible that the aggregated settlements established in the late thirteenth and early fourteenth centuries would have remained unstable, a characteristic of prekatsina cult attempts at aggregation, and that conflict would have developed over unnegotiated land ownership in a dispersed settlement pattern. Pueblo aggregation allowed the focusing of human energy away from conflict and onto arable land resources to produce the food necessary to sustain a population expanding from immigration.

Therefore there are two points that must be highlighted to facilitate understanding the evolution of fourteenth century Pueblo society. First, it is clear from the development of enclosed plazas and the katsina cult in the upper Little Colorado Valley, and elsewhere, that the first choice for leadership was not conflict, but the avoidance of conflict. It may be ironic that aggregation in Pueblo society should be a mechanism for conflict reduction, but in fact it was the successful solution chosen by the prehistoric populations of the Colorado Plateau (Adams 1988). Second, institutional responses to stress resulted in social changes that are manifest in the archaeological record.

This essay is in fact a study of prehistoric social organization. By careful consideration of regional trends in culture change, for example the process of aggregation, on the Colorado Plateau in the thirteenth and fourteenth centuries combined with an ethnological analysis of Pueblo culture, this study has interpreted changes in the archaeological record in terms of what Taylor (1968) might have called the conjunctive approach. That is, what changes at a system level can account for the changing structure of material culture remains? What system-wide adjustments are necessary to ensure survival of a cultural pattern and to explain changes within that pattern? It is at these levels that the context of the katsina cult can be considered.

The katsina cult has been considered in the context of its time and place. Reconstruction of the environmental events of the thirteenth and fourteenth centuries sets the stage for the systemic response of late thirteenth century societies. Interestingly enough the katsina cult model has shown that the cultural response was not in the subsistence system of the culture, but rather in the social system. Stable to declining resources and substantial population increase can be met in two ways: (1) by reducing population, through warfare, starvation, or disease; or (2) by increasing production. Increased production is usually translated by archaeologists into agricultural intensification or some change in the subsistence subsystem. An equally plausible perspective, and one that offers a better chance for understanding culture system change is to consider the social subsystem as well as the subsistence base. What changes in relations between peoples could be utilized as a response to the stress being placed on the culture by environmental deterioration? Social responses at formative level cultures usually involve institutional responses.

Institutional responses to system stress in agricultural societies must result in production of more food per capita. To increase productivity the social system must do one of two things. First, it can grow more complex whereby leaders can control and direct labor for public works programs, such as agricultural intensification using irrigation via dams and canals.

This choice was apparently never made in the Colorado Plateau cultures. The second choice, the one made by the prehistoric Pueblo people, was what has been termed the cooperative model. Instead of becoming vertically more complex, Pueblo society became horizontally more complex. Institutions were developed to crosscut and integrate existing kinship systems. An example of such a horizontal integrator, and the subject of this study, is the katsina cult.

Johnson (1982, 1989) has proposed a similar model for the segmentary lineage cultural systems, such as characterize the prehistoric and historic Pueblos. However, he visualizes the ritual solution to preventing the segmentary tendencies as but a temporary one. Johnson's (1989) analysis of segmentary lineages is too simplified for the Pueblos. The katsina cult worked because it is involved at all levels of Pueblo culture—subsistence, social, and political. The katsina cult mirrors Pueblo society allowing all village members to participate and have a stake in the success of their society, as well as providing a mechanism for the release of tensions (Ortiz 1972). Katsinas can work as tools of the village leadership to accomplish public works projects, such as construction or cleaning of spring-fed terraces, dams, and cisterns (Stephen 1936; Titiev 1944; Wright 1977:44). But more importantly, the cult can redistribute food through ceremonies. The web of integration through cooperation woven by the cult and other cross-kinship social institutions involves subsistence, as noted above; social ties, with each kin unit involved in ensuring the success of the ritual by working with all other units; and political ties, by focusing control of katsinas in leadership hands and giving each leader a role in conduct of the cult. To achieve success at improving subsistence requires the cooperation and support of every other individual in the village through their prayers transmitted by the katsinas to the Pueblo gods.

The elaborate ritual of Pueblo society, as pointed out by Ortiz (1972) has many functions. Not only are Pueblo rituals comprised of solemn processions symbolic of appropriate Pueblo behavior, they are also comprised of raucous events where every rule of Pueblo conduct is broken. These enacted transgressions do not go unpunished and thereby serve their purpose to remind people of what is right and what is wrong. Even war and warfare are depicted but are clearly not suggested as preferred solutions to interpersonal or even intervillage problems. By showing the disruptive nature of such behavior, its impropriety is brought home to the populace.

At all levels in nearly every way Pueblo society emphasizes the importance of proper behavior and of cooperation with other members of society. Rewards of proper behavior can be found in this life and in the promise of afterlife. The katsina cult is the most universal and visible of the institutions developed in Pueblo society, especially western Pueblo society, to make the Pueblo system of cooperation work. The cult provides the most thorough mechanism for crosscutting segmentary kinship units. Development of the cult fostered the aggregation process already in full swing in the late 1200s. By stabilizing the horizontal ties between the kinship units, the cult could maintain the aggregated settlement pattern.

In Pueblo society there are definitely firsts among equals. There is, and probably was prehistorically, a hereditary status system of leadership. As long as each segment of society in an aggregated system reaped benefits that outweighed the disadvantages, the kin group would retain control. The economic benefits could include specialization, diversified trade, and intravillage redistribution. As Lightfoot (1984) notes, advantages of aggregation can extend beyond subsistence to safety. In any conflict situation, a small Pueblo group would be at a severe disadvantage to a large village. Therefore, in the unstable environmental conditions of the fourteenth and fifteenth centuries, safety is a predictable benefit to aggregation.

Greater social stability is an important benefit of the katsina cult. To retain and reinforce this stability, however, religious sanctions may be threatened by the leadership on any recalcitrant groups within the village social unit. The integrative nature of the cult, whereby all individuals and all segments of society are needed to ensure success of a ceremony, would be violated by individuals threatening to leave the village. Disruption of the proper flow of life in the village could be met with by sanctions as strong as death to the transgressor (Ellis 1951). Thus the cult begets and maintains aggregation. The structure of Pueblo society also mitigates against too much accumulation of power. Desire to outdo others can draw its own sanctions (Ellis 1951). Social sanctions against accumulation of power by leaders, in modern Pueblo society, if paralleled in prehistoric Pueblo society, could provide the upper limits to pueblo growth and partly explain why more complex societies did not develop on the Colorado Plateau.

The use of ethnology and the direct historic approach to evaluate change in prehistoric Pueblo culture is nothing new. However, modeling the archaeological record, predicting change, and comparing it to the ethnographic record for fit is a different process. The katsina cult, and its development, is visualized as a socio-cultural process whereby prehistoric Pueblo culture changed "to remain the same." That is, prehistoric Pueblo culture changed to retain its agricultural adaptation and its standard-of-living. Adaptation of new institutions and new public architecture to preserve the old standards are manifest in the archaeological record. These adaptations involved great kivas, enclosed plazas, and the katsina cult, as increments along a scale of more progressive integrative devices. The katsina cult that first developed bore some iconographic and structural similarities to the modern Pueblo cult but also differed in substantial ways. The predicted changes in late thirteenth and fourteenth century Pueblo society, using this initial model of the katsina cult, was tested on the cultural changes and developments at the Homol'ovi Pueblos and found to fit the archaeological record quite well. At this point more speculative aspects of the prehistoric cult were postulated by comparing it to the modern cult. Data are still lacking on some of the specifics of culture change postulated by using the direct historical approach, but the data base is attainable. Finally, the Hopi and the Jornada katsina cults were postulated to account for post-fourteenth century regional and temporal variation in cult iconography in the Pueblo world.

In conclusion, the katsina cult was developed in the upper Little Colorado River Valley during the period 1275–1325. It became visible through its iconography about 1325. The cult was developed out of traits shared with groups primarily to the south extending into northern Mexico. Its purpose was to integrate divergent groups aggregated into large villages whose movement into the upper Little Colorado River area was caused by significant environmental deterioration elsewhere on the Colorado Plateau (as measured by the needs of marginal agriculturalists, such as the Anasazi) beginning about 1275. The cult succeeded remarkably well and spread from its hearth throughout the existent Pueblo world. At Hopi it was elaborated, and out of this elaboration such characteristics as kiva murals appeared. This form of the cult was highly successful in the western Pueblos, and through modification by an influx of Jornada cult elements, became broadly successful in the Rio Grande Valley area, as measured by its prehistoric and modern distribution.

The cooperative enterprise and attitude fostered by the katsina cult in Pueblo society have been keystones to the success of that society. The inner strength of Pueblo culture lies in the thorough integration of every individual player's role in the culture of the village. The incredibly strong sense of us and them fostered by Pueblo culture has secured the continuity of Pueblo culture in its varied forms to the present and beyond. Katsina iconography then and now serves to reinforce this sense. The katsina cult, developed perhaps 700 years ago, provided not the only one, but easily the most visible foundation to modern Pueblo culture. This essay has attempted to outline the early role the katsina cult played in the development of modern Pueblo society and to demonstrate the archaeologist's ability to determine social and other "perishable institutions" from the archaeological record and to apply them successfully to reconstructing prehistoric culture.

Bibliography

ABRUZZI, WILLIAM S.

1981   *Ecological Succession and Mormon Colonization in the Little Colorado River Basin.* Unpublished Ph.D. dissertation, State University of New York, Binghamton.

ADAMS, E. CHARLES

1979a   Native Ceramics from Walpi. *Walpi Archaeological Project, Phase II,* Vol. 3. Museum of Northern Arizona, Flagstaff.

1979b   *Overview: Summary, Walpi Archaeological Project, Phase II,* Vol. 1. Museum of Northern Arizona, Flagstaff.

1980   *An Archaeological Assessment of Homolovi I Ruin.* Prepared for the Bureau of Land Management, Phoenix, by the Museum of Northern Arizona, Flagstaff.

1981a   Cultural and historical causes of ceramic change in ancestral Hopi villages. Paper presented at the seminar on Southwestern Native American ceramics sponsored by the Millicent Rogers Museum, Santa Fe.

1981b   The view from the Hopi Mesas. In *The Protohistoric Period in the North American Southwest, A.D. 1450–1700,* edited by David A. Wilsox and W. Bruce Masse, pp. 321–335. Anthropological Research Papers, No. 24. Arizona State University, Tempe.

1982   *Walpi Archaeological Project: Synthesis and Interpretation.* Ms. on file, Museum of Northern Arizona, Flagstaff.

1988   The Case for Conflict during the Late Prehistoric and Protohistoric Periods in the Western Pueblo Area of the American Southwest. In *Cultures in Conflict: Current Archaeological Perspectives,* edited by Diane Clair Tkaczak and Brian C. Vivian, pp. 103–111. The Archaeological Association of the University of Calgary, Calgary, Alberta.

1989   Homol'ovi III: A Pueblo Hamlet in the Middle Little Colorado River Valley. *Kiva* 54:217–230.

ADAMS, E. CHARLES AND JENNY L. ADAMS

1987   Thirteenth Century Abandonment of the Four Corners: A Reevaluation. Ms. in possession of the authors.

ADAMS, E. CHARLES, DEBORAH DOSH, AND MIRIAM T. STARK

1990   Ceramic Distributions and Ceramic Exchange: The Distribution of Jeddito Yellow Ware and Implications for Social Complexity. Ms. on file, Arizona State Museum Library, Tucson.

ADAMS, JENNY L.

1979   Stone Implements, Miscellaneous Ground Stone, Miscellaneous Stone Artifacts and Natural Objects. In Stone Artifacts, Walpi Archaeological Project, Phase II, Vol. 4, Part I. Museum of Northern Arizona, Flagstaff.

1980   Perishable Artifacts from Walpi. Walpi Archaeological Project, Phase II, Vol. 5, Part I. Museum of Northern Arizona, Flagstaff.

ADLER, MICHAEL A.

1989   Ritual Facilities and Social Integration in Unranked Societies. In The Architecture of Social Integration in Prehistoric Pueblos, edited by William D. Lipe and Michelle Hegmon, pp. 35–52. Occasional Paper, No. 1. Crow Canyon Archaeological Center, Cortez, Colorado.

ANDERSON, FRANK G.

1951   The Kachina Cult of the Pueblo Indians. Unpublished Ph.D. dissertation. Department of Anthropology, University of New Mexico, Albuquerque.

ANDREWS, MICHAEL

1982   An Archaeological Assessment of Homolovi III and Chevelon Ruin, Northern Arizona. Prepared for the Arizona State Land Department, Phoenix, by Northern Arizona University, Flagstaff.

ANYON, ROGER, PATRICIA A. GILMAN, AND STEVEN A. LEBLANC

1981   A Reevaluation of the Mogollon Mimbres Archaeological Sequence. The Kiva 46:209–225.

ANYON, ROGER AND STEVEN A. LEBLANC

1980   The Architectural Evolution of Mogollon–Mimbres Communal Structures. The Kiva 45:253–277.

ARNON, N. AND W. W. HILL

1979   Santa Clara Pueblo. In Southwest, edited by Alfonso Ortiz, pp. 296–307. Handbook of North American Indians, Vol. 9. Smithsonian Institution, Washington, D.C.

BANDELIER, ADOLPH F.

1890–   Final report of investigations among the Indians of the Southwestern United
1892   States, carried on mainly in the years from 1880–1885. 2 volumes.

Archaeological Institute of America Papers, American Series, No. 3 and 4. Cambridge, Mass.

BINFORD, LEWIS

1962   Archaeology as Anthropology. *American Antiquity* 28:217–225.

BISHOP, RONALD L., VALETTA CANOUTS, SUZANNE P. DE ATLEY, ALFRED QOYAWAYMA, AND C. W. AIKENS

1988   The Formation of Ceramic Analytical Groups: Hopi Pottery Production and Exchange, A.D. 1300–1600. *Journal of Field Archaeology* 15:317–337.

BLUHM, ELAINE A.

1957   *The Sawmill Site; a Reserve Phase Village, Pine Lawn Valley, Western New Mexico.* Fieldiana: Anthropology, Vol. 47, No. 1. Field Museum of Anthropology, Chicago.

BOWER, NATHAN W., STEVE FACISCEWSKI, STEPHEN RENWICK, AND STEWART PECKHAM

1986   A Preliminary Analysis of Rio Grande Glazes of the Classic Period Using Screening Electron Microscopy with X-ray Fluorescence. *Journal of Field Archaeology* 13(3):307–315.

BRADFIELD, MAITLAND

1971   The Changing Pattern of Hopi Agriculture. *Royal Anthropological Institute, Occasional Papers*, No. 30. London.

BRANDT, ELIZABETH A.

1979   Sandia Pueblo. In *Southwest*, edited by Alfonso Ortiz, pp. 343–350. Handbook of North American Indians, Vol. 9. Smithsonian Institution, Washington, D.C.

BRETERNITZ, DAVID A.

1966   *An appraisal of Tree-ring Dated Pottery in the Southwest.* Anthropological Papers, No. 10. University of Arizona, Tucson.

BREW, JOHN O.

1937   The First Two Seasons at Awatovi. *American Antiquity* 3:122–137.

1939   Preliminary Report of the Peabody Museum Awatovi Expedition of 1937. *American Antiquity* 5:103–114.

1941   Preliminary Report of the Peabody Museum Awatovi Expedition of 1939. *Plateau* 13(3):37–48.

1943   On the Pueblo IV and on the Kachina–Tlaloc Relations. In *El Norte de México y el Sur de Estados Unidos, Tercera Reunion de Mesa Redonda Sobre Problemas Antropológicos de México y Centro América*, pp. 241–245. Sociedad Mexicana de Antropología.

BRODY, JOHN J.

1977   *Mimbres Painted Pottery*. University of New Mexico Press, Albuquerque.

1989   Site Use, Pictorial Space, and Subject Matter in Late Prehistoric and Early Historic Rio Grande Pueblo Art. *Journal of Anthropological Research* 45:15–28.

BRONITSKY, GORDON

1982   Technological Assessment of Selected Southwest Ceramics: Phase I Research Design. In *Mogollon Archaeology: Proceedings of the 1980 Mogollon Conference*, edited by P. H. Beckett, pp. 229–287. Acoma Books, Ramona, California.

BROOK, VERNON R.

1982   Some effigies of the Jornada Branch. In *Mogollon Archaeology: Proceedings of the 1980 Mogollon Conference*, edited by P. H. Beckett, pp. 211–225. Acoma Books, Ramona, California.

BUNZEL, RUTH L.

1932   Zuni Katcinas. *Annual Report* No. 47, pp. 837–1108. Bureau of American Ethnology, Washington, D.C.

CARLSON, ROY L.

1970   *White Mountain Redware: A Pottery Tradition of East-Central Arizona and Western New Mexico*. Anthropological Papers, No. 19. University of Arizona, Tucson.

1982a   The Mimbres Kachina Cult. In *Mogollon Archaeology: Proceedings of the 1980 Mogollon Conference*, edited by P. H. Beckett, pp. 147–155. Acoma Books, Ramona, California.

1982b   The Polychrome Complexes. In *Southwestern Ceramics: A Comparative Review*, edited by Albert H. Schroeder, pp. 201–234. The Arizona Archaeologist, No. 15. The Arizona Archaeological Society, Phoenix.

CHAPMAN, KENNETH

1938   The Cave Pictographs of the Rito de los Frijoles, New Mexico. In *Pajarito Plateau and Its Ancient People* by Edgar Lee Hewett. University of New Mexico Press, Albuquerque.

CLARK, GEOFFREY A.

1969   Preliminary Analysis of Burial Clusters at the Grasshopper Site, East-Central Arizona. *The Kiva* 35:57–90.

COLE, SALLY J. (SARAH J. COLE)

1989a   Katsina Iconography in Homol'ovi Rock Art. *Kiva* 54:313–329.

1989b   *Rock Art Evidence for the Presence and Social Significance of the Katsina Cult at 13th–14th Century Homol'ovi in the Central Little Colorado River*

Valley, Northeastern Arizona. Unpublished Master's thesis, Vermont College of Norwich University, Norwich.

COLLINS, SUSAN

1975   Prehistoric Rio Grande Settlement Patterns and the Inference of Demographic Change. Unpublished Ph.D. dissertation, Department of Anthropology, University of Colorado, Boulder.

COLTON, HAROLD S.

1956   Pottery Types of the Southwest. Ceramic Series 3C. Museum of Northern Arizona, Flagstaff.

1957   Stoneman's Lake. Plateau 29(3):56–58.

1974   Hopi History and Ethnohistory. Indian Claims Commission Docket 196. Published as Hopi Indians, edited by David A. Horr. Garland Publishing, New York.

1975   Hopi Kachina Dolls—a Key to their Identification. University of New Mexico Press, Albuquerque.

COLTON, HAROLD S. AND LYNDON L. HARGRAVE

1937   Handbook of Northern Arizona Pottery Wares. Bulletin, No. 11. Museum of Northern Arizona, Flagstaff.

COLTON, MARY RUSSELL-FARRELL AND HAROLD S. COLTON

1931   Petroglyphs, the Record of a Great Adventure. American Anthropologist 33:31–37.

CORDELL, LINDA S.

1979   Prehistory: Eastern Anasazi. In Southwest, edited by Alfonso Ortiz, pp. 131–151. Handbook of North American Indians, Vol. 9. Smithsonian Institution, Washington, D.C.

1984   Prehistory of the Southwest. Academic Press, New York.

COSGROVE, C. B., JR.

1934   Report on Excavation, Repair, and Restoration of Agate House and Other Sites. CWA Report, Winter 1933–34, Petrified Forest National Monument. Ms. on file, Museum of Northern Arizona, Flagstaff.

1947   Caves of the Upper Gila and Hueco Areas in New Mexico and Texas. Papers of the Peabody Museum of American Archaeology and Ethnology, Vol. 24, No. 2, Harvard University, Cambridge.

COUES, ELLIOT (ED.)

1900   On the Trail of a Spanish Pioneer: The Diary and Itinerary of Francisco Garces (Missionary Priest) in his Travels through Sonora, Arizona and California, 1775–1776. Frances P. Harper, New York.

COURLANDER, HAROLD

1971   The Fourth World of the Hopi. Crown Publishers, New York.

CROTTY, HELEN
    1987   Masks Portrayed in Pueblo IV Kiva Murals and New Evidence for the Origins of Pueblo Ceremonialism. Ms. in possession of the author.

CROWN, PATRICIA L.
    1981   *Variability in Ceramic Manufacture at the Chodistas Site, East-Central Arizona.* Ph.D. dissertation, University of Arizona, Tucson. University Microfilms, Ann Arbor.

CROWN, PATRICIA L., LARRY A. SCHWALBE, AND J. RONALD LANDON
    1985   Gila Polychrome at Homolovi: An X-ray Fluorescence Analysis. In *Excavation and Surface Collection of Homolovi II Ruin,* edited by Kelley A. Hays and E. Charles Adams, Appendix B. Ms. on file, Arizona State Museum, University of Arizona, Tucson.

CUMMINGS, BYRON
    1940   *Kinishba, A Prehistoric Pueblo of the Great Pueblo Period.* Hohokam Museum Association and the University of Arizona, Tucson.
    1953   *First Inhabitants of Arizona and the Southwest.* Cummings Publication Council, Tucson.

CUSHING, FRANK
    1896   Outlines of Zuni Creation Myths. *Annual Report,* No. 13. Bureau of American Ethnology, Washington, D.C.

DANSON, EDWARD B.
    1957   *An Archaeological Survey of West Central New Mexico and East Central Arizona.* Papers of the Peabody Museum of Archaeology and Ethnology, Vol. 44, No. 1. Harvard University, Cambridge.
    1966   Six Startling Statuettes Added to Museum Here. *The Sun,* Friday, August 26:11.

DE ATLEY, SUZANNE P. AND FRANK J. FINDLOW
    1982   Regional Interpretations of the Northern Casas Grandes Frontier. In *Mogollon Archaeology: Proceedings of the 1980 Mogollon Conference,* edited by P. H. Beckett, pp. 263–277. Acoma Books, Ramona, California.

DEAN, JEFFREY S., ROBERT C. EULER, GEORGE J. GUMERMAN, FRED PLOG, RICHARD H. HELEY, AND THOR N. V. KARLSTROM
    1985   Human Behavior, Demography and Paleoenvironment on the Colorado Plateaus. *American Antiquity* 50:537–554.

DEAN, JEFFREY S. AND WILLIAM J. ROBINSON
    1978   *Expanded Tree-Ring Chronology for the Southwestern U.S.* Chronology Series III, Laboratory of Tree-Ring Research, Tucson.

1982   Dendrochronology of Grasshopper Pueblo. In *Multidisciplinary Research at Grasshopper Pueblo, Arizona*, edited by William A. Longacre, Sally J. Holbrook, and Michael W. Graves, pp. 46–60. Anthropological Papers, No. 40, University of Arizona, Tucson.

DI PESO, CHARLES
1950   Painted Stone Slabs of Point of Pines, Arizona. *American Antiquity* 16:57–65.
1951   *The Babocomari Village Site on the Babocomari River*. The Amerind Foundation Series, No. 5, pp. 195–209. Dragoon, Arizona.
1958   *The Reeve Ruin of Southeastern Arizona*. The Amerind Foundation Series, No. 9. Northland Press, Flagstaff, Arizona.
1974   *Casas Grandes: A Fallen Trading Center of the Gran Chichimeca*. 3 vols. Northland Press, Flagstaff, Arizona.

DI PESO, CHARLES, JOHN B. RINALDO, AND GLORIA FENNER
1974   *Casas Grandes: A Fallen Trading Center of the Gran Chichimeca*. 8 vols. Northland Press, Flagstaff, Arizona.

DITTERT, ALFRED E, JR.
1959   *Culture Change in the Cebolleta Mesa Region, Central Western New Mexico*. Unpublished Ph.D. dissertation, Department of Anthropology, University of Arizona, Tucson.
1976   Comments on papers. In The 1976 Salado Conference. Edited by D. E. Doyel and E. W. Haury. *The Kiva* 42:126–127.

DIXON, KEITH A.
1963   The Interamerican Diffusion of a Cooking Technique: The Culinary Shoe-Pot. *American Anthropologist* 65:593–619.
1976   Shoe-Pots, Patajos, and the Principal of Whimsy. *American Antiquity* 41:386–391.

DOCKSTADER, FREDERICK J.
1954   *The Kachina and the White Man: A Study of the Influences of White Culture on the Hopi Kachina Cult*. Cranbrook Institute of Science, Bulletin No. 35. Bloomfield Hills, Michigan.

DOSH, STEVEN G.
1982   *The Emergency Protection of Homolovi I Ruin*. Final Report Submitted to the Bureau of Land Management, Phoenix, by the Museum of Northern Arizona, Flagstaff.

DOYEL, DAVID E.
1972   *Cultural and Ecological Aspects of Salado Prehistory*. Master's thesis, Department of Anthropology, California State University, Chico.

DOYEL, DAVID E. AND EMIL W. HAURY
1976   Summary of Conference Discussion. In The 1976 Salado Conference, edited by D. E. Doyel and E. W. Haury, The Kiva 42:127–134.

DOZIER, EDWARD P.
1970   The Pueblo Indians of North America. Holt, Rinehart, and Winston, New York.

DUTTON, BERTHA
1963   Sun Father's Way: The Kiva Murals of Kuaua. University of New Mexico Press, Albuquerque.

EDELMAN, SANDRA A.
1979   San Ildefonso Pueblo. In Southwest, edited by Alfonso Ortiz, pp. 308–316. Handbook of North American Indians, Vol. 9. Smithsonian Institution, Washington, D.C.

EDELMAN, SANDRA A. AND ALFONSO ORTIZ
1979   Tesuque Pueblo. In Southwest, edited by Alfonso Ortiz, pp. 330–335. Handbook of North American Indians, Vol. 9. Smithsonian Institution, Washington, D.C.

EGGAN, FRED
1950   The Social Organization of the Western Pueblos. University of Chicago Press, Chicago.
1979   Pueblos: Introduction. In Southwest, edited by Alfonso Ortiz, pp. 224–235. Handbook of North American Indians, Vol. 9. Smithsonian Institution, Washington, D.C.

ELLIS, FLORENCE H.
1951   Patterns of Aggression and the War Cult. Southwestern Journal of Anthropology 7(2):177–201.
1978   Small Structures Used by Historic Pueblo People and Their Immediate Ancestors. In Limited Activity and Occupation Sites: A Collection of Conference Papers, edited by Albert E. Ward, pp. 59–68. Contributions to Anthropological Studies, Vol. 1. Center for Anthropological Studies, Albuquerque.
1979   Laguna Pueblo. In Southwest, edited by Alfonso Ortiz, pp. 438–449. Handbook of North American Indians, Vol. 9. Smithsonian Institution, Washington, D.C.

ELLIS, FLORENCE H. AND LAURENS HAMMACK
1968   The Inner Sanctum of Feather Cave, a Mogollon Sun and Earth Shrine Linking Mexico and the Southwest. American Antiquity 33:25–44.

ERICKSON, J. T.
1977   Kachinas, an Evolving Hopi Art Form? Heard Museum, Phoenix Arizona.

EULER, ROBERT C., GEORGE J. GUMERMAN, THOR N. V. KARLSTROM,
JEFFREY S. DEAN, AND RICHARD HEVLY
1979   The Colorado Plateaus: Cultural Dynamics and Paleoenvironment.
        Science 205:1089–1101.

FERDON, E. N., JR.
1955   *A Trial Survey of Mexican–Southwestern Architectural Parallels.* Re-
        search Monographs, No. 21. School of American Research, Santa Fe.

FERG, ALAN
1982   14th Century Kachina Depiction on Ceramics. In *Collected Papers in
        Honor of John W. Runyon,* edited by Gerald X. Fitzgerald, pp. 13–29.
        Papers of the Archaeological Society of New Mexico, No. 7. Albu-
        querque.

FEWKES, J. WALTER
1896   Preliminary Account of an Expedition to the Cliff Villages of the Red
        Rock Country and the Tusayan Ruins of Sikyatki and Awatobi, Ari-
        zona, in 1895. *Annual Report of the Smithsonian Institution for 1895,* pp.
        557–588. Washington, D.C.
1898   Preliminary Account of an Expedition to the Pueblo Ruins near Wins-
        low, Arizona in 1896. *Annual Report of the Smithsonian Institution for
        1896,* pp. 517–540. Washington, D.C.
1903   Hopi Katcinas Drawn by Native Artist. *Annual Report for 1899–1900,*
        No. 21, pp. 3–126. Bureau of American Ethnology, Washington, D.C.
1904   Two Summers Work in Pueblo Ruins. *Annual Report for 1899–1900,*
        No. 22, pt. 1, pp. 3–195. Bureau of American Ethnology, Washington,
        D.C.
1919   Designs on Prehistoric Hopi Pottery. *Annual Report for 1911–1912,*
        No. 33, pp. 207–284. Bureau of American Ethnology, Washington,
        D.C.

FINDLOW, FRANK J. AND MARISA BOLOGNESE
1982   A Preliminary Analysis of Prehistoric Obsidian Use within the
        Mogollon Area. In *Mogollon Archaeology: Proceedings of the 1980
        Mogollon Conference,* edited by Patrick H. Beckett, pp. 297–315. Acoma
        Books, Ramona, California.

FORD, RICHARD I., ALBERT H. SCHROEDER, AND STEWART L. PECKHAM
1972   Three Perspectives on Puebloan Prehistory. In *New Perspectives on the
        Pueblos,* edited by Alfonso Ortiz, pp. 19–39. University of New Mexico
        Press, Albuquerque.

FORDE, C. DARYLL
1931   Hopi Agriculture and Land Ownership. *Journal of the Royal Anthropo-
        logical Institute* 41(4):357–405. London.

FRISBIE, THEODORE
1978   High Status Burials in the Great Southwest. In *Across the Chichimeca Sea*, edited by Carroll Riley and Basil Hedrick, pp. 202–227. Southern Illinois University Press, Carbondale.

GODFREY, ANTHONY
1988   *Hopi Agricultural Report, 1540–1934*. Report prepared for the Hopi Tribe for the Adjudication of the 1934 Boundary Dispute. The Hopi Tribe, Kykotsmovi, Arizona.

GOLDFRANK, ESTHER S.
1927   *The Social and Ceremonial Organization of Cochiti*. American Anthropological Association, Memoirs No. 33. Washington, D.C.

GRATZ, KATHLEEN E. AND PETER J. PILLES, JR.
1979   Sinagua Settlement Patterns and Organizational Models: A Trial Survey. Paper presented at 1979 Annual Meeting of the Southwestern Anthropological Association, Santa Barbara, California.

GRAVES, MICHAEL W., SALLY J. HOLBROOK, AND WILLIAM A. LONGACRE
1982   Aggregation and Abandonment at Grasshopper Pueblo: Evolutionary Trends in the late Prehistory of East-Central Arizona. In *Multidisciplinary Research at Grasshopper Pueblo, Arizona*, edited by W. A. Longacre, S. J. Holbrook, and M. W. Graves, pp. 110–121. Anthropological Papers, No. 40. University of Arizona, Tucson.

GRIFFIN, P. BOIN
1967   A High Status Burial from Grasshopper Ruin, Arizona. *The Kiva* 33:37–53.

GUMERMAN, GEORGE J. AND JEFFREY S. DEAN
1989   Prehistoric Cooperation and Competition in the Western Anasazi Area. In *Dynamics of Southwestern Prehistory*, edited by Linda S. Cordell and George J. Gumerman, pp. 99–148. Smithsonian Institution Press, Washington, D.C.

GUMERMAN, GEORGE J. AND EMIL W. HAURY
1979   Prehistory: Hohokam. In *Southwest*, edited by Alfonso Ortiz, pp. 75–90. Handbook of North American Indians, Vol. 9. Smithsonian Institution, Washington, D.C.

GUMERMAN, GEORGE J. AND S. ALAN SKINNER
1968   A Synthesis of the Prehistory of the Central Little Colorado Valley, Arizona. *American Antiquity* 33:185–199.

HAASE, WILLIAM R.
1985   Domestic Water Conservation among the Northern San Juan Anasazi. *Southwestern Lore* 51(2):15–27.

HACK, JOHN T.

    1942a   *The Changing Physical Environment of the Hopi Indians of Arizona.* Papers of the Peabody Museum of American Archaeology and Ethnology, Vol. 35, No. 1. Harvard University, Cambridge.

    1942b   *Prehistoric Coal Mining in the Jeddito Valley, Arizona.* Papers of the Peabody Museum of American Archaeology and Ethnology, Vol. 35, No. 2. Harvard University, Cambridge.

HACKETT, CHARLES W.

    1937   *Historical Documents Relating to New Mexico, Nueva Vizcaya, and Approaches Thereto, to 1773. Collected by Adolph F. A. Bandelier and Fanny R. Bandelier.* Carnegie Institution of Washington, Publication 330, Vol. 3, Washington, D.C.

HACKETT, CHARLES W. AND C. C. SHELBY

    1970   *Revolt of the Pueblo Indians of New Mexico and Otermin's Attempted Reconquest, 1680 to 1692.* 2 vols. University of New Mexico Press, Albuquerque.

HAMMACK, LAURENS C., STANLEY D. BUSSEY, AND RONALD ICE

    1966   *The Cliff Highway Salvage Project: A Preliminary Report Describing the Archaeological Investigations at Three Sites Located Within the Right-of-Way of S1165(18).* Museum of New Mexico, Santa Fe.

HAMMOND, GEORGE P. AND AQUPITA REY, (EDS. AND TRANSLATORS)

    1928   *Obregon's History of Sixteenth Century Explorations in Western America, Entitled: Chronicle, Commentary, or Relation of the Ancient and Modern Discoveries in New Spain, New Mexico and Mexico, 1584.* Wetzel, Los Angeles.

HANTMAN, JEFFREY L.

    1982   *A Long Term Management Plan for Significant Sites in the Vicinity of Winslow, Arizona.* Prepared for the Arizona State Land Department, Phoenix, by Soil Systems, Inc., Phoenix.

HARGRAVE, LYNDON L.

    1931   Recently Dated Pueblo Ruins: Excavations at Kin Tiel and Kokopnyama. In *Recently Dated Pueblo Ruins in Arizona*, by Emil W. Haury and Lyndon L. Hargrave, pp. 80–120. Smithsonian Miscellaneous Collection 82, No. 11, Washington, D.C.

HARRY, KAREN G.

    1989   The Obsidian Assemblage from Homol'ovi III: Social and Economic Implications. *Kiva* 54:285–296.

HARVEY, BYRON III

    1963   Masks at a Maskless Pueblo: The Laguna Colony Kachina Organization at Isleta. *Ethnology* 2:478–489.

1972   An Overview of Pueblo Religion. In *New Perspectives on the Pueblos,* edited by Alfonso Ortiz, pp. 192–217. University of New Mexico Press, Albuquerque.

HAURY, EMIL W.

1934   *The Canyon Creek Ruin and the Cliff Dwellings of the Sierra Ancha.* Medallion Papers No. 14. Gila Pueblo, Globe, Arizona.

1945   *The Excavation of Los Muertos and Neighboring Ruins in the Salt River Valley, Southern Arizona.* Papers of the Peabody Museum of American Archaeology and Ethnology, Vol. 24, No. 1. Harvard University, Cambridge.

1958   Evidence at Point of Pines for a Prehistoric Migration from Northern Arizona. In *Migrations in New World Culture History,* edited by Raymond H. Thompson. University of Arizona Bulletin 29:2, Social Science Bulletin 27:1–8, Tucson.

1976   *The Hohokam: Desert Farmers and Craftsmen.* University of Arizona Press, Tucson.

1985   *Mogollon Culture in the Forestdale Valley, East-Central Arizona.* University of Arizona Press, Tucson.

HAWLEY, FLORENCE M.

1936   *Field Manual of Prehistoric Southwestern Pottery Types.* Anthropological Series, Vol. 1, No. 4. University of New Mexico Bulletin, Albuquerque.

HAYES, ALDEN

1981   A Survey of Chaco Canyon Archaeology. In *Archeological Surveys of Chaco Canyon, New Mexico,* pp. 1–68. Publications in Archeology 18A, Chaco Canyon Series. National Park Service, Washington, D.C.

HAYES, ALDEN C.

1981   *Contributions to Gran Quivira Archeology.* Publications in Archeology, No. 17. National Park Service, Washington, D.C.

HAYES, ALDEN C., JON NATHAN YOUNG, AND A. HELENE WARREN

1981   *Excavation of Mound 7, Gran Quivira National Monument, New Mexico.* Publications in Archeology, No. 16. National Park Service, Washington, D.C.

HAYS, KELLEY A.

1985   Ceramics. In *Excavation and Surface Collection of Homolovi II Ruin,* edited by Kelley A. Hays and E. Charles Adams, pp. 16–41. Final Report Submitted to the Arizona State Land Department, Phoenix, by Arizona State Museum, Tucson.

1989   Katsina Depictions on Homol'ovi Ceramics: Toward a Fourteenth-Century Pueblo Iconography. *Kiva* 54:297–311.

HAYS, KELLEY A. AND E. CHARLES ADAMS (EDS.)
1985 *Excavation and Surface Collection of Homolovi II Ruin.* Final Report Submitted to the Arizona State Land Department, Phoenix, by Arizona State Museum, Tucson.

HEDRICK, BASIL C., J. CHARLES KELLEY, AND CARROLL L. RILEY (EDS.)
1974 *The Mesoamerican Southwest.* Southern Illinois University Press, Carbondale.

HEREFORD, RICHARD
1984 Climate and Ephemeral-Stream Processes: Twentieth-Century Geomorphology and Alluvial Stratigraphy of the Little Colorado River, Arizona. *Geological Society of America Bulletin* 95:654–668.

HERRINGTON, LAVERNE
1982 Water Control Systems of the Mimbres Classic Phase. In *Mogollon Archaeology: Proceedings of the 1980 Mogollon Conference,* edited by Patrick H. Beckett, pp. 75–90. Acoma Books, Ramona, California.

HEWETT, EDGAR L.
1938 *Pajarito Plateau and Its Ancient People.* University of New Mexico Press, Albuquerque.

HIBBEN, FRANK C.
1955 Excavations at Pottery Mound, New Mexico. *American Antiquity* 21:179–180.
1960 Prehispanic Paintings at Pottery Mound. *Archaeology* 21:267–274.
1966 A Possible Pyramidal Structure and Other Mexican Influences at Pottery Mound, New Mexico. *American Antiquity* 31:522–529.
1967 Mexican Features of Mural Painting at Pottery Mound. *Archaeology* 20:84–87.
1975 *Kiva Art of the Anasazi at Pottery Mound.* K.C. Publishing, Las Vegas.

HILL, JAMES N.
1970 *Broken K Pueblo: Prehistoric Social Organization in the American Southwest.* Anthropological Papers, No. 18. University of Arizona, Tucson.

HODDER, IAN
1982 *Symbols in Action: Ethnoarchaeological Studies of Material Culture.* Cambridge University Press, Cambridge.

HOUGH, WALTER
1903 Archaeological Field Work in Northeastern Arizona. The Museum-Gates Expedition, 1901. *Annual Report for 1901,* pp. 279–358. U.S. National Museum, Washington, D.C.

JENNINGS, CALVIN H.

1980   *Further Investigations at the Puerco Site, Petrified Forest National Park, Arizona.* Laboratory of Public Archaeology, Colorado State University, Fort Collins.

JOHNSON, ALFRED E.

1965   *The Development of Western Pueblo Culture.* Unpublished Ph.D. dissertation, Department of Anthropology, University of Arizona, Tucson.

JOHNSON, ALFRED E. AND RAYMOND H. THOMPSON

1963   The Ringo Site, Southeastern Arizona. *American Antiquity* 28(4): 465–481.

JOHNSON, GREGORY

1982   Organizational Structure and Scalar Stress. In *Theory and Explanation in Archaeology: The Southhampton Conference,* edited by Colin Renfrew, Michael J. Rowlands, and Barbara A. Segraves, pp. 389–421. Academic Press, New York.

1989   Dynamics of Southwestern Prehistory: Far Outside—Looking In. In *Dynamics of Southwestern Prehistory,* edited by Linda S. Cordell and George J. Gumerman, pp. 371–389. Smithsonian Institution Press, Washington, D.C.

JUDD, NEIL M.

1954   The Material Culture of Pueblo Bonito. *Smithsonian Miscellaneous Collections,* No. 124. Washington, D.C.

JUDGE, W. JAMES

1975   *The Excavation of Tijeras Pueblo 1971–1973: Preliminary Report.* Archeological Report No. 3. USDA Forest Service, Southwest Region, Albuquerque.

KABOTIE, FRED

1949   *Designs from the Ancient Mimbrenos with a Hopi Interpretation.* Grabhorn Press, San Francisco.

KELLEY, J. CHARLES

1966   Mesoamerica and the Southwestern United States. In *Archaeological Frontiers and External Connections,* edited by G. F. Ekholm and G. K. Willey, pp. 95–110. Handbook of Middle American Indians, Vol. 4. University of Texas Press, Austin.

KENAGHY, SUSAN G.

1986   *Ritual Pueblo Ceramics: Symbolic Stylistic Behavior as a Medium of Information Exchange.* Unpublished Ph.D. dissertation, Department of Art History, University of New Mexico, Albuquerque.

KENNARD, EDWARD A. AND EDWIN EARLE

1938   *Hopi Kachinas.* J. J. Augustin, New York.

KENT, KATE PECK

1957   *The Cultivation and Weaving of Cotton in the Prehistoric Southwestern U.S.* Transactions of the American Philosophical Society, Vol. 47, No. 3. Philadelphia.

1983   *Prehistoric Textiles of the Southwest.* School of American Research Press, Santa Fe.

KESSEL, JOHN L.

1979   *Kiva, Cross, and Crown: The Pecos Indians and New Mexico, 1540–1840.* National Park Service, Washington, D.C.

KIDDER, ALFRED V.

1932   *The Artifacts of Pecos.* Papers of the Phillips Academy Southwestern Expedition, No. 5. Yale University Press, New Haven.

KINTIGH, KEITH W.

1984   *Settlement, Subsistence and Society in Late Zuni Prehistory.* Anthropological Papers, No. 44. University of Arizona, Tucson.

1990   Chaco, Communal Architecture, and Cibolan Aggregation. Paper presented at the Second Southwest Symposium, Albuquerque.

KOLBE, THOMAS

1990   *The Geomorphology and Alluvial Chronology of the Middle Little Colorado River Valley, Arizona.* Unpublished Master's thesis, Department of Quaternary Studies, Northern Arizona University, Flagstaff.

LANGE, CHARLES H. (ASSEMBLER)

1968   *The Cochiti Dam Archaeological Salvage Project; Part 1: Report on the 1963 Season.* Museum of New Mexico Research Records, No. 6. University of New Mexico Press, Santa Fe.

LANGE, RICHARD C.

1989   A Survey of the Homolovi Ruins State Park. *Kiva* 54:195–216.

LANGE, RICHARD C., LISA C. YOUNG, AND LEE FRATT

1986   *The First Season's Survey by the Arizona State Museum in the Vicinity of the Homolovi Ruins.* Report submitted to the Arizona State Historic Preservation Office, Phoenix.

LANGE, RICHARD C., MIRIAM T. STARK, LEE FRATT, LISA C. YOUNG, AND SARA C. SEIBERT

1987   *The Second Season's Survey of the Homolovi Ruins State Park, Northeastern Arizona.* Report Submitted to the Arizona State Historic Preservation Office, Phoenix.

LEBLANC, STEVEN A.

1976   Mimbres Archaeological Center: Preliminary Report of the Second Season, 1975. *Journal of New World Archaeology* 1(6).

1980   The Dating of Casas Grandes. *American Antiquity* 45:799–806.

1983   *The Mimbres People: Ancient Pueblo Painters of the American Southwest.* Thames and Hudson, New York.

LEBLANC, STEVEN A. AND BEN NELSON

1976   The Salado in Southwestern New Mexico. *The Kiva* 42:71–79.

LEKSON, STEVEN H.

1982   Architecture and Settlement Plan in the Redrock Valley of the Gila River, Southwestern New Mexico. In *Mogollon Archaeology: Proceedings of the 1980 Mogollon Conference,* edited by Patrick H. Beckett, pp. 61–73. Acoma Books, Ramona, California.

LIGHTFOOT, KENT G.

1984   *Prehistoric Political Dynamics: A Case Study from the American Southwest.* Northern Illinois University Press, De Kalb.

LIGHTFOOT, KENT G. AND GARY M. FEINMAN

1982   Social Differentiation and Leadership Development in Early Pithouse Villages in the Mogollon region of the American Southwest. *American Antiquity* 47:64–86.

LIGHTFOOT, KENT G. AND ROBERTA JEWETT

1984   Late Prehistoric Ceramic Distributions in East-Central Arizona: An Examination of Cibola Whiteware, White Mountain Redware, and Salado Redware. In *Regional Analysis of Prehistoric Ceramic Variation: Contemporary Studies of the Cibola Whitewares,* edited by Alan P. Sullivan and Jeffrey L. Hantman, pp. 36–73. Anthropological Research Papers, No. 31. Arizona State University, Tempe.

LIGHTFOOT, KENT G. AND FRED PLOG

1984   Intensifications Along the North Side of the Mogollon Rim. In *Prehistoric Agricultural Strategies in the Southwest,* edited by Suzanne K. Fish and Paul R. Fish, pp. 179–195. Anthropological Research Papers, No. 33. Arizona State University, Tempe.

LIPE, WILLIAM D.

1983   The Southwest. In *Ancient North Americans,* edited by Jesse D. Jennings, pp. 421–493. W. H. Freeman, San Francisco.

LONGACRE, WILLIAM A.

1964   A Synthesis of Upper Little Colorado Prehistory, Eastern Arizona. In *Chapters in the Prehistory of Arizona, II.* Assembled by Paul S. Martin, pp. 201–215. Fieldiana: Anthropology, Vol. 55. Field Museum of Anthropology, Chicago.

1970   *Archaeology as Anthropology: A Case Study.* Anthropological Papers, No. 17. University of Arizona, Tucson.

MALOTKI, EKKEHART
1990   *Language as a Key to Cultural Understanding: New Interpretations of Central Hopi Concepts.* Ju-Baessler Archiv, Neue Folge, Vol. 38.

MARTIN, PAUL S.
1979   Prehistory: Mogollon. In *Southwest,* edited by Alfonso Ortiz, pp. 61–74. Handbook of North American Indians, Vol. 9. Smithsonian Institution, Washington, D.C.

MARTIN, PAUL S., WILLIAM A. LONGACRE, AND JAMES N. HILL
1967   *Chapters in the Prehistory of Eastern Arizona III.* Fieldiana: Anthropology Vol. 57. Field Museum of Natural History, Chicago.

MARTIN, PAUL S. AND FRED PLOG
1973   *The Archaeology of Arizona.* Doubleday, New York.

MARTIN, PAUL S. AND JOHN B. RINALDO
1960   *Table Rock Pueblo, Arizona.* Fieldiana: Anthropology Vol. 51, No. 2. Field Museum of Natural History, Chicago.

MARTIN, PAUL S., JOHN B. RINALDO, ELAINE A. BLUHM, AND HUGH C. CUTLER
1956   *Higgins Flat Pueblo, Western New Mexico.* Fieldiana: Anthropology, Vol. 45. Field Museum of Natural History, Chicago.

MARTIN, PAUL S., JOHN B. RINALDO, AND WILLIAM A. LONGACRE
1961   *Mineral Creek Site and Hooper Ranch Pueblo, Eastern Arizona.* Fieldiana: Anthropology Vol. 52. Field Museum of Natural History, Chicago.

MARTIN, PAUL S., JOHN B. RINALDO, WILLIAM A. LONGACRE, CONSTANCE CRONIN, LESLIE G. FREEMAN, JR., AND JAMES SCHOENWETTER
1962   *Chapters in the Prehistory of Eastern Arizona I.* Fieldiana: Anthropology Vol. 53. Field Museum of Natural History, Chicago.

MARTIN, PAUL S., JOHN B. RINALDO, WILLIAM A. LONGACRE, LESLIE G. FREEMAN, JR., JAMES A. BROWN, RICHARD H. HEVLY AND M. E. COOLEY
1964   *Chapters in the Prehistory of Eastern Arizona II.* Fieldiana: Anthropology Vol. 55. Field Museum of Natural History, Chicago.

MARTIN, PAUL S. AND ELIZABETH S. WILLIS
1940   *Anasazi Painted Pottery in the Field Museum of Natural History.* Anthropology Memoirs, No. 5. Field Museum of Natural History, Chicago.

MARTYNEC, RICHARD J.
1985   *A Synthesis of Petrified Forest National Park Rock Art and Ceramics.* Bulletin, No. 45. Museum of Northern Arizona, Flagstaff.

MCCLUSKEY, STEVEN
1982   Historical Archaeoastronomy: The Hopi Example. In *Archaeoastronomy in the New World*, edited by A. F. Aveni, pp. 31–57. Cambridge University Press, Cambridge.

MCGREGOR, JOHN C.
1940   Burial of an Early American Magician. *Proceedings of the American Philosophical Society.* Vol. 86, No. 2. Philadelphia.

MCGUIRE, RANDALL H.
1980   The Mesoamerican Connection. *The Kiva* 46:3–38.

MICHAELIS, HELEN
1981   Willowsprings: A Hopi Petroglyph Site. *Journal of New World Archaeology* 4(2):3–23.

MIKSICEK, CHARLES
1985   Paleoethnobotany of a Fourteenth Century Hopi Site: Homolovi II. In *Excavation and Surface Collection of Homolovi II Ruin*, edited by Kelley A. Hays and E. Charles Adams, pp. 93–106. Ms. on file, Homol'ovi Research Program, Arizona State Museum, Tucson.
1989   *Paleoethnobotany of Homol'ovi III.* Ms. on file, Homol'ovi Research Program, Arizona State Museum, Tucson.

MINDELEFF, VICTOR
1891   A Study of Pueblo Architecture, Tusayan and Cibola. *Annual Report No. 8.* Bureau of American Ethnology, Washington, D.C.

MOULARD, BARBARA
1984   *Within the Underworld Sky: Mimbres Ceramics Art in Context.* Twelve Trees Press, Pasadena, California.

NAGATA, SHUICHI
1970   *Modern Transformations of Moenkopi Pueblo.* Illinois Studies in Anthropology, No. 6. Urbana.

NEQUATEWA, EDMUND
1936   *Truth of a Hopi.* Bulletin, No. 8. Museum of Northern Arizona, Flagstaff.

NICKENS, PAUL
1975   Prehistoric Cannibalism in the Mancos Canyon, Southwest Colorado. *The Kiva* 40:283–293.

ORTIZ, ALFONSO
1969   *The Tewa World: Space, Time, Being and Becoming in a Pueblo Society.* University of Chicago Press, Chicago.

1972   *New Perspectives on the Pueblos.* University of New Mexico Press, Albuquerque.

PAGE, GORDON
1940   *Hopi Agricultural Notes.* U.S. Department of Agriculture, Soil Conservation Service, Washington, D.C.

PAGE, JAKE
1982   Inside the Sacred Hopi Homeland. *National Geographic Magazine* 162:607–629.

PARSONS, ELSIE C.
1930   Spanish elements in the Kachina Cult of the Pueblos. *Proceedings of the 23rd International Congress of Americanists,* pp. 582–603.
1932   Isleta, New Mexico. In *Annual Report,* No. 47, pp. 193–466. Bureau of American Ethnology, Washington, D.C.
1933   Some Aztec and Pueblo Parallels. *American Anthropologist* 35:611–631.
1936   Supplementary sections with Crow Wing. In *Hopi Journal of A. M. Stephen.* Columbia University Press, New York.
1939   *Pueblo Indian Religion,* 2 vols. University of Chicago Press, Chicago.

PECKHAM, BARBARA A.
1981   Pueblo IV Murals at Mound 7. In *Contributions to Gran Quivira Archaeology,* edited by Alden C. Hayes, pp. 15–38. Publications in Archeology, No. 17. National Park Service, Washington, D.C.

PETERSON, CHARLES S.
1973   *Take Up Your Mission: Mormon Colonizing along the Little Colorado River, 1870–1900.* University of Arizona Press, Tucson.

PILLES, PETER J., JR.
1975   Petroglyphs of the Little Colorado River Valley, Arizona. *American Indian Rock Art,* No. 1, edited by Shari T. Grove. San Juan County Museum, Farmington, New Mexico.
1976   Sinagua and Salado Similarities as seen from the Verde Valley. In The 1976 Salado conference, edited by David E. Doyel and Emil W. Haury. *The Kiva* 42:113–124.
1979   Sunset Crater and the Sinagua: a New Interpretation. In *Volcanic Activity and Human Ecology,* edited by Payson Sheets and Donald Grayson, pp. 459–485. Academic Press, New York.
1982   Review of "Ethnohistory and Rock Art: Introduction" by Clement W. Meighan, "Willow Springs: A Hopi Petroglyph Site" by Helen Michaels, and "Kachinas in Rock Art" by Polly Schaafsma in *Journal of New World Archaeology,* Vol. 4, No. 2.

1987   Hisatsinom: The Ancient People. In *Earth Fire: A Hopi Legend of the Sunset Crater Eruption*, edited by Ekkehart Malotki with Michael Lomatuway'ma, pp. 105–119. Northland Press, Flagstaff.

PLOG, FRED (ED.)

1978   *An Analytical Approach to Cultural Resource Management: The Little Colorado Planning Unit.* Anthropological Research Papers, No. 13. Arizona State University, Tempe.

PLOG, FRED, STEADMAN UPHAM, AND PHIL C. WEIGAND

1982   A Perspective on Mogollon–Mesoamerican Interaction. In *Mogollon Archaeology: Proceedings of the 1980 Mogollon Conference*, edited by Patrick H. Beckett, pp. 227–238. Acoma Books, Ramona, California.

POND, GORDON G.

1966   A Painted Kiva near Winslow, Arizona. *American Antiquity* 31:555–558.

RAVESLOOT, JOHN C., JEFFREY S. DEAN, AND MICHAEL S. FOSTER

1986   A New Perspective on the Casas Grandes Tree-Ring Dates. Paper presented at the Fourth Annual Mogollon Conference, University of Arizona, Tucson.

REED, ERIK K.

1948   The Western Pueblo Archaeological Complex. *El Palacio* 55(1):9–15.

1956   Types of Village-Plan Layouts in the Southwest. In *Prehistoric Settlement Patterns in the New World*, edited by Gordon R. Willey, pp. 11–17. Viking Fund Publications in Anthropology, No. 23. New York.

REID, J. JEFFERSON AND IZUMI SHIMADA

1982   Pueblo Growth at Grasshopper: Methods and Models. In *Multidisciplinary Research at Grasshopper Pueblo, Arizona*, edited by William A. Longacre, Sally J. Holbrook, and Michael W. Graves, pp. 12–18. Anthropological Papers, No. 40. University of Arizona Press, Tucson.

REID, J. JEFFERSON AND STEPHANIE WHITTLESEY

1982   Households at Grasshopper. *American Behavioral Scientist* 25(6): 687–703.

RENFREW, COLIN

1986   Introduction: Peer Polity Interaction and Socio-Political Change. In *Peer Polity Interaction and Socio-Political Change*, edited by Colin Renfrew and John F. Cherry, pp. 1–18. Cambridge University Press, Cambridge.

REYMAN, JONATHAN

1978   Pochteca Burials at Anasazi Sites? In *Across the Chichemec Sea*, edited by C. Riley and B. Hedrick, pp. 242–254. Southern Illinois University Press, Carbondale.

RILEY, CARROLL L.
1975   The Road to Hawikuh: Trade and Trade Routes to Cibola-Zuni during the late Prehistoric and Early Historic Times. *The Kiva* 41:137–159.
1987   *The Frontier People: The Greater Southwest in the Protohistoric Period.* University of New Mexico Press, Albuquerque.

RINALDO, JOHN B.
1959   *Foote Canyon Pueblo, Eastern Arizona.* Fieldiana: Anthropology Vol. 49, No. 2. Field Museum of Natural History, Chicago.

ROSE, MARTIN R., JEFFREY S. DEAN, AND WILLIAM J. ROBINSON
1981   *The Past Climate of Arroyo Hondo, New Mexico, Reconstructed from Tree Rings.* Arroyo Hondo Archaeological Series, Vol. 4. School of American Research Press, Santa Fe.

SCHAAFSMA, POLLY
1965   Kiva murals from Pueblo del Encierro (LA70). *El Palacio* 72:7–16.
1972   *Rock Art in New Mexico.* State Planning Office, Santa Fe.
1980   *Indian Rock Art of the Southwest.* School of American Research and University of New Mexico Press, Santa Fe and Albuquerque.
1981   Kachinas in Rock Art. *Journal of New World Archaeology* 4(2):24–31.

SCHAAFSMA, POLLY AND CURTIS F. SCHAAFSMA
1974   Evidence for the Origin of the Pueblo Katchina Cult as Suggested by Southwestern Rock Art. *American Antiquity* 39:535–545.

SCHROEDER, ALBERT
1961   Puerco Ruin Excavations, Petrified Forest National Monument, Arizona. *Plateau* 33(4):93–104.
1979a   Pecos Pueblo. In *Southwest,* edited by Alfonso Ortiz, pp. 430–437. Handbook of North American Indians, Vol. 9. Smithsonian Institution, Washington, D.C.
1979b   Pueblos Abandoned in Historic Times. In *Southwest,* edited by Alfonso Ortiz, pp. 236–254. Handbook of North American Indians, Vol. 9. Smithsonian Institution, Washington, D.C.

SCHWARTZ, DOUGLAS
1981   Foreword. In *The Past Climate of Arroyo Hondo, New Mexico, Reconstructed from Tree Rings,* Arroyo Hondo Archaeological Series, Vol. 4, by Martin R. Rose, J. S. Dean, and W. J. Robinson, pp. IX–XV. School of American Research, Santa Fe.

SHEPARD, ANNA O.
1971   Technological Note on Awatovi Pottery. In *Painted Ceramics of the Western Mound at Awatovi,* by Watson Smith, pp. 170–184. Papers of

the Peabody Museum of American Archaeology and Ethnology, No. 39. Harvard University, Cambridge.

SIMMONS, MARC

1979   History of Pueblo-Spanish Relations to 1821. In Southwest, edited by Alfonso Ortiz, pp. 178–193. Handbook of North American Indians, Vol. 9. Smithsonian Institution, Washington, D.C.

SISSON, EDWARD B.

1975   Of Shoe-form Vessels and Ethnographic Analogy. American Antiquity 40:475–476.

SMILEY, TERAH L.

1952   Four Late Prehistoric Kivas at Point of Pines, Arizona. University of Arizona Social Science Bulletin, No. 4. Tucson.

SMITH, WATSON

1952   Kiva Mural Decorations at Awatovi and Kawaika-a, with a Survey of Other Wall Paintings in the Pueblo Southwest. Papers of the Peabody Museum of American Archaeology and Ethnology, No. 37. Harvard University, Cambridge.

1971   Painted Ceramics of the Western Mound at Awatovi. Papers of the Peabody Museum of American Archaeology and Ethnology, Vol. 38. Harvard University, Cambridge.

1972   Prehistoric Kivas of Antelope Mesa, Northeastern Arizona. Papers of the Peabody Museum of Archaeology and Ethnology, Vol. 39, No. 1. Harvard University, Cambridge.

1980   Mural Decoration from Ancient Hopi Kivas. In Hopi Kachina: Spirit of Life, edited by Dorothy K. Washburn, pp. 29–38. California Academy of Sciences, University of Washington Press, Seattle.

SMITH, WATSON, RICHARD B. WOODBURY, AND NATALIE F. S. WOODBURY

1966   The Excavation of Hawikuh by Frederick Webb Hodge; Report of the Hendricks-Hodge Expedition, 1917–1923. Contributions from the Museum of the American Indian, Heye Foundation, No. 20. New York.

SNOW, DAVID H.

1976   Archaeological Excavations at Pueblo del Encierro, LA 70, Cochiti Dam Salvage Project, Cochiti, New Mexico, Final Report: 1964–1965 field seasons. Laboratory of Anthropology Notes, No. 78. Museum of New Mexico, Santa Fe.

1981   Protohistoric Rio Grande Pueblo Economics: a Reviw of Trends. In The Protohistoric Period in the North American Southwest, A.D. 1450–1700, edited by David R. Wilcox and W. Bruce Masse, pp. 354–377. Anthropological Research Papers, No. 24. Arizona State University, Tempe.

1982   The Rio Grande Glaze, Matte-Paint, and Plainware Tradition. In *Southwestern Ceramics: A Comparative Review*, edited by Albert H. Schroeder, pp. 235–278. The Arizona Archaeologist, No. 15. The Arizona Archaeological Society, Phoenix.

STALLINGS, W. S., JR.

1931   *El Paso Polychrome*. School of American Research Series Bulletin No. 3, Sante Fe.

STEPHEN, ALEXANDER M.

1936   *Hopi Journal of Alexander M. Stephen*. Edited by E. C. Parsons. 2 vols. Columbia University Press, New York.

STEVENSON, MATILDA COXE

1887   The Religious Life of the Zuni Child. *Annual Report*, No. 5, pp. 533–555. Bureau of American Ethnology, Washington, D.C.

1904   The Zuni Indians: Their Mythology, Esoteric Fraternities, and Ceremonies. *Annual Report*, No. 23, pp. 3–635. Bureau of American Ethnology, Washington, D.C.

STUART, DAVID E. AND RORY E. GAUTIER

1981   *Prehistoric New Mexico: Background for Survey*. Historic Preservation Bureau, Santa Fe.

STUBBS, STANLEY A.

1950   *Bird's-eye View of the Pueblos*. University of Oklahoma Press, Norman.

TAYLOR, WALTER

1968   *A Study of Archaeology*. Reprinted by Southern Illinois University Press, Carbondale.

TEDLOCK, DENNIS

1979   Zuni Religion and World View. In *Southwest*, edited by Alfonso Ortiz, pp. 499–508. Handbook of North American Indians, Vol. 9. Smithsonian Institution, Washington, D.C.

TITIEV, MISCHA

1944   *Old Oraibi: A Study of the Hopi Indians of Third Mesa*. Papers of the Peabody Museum of American Archaeology and Ethnology, Vol. 22. Harvard University, Cambridge.

TURNER, CHRISTY G., II

1963   *Petroglyphs of the Glen Canyon Region: Styles, Chronology, Distribution and Relationships from Basketmaker to Navajo*. Bulletin, No. 38. Museum of Northern Arizona, Flagstaff.

1970   A Massacre at Hopi. *American Antiquity* 35:320–331.

UPHAM, STEADMAN
1978   Final Report on Archaeological Investigations at Chavez Pass Ruin, Coconino National Forest, Arizona: The 1978 Field Season. On file, USDA
Forest Service, Coconino National Forest, Flagstaff, Arizona.
1982   Polities and Power: An Economic and Political History of the Western
Pueblo. Academic Press, New York.

VIVIAN, R. GORDON
1964   Excavations in a 17th-Century Jumano Pueblo, Gran Quivira. Archaeological Research Series, No. 8, National Park Service, Washington,
D.C.

WADE, EDWIN L. AND LEA S. MCCHESNEY
1980   America's Great Lost Expedition: The Thomas Keam Collection of Hopi
Pottery from the Second Hemenway Expedition, 1890–1894. The Heard
Museum, Phoenix.
1981   Historic Hopi Ceramics: The Thomas V. Keam Collection of the Peabody
Museum of Archaeology and Ethnology, Harvard University. Peabody
Museum Press, Cambridge.

WEAVER, DONALD E., JR., STEVEN G. DOSH, AND KEITH E. MILLER
1982   An Archaeological Assessment of Homolovi II Ruin, NA953, Near
Winslow, Navajo County, Arizona. Ms. on file, Museum of Northern
Arizona, Flagstaff.

WENDORF, FRED AND ERIC REED
1955   An Alternative Reconstruction of Northern Rio Grande Prehistory.
El Palacio 62(5–6):131–173.

WHITE, LESLIE A.
1932   The Acoma Indians. In Annual Report, No. 47, pp. 17–192. Bureau of
American Ethnology, Washington, D.C.
1934   Masks in the Southwest. American Anthropologist 36:626–628.

WHITELY, PETER M.
1985   Unpacking Hopi "Clans": Another Vintage Model out of Africa?
Journal of Anthropological Research 41:359–374.
1986   Unpacking Hopi "Clans", II: Further Questions About Hopi Descent
Groups. Journal of Anthropological Research 42:69–79.

WHITING, ALFRED F.
1939   Ethnobotany of the Hopi. Bulletin, No. 15. Museum of Northern Arizona, Flagstaff.
1964   Hopi Kachinas. Plateau 37(1):1–7.

WOODBURY, RICHARD B. AND NATALIE F. S. WOODBURY
1966   Decorated Pottery of the Zuni Area. In The Excavation of Hawikuh by
Frederick Webb Hodge. Report of the Hendricks-Hodge Expedition, 1917–

1923 (with W. Smith), Appendix II. Contributions from the Museum of the American Indian, Heye Foundation, No. 20. New York.

WRIGHT, BARTON

1977   *Hopi Kachinas: The Complete Guide to Collecting Kachina Dolls.* Northland Press, Flagstaff, Arizona.

1985   *Kachinas of the Zuni.* Northland Press, Flagstaff, Arizona.

YAVA, ALBERT

1981   *Big Falling Snow: A Tewa-Hopi Indian's Life and Times and the History and Traditions of His People.* Edited and annotated by Harold Courlander. University of New Mexico Press, Albuquerque.

YOUNG, JON NATHAN

1967   *The Salado Culture in Southwestern Prehistory.* Unpublished Ph.D. dissertation, Department of Anthropology, University of Arizona, Tucson.

YOUNG, LISA C.

1989   Mobility and Farmers: Adaptive Diversity in the American Southwest. NSF Dissertation Improvement Proposal, Arizona State Museum, Tucson.

1990   *Preliminary Report on the Excavation of Two Field Houses in the Homol'ovi Area.* Ms. on file, Homol'ovi Research Program, Arizona State Museum, University of Arizona, Tucson.

YOUNG, M. JANE AND NANCY L. BARTMAN

1981   *Rock Art of the Zuni-Cibola Region.* Published by M. Jane Young.

Index

Hopi, 88, 90, 120, 171; agriculture, 153, 171, 180, 182; ancestral villages, 55; chief katsina, 8–9, 55; clan, 8, 55, 157; cotton production, 180; crafts, 159; definition, 150, 155; deities, 8; diet, 80; dolls, 6, 8, 159; ethnography, 20, 82; Fourth World, 8; homeland, 66; katsina dances, 3, 7, 19, 20; katsina masks, 7; katsina ritual, 4, 7, 159; katsina season, 7, 8; murals, 34, 47; Nimanywu (Katsina Going Home), 8–9; oral tradition, 60, 72–73, 120, 163, 177; Patsavu (Katsina Initiation), 9; piki at, 80; political organization, 13, 157; Powamuya (Bean Dance), 7, 157; social organization, 13, 159; Soyalang (Winter Solstice), 8–9, 37; Third World (underworld), 8, 66, 155; visitation/travel, 66; war chief, 37, 156
Hopi area. See Hopi; Hopi Mesas
Hopi Buttes, 84, 107, 108
Hopi Katsina Cult. See Hopi style cult
Hopi Mesas: area, 24, 51, 52, 65, 67–75, 82, 111–112, 124, 131, 142, 160; ceramics, 36, 50, 68, 93, 107, 128, 135, 159; enclosed plazas, 103, 125, 135, 146; and katsina cult, 134, 141, 146, 148, 149, 155, 184; kiva murals, 33, 37, 66, 77, 78, 135–136, 146; people/culture, 57, 73, 87, 90; pueblos, 47, 65, 66, 67, 72, 73, 74, 77, 78, 81, 84, 110; rock art, 73–74, 77, 111–112, 132, 135, 146; street-oriented plazas, 103; trade, 160, 183, 184. See also Hopi
Hopi style cult, 120–121, 135–138, 142–143, 147, 148, 190; ceramics, 36, 136–137, 142, 147; at Homol'ovi, 136; and Jornada style, 143–144, 147–148, 190; on kiva murals, 76, 136, 142, 147; at Pottery Mound, 136, 143; as a rain cult, 142–143, 186; rock art, 111–112; at Zuni, 136–137
Hough, Walter, 54, 67
Hu (Whipper) Katsina, 63, 74, 90, 91, 118, 155, 156, 157
Huckovi Black-on-orange, 69

Hueco Tanks, 26, 117, 122. See also El Paso
Huitzilopochtli cult, 143
Humanas area, 148. See also Las Humanas

Icon. See Iconography
Iconography: age of, 124; bird/feather, 98, 100, 127, 131, 132, 134, 136, 142, 154; for clans, 177; Hopi, 121; katsina mask/figure, 5, 12, 18, 21, 23, 24, 29, 63, 78, 98, 123, 131, 145, 146, 148, 154, 162, 165, 166, 190; of katsina cult, 78, 82, 121, 124, 127, 134, 178; Mexican, 122, 123, 153, 154; private, 161, 165; public, 154, 161, 165, 184, 186; as symbolism, 12, 14, 15–16, 18, 78, 101, 141, 154, 155, 161, 162, 177, 178, 179, 184, 186. See also Ceramics; Murals, kiva; Rock art
Immigration, 94, 126, 128, 145, 151, 153, 155, 160, 164–165, 166, 170, 172, 173, 176, 177, 179, 186; as labor, 145
Inhumation, 43, 80, 94, 163
Inscription Point, 74
Integration, 126, 147, 153, 154, 155, 157, 161, 165, 176, 177, 184, 186, 188, 189; structures for, 152, 168, 171, 174
Isleta Pueblo, 10, 19

Jeddito Black-on-orange, 68, 107
Jeddito Black-on-yellow, 41, 43, 51, 55, 57, 58, 66, 68, 69, 96, 97
Jeddito Engraved, 68
Jeddito Orange Ware, 57, 171
Jeddito Polychrome, 68, 107, 128, 129
Jeddito Stippled, 58
Jeddito Valley/Wash, 67, 68, 74
Jeddito Yellow Ware, 43, 52, 58, 60, 65, 66, 72, 73, 75, 81, 96, 134, 136–137, 159, 160, 171, 173, 175, 179, 183; coal fired, 68; color source, 67; for dating, 171, 173; decoration, 68–69; form, 70; technology, 70–71; at Zuni, 43
Jemez Mountains, 142
Jemez Pueblo, 11, 12, 13, 148; katsina dances, 19

About the Author

E. Charles Adams, Associate Curator of Archaeology, Arizona State Museum, University of Arizona, is the author of numerous articles on the archaeology of Pueblo cultures of the Southwest. Adams has directed the Homol'ovi Research Program for the Arizona State Museum since 1985. This project has focused on several fourteenth-century pueblos in northeastern Arizona believed ancestral to the Hopi Indians. Previously, Adams was Director of Research for the Crow Canyon Archaeological Center near Cortez, Colorado, and Senior Archaeologist for the Museum of Northern Arizona, Flagstaff. From 1975 to 1982, while at the Museum of Northern Arizona, he directed the Walpi Archaeological Project which included excavations of the historic First Mesa Hopi village of Walpi.

Adams has spent much of his professional life working closely with Native Americans, especially the Hopi, trying to improve dialogue between Native American groups and the larger community on a wide range of issues.